CW00517122

FUN in Just One Lifetime

FUN

in

Just One Lifetime

Memoirs and Travel Journal
of

Theodore G. Budrow

Honeycomb House Publishing
New Cumberland, Pennsylvania

FUN in Just One Lifetime
Published by Honeycomb House Publishing

© 2021 Theodore G. Budrow

Printed in the United States of America
ISBN (paperback): 978-0-9753934-3-7

I want to have fun in just one lifetime,
I want to have fun before it's done.
I'll find some friends that I can trust,
And on my way, I know I must
Find Love with just one someone,
To raise with me a family.
And let me write a song
For the world to sing, and I'll have

FUN

*IN JUST ONE LIFETIME!**

*From the song "Fun in Just One Lifetime," Words and Music by Frank Marzocco and Joe Liles, Arrangement by Joe Liles. Copyright 2016 by Frank Marzocco and Joe Liles

Contents

Part 1

Budrow Memories

Introduction

A Lifetime of *FUN*

During my childhood I remember how good it was to come home from church on Sundays to the delightful and mouth-watering smell of roast meat wafting from the kitchen, and the sight of a dinner table all set with silverware, napkins and glasses, waiting for the food to be placed upon it.

One Thanksgiving Day, around 1942, my mother suggested we all take turns saying sentence prayers around the table, instead of Dad or Grandpa saying the blessing. So we did that. I cannot remember what mine was, or any of the others, for that matter, but I do recall that Grandpa almost burst out crying when he said, "I thank You for a Savior."

I didn't think much of it then, but now I can see that the memory of that prayer was imprinted on my brain by my heavenly Father, so that I could praise Him for it now.

Fast forward to 2014, when my wife Maralou and I hosted a Thanksgiving dinner at our home in Landisville, PA for twenty-seven people and four dogs. It was a small house—one floor, two bedrooms, a dining area, a living room and a carport (turned into a family room)—and with that many people, we were packed in like sardines. There were five small children, and the four dogs who had never met one another before.

Yet, in spite of all that, the day was perfect. There were:

NO spills

NO discipline needed

NO crying

NO barking—not even a growl—from the dogs!

Everyone there was a Christian, in every sense of the word, except for one Orthodox Jew, who led us in a Hebrew Thanksgiving prayer. We read Deuteronomy 8:7-10, praised God, and had a very wonderful time, because the Spirit of the Lord was there with us, and where He is, is peace.

Let me tell you how this wonderful lifetime of FUN began:

1

Early *FUN*

I was born on Christmas Day, 1932, in Niagara Falls, New York. My earliest recollections are of our house at 779 Ridge Road in Lewiston, New York, a village located along the Niagara River, some five miles north of Niagara Falls. I had one sibling, my sister Jane, who was less than a year older (born January 7, 1932).

Our growing-up years were marked by many activities and events experienced together. Since we were so close in age, Mom raised us like twins. Jane was always the loving older sister, though, and I was the teasing, obnoxious little brother. She would hug and kiss me, which "grossed me out," so I would turn my face and lick her face, which grossed her out! This happened once too often, and she went crying to Mom. Mom caught me by the shoulders and held me against the wall while Jane licked my face repeatedly. Ugh! The face-licking was never repeated!

But as teenagers we were close, going to all the church activities, skiing together, square dancing, beach bathing with our parents, and taking long trips in the summers to visit relatives. And, of course, going to school together.

We began our education at Hickory College, a one-room grade school situated in a grove of hickory trees. It was built in 1842, and continued in operation until 1941. Edith Breckon was the teacher of all twelve grades when Jane started first grade there. Jane was a quick learner, and would come home to tell me all she was being taught, so it was determined that since I had been so nicely taught by my older sibling, that I would skip first grade and join Jane in second grade. We stayed together for third and fourth also, then the school was closed and all the students went to the consolidated school in Lewiston. I repeated fourth grade, to place me more in line with my age group, and Jane went on to fifth grade.

We stayed there for two years, then our parents decided that Niagara Falls had a more advanced school system, so they paid the tuition required and we started riding the commercial bus up the hill to school daily. I was in the sixth grade at Maple Avenue School, and Jane went to North Junior High. We graduated from that school system—Jane in 1949, and I in 1950.

2

$\mathcal{FUN}$ with Family (Part 1)

There are several events that happened during my childhood that are especially nice to recall. One of them is a picnic—in the middle of the winter!

On the Canadian side of the Niagara River, just north of the Whirlpool, there is a trail down to the water, where an island, undercut by the river, collapsed into the gorge. The Canadian Park Service turned it into a park, known as the Glen, with trails and a picnic pavilion. We went there frequently. My mother, always looking for new ways to have fun, came up with the idea of a winter picnic, so down we went on the slippery trail, and had fun in the snow at the bottom. Then we feasted on hot fried chicken and mashed potatoes (Mom packed the meal in a roasting pan, and wrapped everything in blankets). What fun! But the Park Service put a stop to that practice; the Glen is now closed to visitors in the winter.

On Sundays, in the summer, we many times went to the beach instead of to church. But during the week, on a hot day, that trip was too far to travel. There was a quarry within a few miles of home where the company had dumped sand all around a large pond and allowed swimming. The entrance fee was not too much, and many times we swam there, at Sandhurst. Mom often had a car full of children, and sometimes another mother, too.

My mother was a lover of classical music, and she made sure that my sister and I were well schooled in it. She took us to all the Civic Music Association concerts, which occurred three or four times a year, always with a visiting soloist. She also had the radio on every Sunday for the Mormon Tabernacle Choir and the New York Philharmonic, and every Saturday for the Metropolitan Opera. She would take a nap on the living room couch then, and woe to the child who stomped through the house and disturbed her!

The biggest department store in Buffalo, New York was Kleinhans; the family that owned the business funded the building of Kleinhans Music Hall. An architectural first for Buffalo, it was acoustically perfect. No amplification was needed; every seat in the house (it seated about 500) was assured of hearing every note.

13

My recollection of a concert there is one of great pleasure. We arrived for a performance by Andrés Segovia to see a stage with no curtains, large enough for a full symphony orchestra, with just a chair and a low stool in the center. Then Segovia came out, sat in the chair, put his foot upon the stool, cradled his guitar like embracing a lover, and filled the hall with the most thrilling and beautiful music I had ever heard. While I wasn't inspired to learn guitar, I still consider it one of my favorite instruments to hear.

The summer when Jane and I were 12 and 11, respectively, our family spent a week in Canada, camping on the north shore of Lake Erie. When Sunday came around, we went to a church service in a small country church nearby.

The building was distinctively different from the church we attended, a large cathedral-type church, St. Paul's Methodist, in Niagara Falls. There were "box pews," with doors on the aisles to gain entrance to the benches. The pulpit was up on the wall, like a little balcony, with a set of stairs, also on the wall, to get there. On the raised floor in front was the lectern and a piano.

The floor was covered with a dark green carpet which had a black pattern running through it, and which continued up the walls to a height of four feet or so, ending in a dark brown chair rail molding. Above that, the walls were a light blue. The ceiling was also light blue, with large patterns of white molding. The windows were of old-fashioned glass (irregular with air bubbles) in pastel shades of white and amber, outlined with white molding.

My mother remarked at the beauty of the sanctuary, with the light blue walls above the dark green carpeting. My beautiful twelve-year-old sister, whose thinking (as I can now see it) was already being influenced by the Christian values taught by our parents, said, "But Mom, didn't God put the blue sky over the green trees?"

Whenever I rise in the morning to see the trees covered by beautiful sunshine in a blue sky, I thank my heavenly Father for another "Jane Day."

3

FUN Traveling

Right after the war, my folks bought a brand new car, a 1946 Mercury four-door sedan. There was so much chrome on that car it was hard to see the paint! We packed up, and Mom drove that car all the way west to Oregon. She gave Jane and me the road maps, and told us that we were the navigators, and she would follow our directions explicitly. We were to tell her which roads to take, and she would not turn left or right unless we said so. So we had to read road signs and route signs, and figure our way through cities, etc. It was a great way to teach us, and a lot of fun to learn.

We also read all the Burma-Shave signs. (Burma-Shave was an American brand of brushless shaving cream, famous for its advertising gimmick of posting humorous rhyming poems on small sequential highway roadside signs.) In the 1940s these series of little red and white signs along the highway, each set displaying a funny poem, were quite famous from coast to coast.

Car in Ditch
Driver in Tree
Moon was Full
And So Was He
Burma-Shave

That was a set of five signs we saw more than once.

Don't Stick Your Arm
Out Too Far
It May Go Home
In Another Car
Burma-Shave

. . . was another.

His Beard Was Long
And Strong And Tough
He Lost His Chicken
In The Rough
Burma-Shave

. . . was yet another.

That last little ditty had multiple meanings, with slang phrases that were popular at the time. "Chicken" can refer to a girlfriend; "chicken in the rough" means eating fried chicken with your fingers; and of course "the rough" can also mean the longer grass next to the fairway on a golf course (in this case, a metaphor for the man's thick beard).

4

$\mathcal{FUN}$ with Gerda

Following WWII, my mother said that we, being the victors, had to win the peace, even as we had won the war. So she made inquiries with the Red Cross, the Quakers, and other international groups, and we ended up corresponding with the Rollett family in Austria. The father was a chemist, as my father was, and was trying to get a small chemical factory back into production. They had two adult daughters and two boys of grade-school age.

The oldest daughter, Irmgard, nicknamed Gerda, obtained a grant from the US Army, and with us to sponsor her, came to the USA. She was the first student in all of Austria to study outside the country, and had a write-up and her picture in all the papers there. She lived with us for a little more than a year, taking courses at Niagara University.

This was the first of over seventy persons to stay with us in world-famous Niagara Falls. We entertained people, mostly students, from Europe, South America and Asia.

Gerda was a lively girl, never at rest for very long. She came bounding down the stairs one morning, all excited, and announced with great joy that she had dreamed in English!

During the summer, we often went on a sunny Sunday to the beach rather than church. The beaches on the north shore of Lake Erie in Canada were wide and unrestricted. You could drive your car right onto the beach, and the lake bottom was sandy away out, until the water was over your head.

The first time we took Gerda, we were driving on the beach looking for a place to park, when Gerda erupted into laughter.

"What's so funny?" we asked.

She had seen a little girl, probably two or three years old, in a two-piece bathing suit. In Europe, the children under five or six don't wear anything at all on the beaches. She might have thought nothing of a child that age wearing a diaper, but a two-piece bathing suit? Hilarious!

Over the years, our family and the Rolletts maintained contact. Gerda's younger sister Doris ("Dorli"), came to Wellsley College for a year, and

Jane took her junior year of college at the University of Graz in Austria, where the Rolletts lived. Their two sons, Horst and Gunther, have visited; Gerda's daughter, Ruth, has likewise been here; and Ruth Steller, Gerda's best friend, has been here, too. I visited the Rolletts during my 1954 European motorcycle tour, and my son, Alfred, visited them in 1980.

5

$\mathcal{FUN}$ with "The Perfect Squelch"

My parents were brought up knowing what it was to work. They both worked their own way through college. Mom sold farming books to farmers in southern Canada and worked as a maid. Dad was variously a tinker, a shepherd, an ice cream maker, a logger, etc.

So when I wanted some money as a teenager, I was told, "Get a job." I mowed lawns, picked produce (tomatoes were the hardest), tied up grape vines, hoed weeds in an orchard, and pumped gas at Al Marshall's service station.

The first thing I did with all that lucre was to order an English bicycle through the Montgomery Ward catalog. It had skinny tires, hand brakes and a gear shift in the rear hub.

To my knowledge, it was the first such bike in Lewiston. When it arrived, I discovered it was a girl's bike! But I didn't care; I was so delighted with the idea of having a gear shift!

I immediately put it together (the pedals and handlebars needed to be attached) and went for a ride. Since it was a warm summer day, I decided to go for a swim in the Cyanamid Pool. (The Cyanamid chemical factory in Canada was built near a stream, which the company dammed up to form a pool, then built a park around it and made the facilities free to the public.)

To get there, I crossed the Niagara River at Lewiston and went up the hill at Brock's Monument Park to get to the River Road, which goes from beginning to end along the river in Canada. The road up the hill was steep enough so that an ordinary bicycle had to be walked up. About halfway up the hill was a shelter with benches; a group of young people were there, resting before resuming their climb. I passed them triumphantly, sitting down, with my bike in low gear, and they watched me in astonishment. "How can you do that?" they called.

I smugly replied, "I ate my Wheaties this morning!" Once in a while you have the perfect rejoinder!

Later in life, when Maralou and I were building on Bairs Road, my friend Bob Nichols and his wife were visiting, and we were showing them the new house. Some of the lighting fixtures had already been installed, and the one for the study corner in Alfred's room was a ceiling fixture which looked like a huge light bulb. Bob looked at it and said, sort of in awe, "Jesus Christ!"

I replied, "Oh, no, Bob! Jesus is the Light of the World! This only lights up part of one room!" Bob was speechless. Yes, once in a while you do have the perfect rejoinder!

6

$\mathcal{FUN}$ with Dancing (Part 1)

My mother was the "social secretary" in our house, and often selected the entertainment for the family. She came up with the idea in 1945 of square dancing, and talked with her many friends about teaching it to all the children. So we purchased some phonograph records and taught ourselves from them. We had a lot of dance parties, doing the Virginia Reel and basic square-dance patterns. There were also square dances in Lewiston and Youngstown (a village just north of Lewiston) on alternate Saturdays, with bands and a caller.

Once, the Girl Scout troop in LaSalle (a suburb of Niagara Falls) decided to hold a square dance, and every girl had to invite a boy, just so there would be an equal number of each gender. The mothers did most of the asking, as many of the girls were too shy (this was around 1945, and young teens weren't as bold as they are today). Mom got a call—one of the girls was too shy to ask a boy, and I was recruited to fill in for the missing boy. So off I went, danced every dance and had a lot of fun.

When it was time for refreshments, each boy got a lunch box and had to find the girl who had prepared it, to eat with her. When I stepped up to the counter, I was handed a "special" lunch, made up by one of the mothers, because the "missing" boy had finally been asked, so I was now an extra—the odd man out, so to speak. My disappointment was great, but I didn't let anyone know. However, I made sure that when the caller said, "Form your squares" I was the very first one on the floor, with a partner and ready to go! I wasn't going to be the one guy left out; let someone else sit by himself, not me!

I cried bitter tears when I got home, and Mom comforted me. But since then I have always been aware of those who might feel left out, and I have done my best to include them. That is the Christian way, and it's why I like dancing where you change partners. It's also why the Syracuse Outing Club and St. Paul's Young Adults were "my cup of tea," as an English friend of mine used to say.

I mentioned earlier that there were square dances on alternate Saturdays in Lewiston and Youngstown, so the young people were used to this entertainment. One Hallowe'en about 1945, the folks in Lewiston, hoping to prevent the soaping of windows and other pranks, held a community Hallowe'en party, with a local band for dancing. That was fine for the older folks, but the younger ones wanted something more lively, and asked for a square dance. No one had anticipated this, so no caller had been hired.

Teddy to the rescue! I went to the band, asked if they could play "Hot Time in the Old Town Tonight," "Darling Nellie Gray" and "Golden Slippers." They could, so I got behind the microphone and called my first square dance. It wasn't hard; all I had to do was sing square dance calls instead of the original song words, and the patterns were familiar to the people, so it all went very well.

Later, in college, I acquired a sound system and had a collection of lively music and folk dance records, and did quite a bit of square dance calling and teaching.

During our time in high school, Jane and I were introduced to folk dancing by our good friend Julie Heilborn. We danced in the Greystone Ballroom in an old hotel owned by Nan Shipston. She ran a gas station single-handedly, including car repair, but donned a skirt to dance. Frank Giorgi was the instructor. I discovered that teaching my feet to do intricate steps was a lot of fun, and I pursued that form of exercise and entertainment until my legs quit in my old age.

7

ℱ𝒰𝒩 in School

During my junior and senior high school years, there were a few teachers who stood apart from the rest.

Miss Johnson was my homeroom teacher; I also had her for English and Math. As I look back on it, I realize that she must have been frustrated to have such an outspoken student as me in her class. We didn't get along very well, so I went to the principal and asked to change homerooms. "Teddy," she said, "You will be taking a demotion, you know. You are in the 7-A-1 class, and if you go to Miss Malcomb's homeroom, which is the only one available, you will be in the 7-A-3 class." Well, that was OK with me, so I solved part of the problem. I still had Miss Johnson for the same subjects as before, but the pressure was not so great.

In her English class, we were given The Yearling to read. The next day in class she asked how many had started the book. Several hands went up, including mine. She asked how far into the book each had read. One chapter? Two? More? My hand was still up, so she asked how many chapters, and I had to say, "The whole book." That was a shock to her. I had fashioned a flashlight with a battery and a wire, and stayed awake all night, reading beneath the covers!

We had a little set-to in Math, too. The problem given was to draw the dimension for a building lot 40 by 100 feet, and calculate the square footage. I drew the diagram as 100 feet wide and 40 feet deep, and Miss Johnson marked it wrong, saying it should be 40 feet wide and 100 feet deep. I argued that the answer was exactly the same, 4000 square feet, but she wouldn't budge. My parents smiled indulgently and sympathized, but wouldn't try to alter the outcome.

Mrs. Holcomb was the music teacher at North Junior High, and both my sister Jane and I were in the chorus. I was one of many boys who "graduated" from soprano to tenor or bass during my stay at North Junior. Mrs. Holcomb heard something in my voice which I didn't, and had me sing "On The Road To Mandalay" in front of the class. My mother must have heard something in my voice too, because she had me take voice lessons in both high school and college.

The junior high school normally was for grades seven, eight and nine, but in 1946 there were so many pupils that they sent the ninth graders on to the senior high school. My sister was a year ahead of me, so I accompanied her to Niagara Falls High School that year. This was great, because we both tried out for the famed A Cappella Choir and were accepted. Jane sang alto and I sang tenor. The director, **Warren Scotchmer**, was very good at getting the correct sounds out of us.

We sang at various places outside of school, and one was at our church, St. Paul's Methodist, for one of the special mid-week Lenten services. At that time, Catholic students weren't allowed to take part in a Protestant service, so "officially" we "gave a concert" before the service commenced. Those four years of singing without accompaniment trained my ear to hear and blend with the harmonies of other voices; I especially liked to be in vocal harmony with my sister Jane. This experience served me well later in life, when I sang barbershop.

Miss Cox was my tenth grade English teacher. She was not a bad teacher, but she was a busybody. One day she watched me as I cut across the corner behind the bush planted where the walk from the school met the sidewalk; of course, that meant walking on the grass, which was a no-no. She caught me up on that misdemeanor the next day after class, and was quite vociferous about it. That upset me, but as usual I was not intimidated by any teacher. I told her, "I try to be nice to you, but you're not nice to me!" That set her back, and she never gave me grief again.

I was not shy, so getting up in front of people to speak, sing, or act was never a problem. I was also not afraid to talk to those in charge when I had a question or problem. This was great, because my English teacher in 1949, Mr. Fabiano, focused his class on public speaking. There was very little written work, but always oral answers and reports. As usual, we were given a book of poetry to read and report on—orally, of course. While curiously poking around at home, I came across a college notebook of my mother's, with a lot of silly poems inside. So when it was my turn to report on the book given us, I "made history," as it were, to the delight and awe of my classmates. There was only one poem in the assigned book that I thought was any good, and I recited it. But then I told them of the kind of poems that I liked, with rhyme and humor, and recited many of them. Their response was very favorable.

I had checked previously with Mr. Fabiano, and so recited my last poem, fearing no recriminations:

> "So I asked Fabiano, "What do you sell?"
> "Brains," he said, "If I must tell."
> "Well," I said, "You're quite an example ---
> "The first salesman I've seen that didn't carry any sample!"

The class was shocked into silence!! Mr. Fabiano had a good laugh watching the class's reaction. The upshot was that he asked me to be on his weekly radio show—minus that last poem, of course!

Mark R. Bedford was my physics teacher. He spoke with his mouth barely open, and always addressed the students as "Miss" or "Mr." As a singer, I wondered why he hardly opened his mouth, so in my usual forthright way, asked him why. He replied that yes, he didn't open his mouth, but that he spoke very distinctly.

He was also the faculty advisor for the Forensic Society, the public speaking club in school. An audition was required to join; I selected a topic from the list given me, and spoke extemporaneously about that topic after a fifteen-minute study. That experience earned me a pass; when in college, I was exempted from a required public speaking class.

8

$\mathcal{FUN}$ with Dickey

The summer of 1950 found Jane and I working at the same Howard Johnson's restaurant. At eighteen, she was eligible to serve drinks; I was seventeen, and worked behind the counter. I was technically a waiter, so I was eligible to collect tips. Jane, working in the dining room, averaged $5 a night in tips, but I only received a single dime all summer!

Mrs. Waverly was the manager of the Howard Johnson's. Her nephew was the short-order cook, and he was a nice guy, about thirty years old. Her other nephew was fifteen, and a spoiled child. I don't think the two were brothers.

I had some regular customers. One was a nice little old lady from England. We got to talking, and I tested her about her tea. No matter how I prepared it for her, she could tell by the taste exactly how I did it. Did I use a teabag, or loose tea? Did I add hot water to the bag in the cup, or did I add the bag after the water? Was the water boiling, or just hot? Did I warm the cup before preparing the tea or not? She never failed to amaze me.

One evening after work (we closed at 10 p.m.), the chef, dishwasher and short-order cook (Mrs. Waverly's nephew) got hot dogs and potato salad, and asked me to join them for a picnic and swim on the shore of Lake Ontario. We were out at the lake until 1 a.m.! They dropped me off at home, and as I walked up the driveway, I heard voices from the back yard. There were my parents and Jane lying on their backs watching a sky full of Northern Lights.

Nobody at work liked Dickey, the spoiled fifteen-year-old who, in a pinch, would be called in to run the cash register. He was supposed to help me wait on the counter customers, too, but he rarely did.

I have said that at that time I was doing folk dancing, and our friends, the Macdonalds, were having a folk dance party on their lawn. It was a Saturday evening, at the end of summer, and I wanted to be there. I determined my escape from the restaurant: I called to Dickey to "hold the fort" while I went to the rest room. I quickly changed out of my uniform and into my street clothes, then went out the back door and caught the bus, which would take me right to the Macdonalds' driveway. When I went in to collect my final pay, Mrs. Waverly read me the riot act, but I never let that bother me. Dickey got what he deserved, and I had a good time dancing!

In the Niagara Falls area, it was not uncommon to have an ice storm in the winter. Everything would be coated with ice, and the driving was quite tricky. But as young teen-age drivers, we found a new sport with such a situation.

In 1945, the government decided to build a new armaments plant in the area near Lewiston, but the war ended before it was ready to go into production. The building was there—empty—and the parking lot was paved. In 1948 we had a really good ice storm, and that parking lot was like an ice skating rink. We teen-age guys would drive into the ordnance plant parking lot, get our cars up to about 30 mph, hit the brakes hard while swerving sharply left or right, and set the car to spinning round and round. Great fun!

9

FUN in College Classes (Part 1)

It never occurred to either Jane or me not to go on with or education after high school—didn't everybody? My parents both had degrees, and my mother's parents both had degrees. Their Sunday School class membership consisted mostly of chemists, engineers, doctors and other professional people. These were the folks my parents socialized with, and their children were the kids Jane and I socialized with, so didn't everyone go to college? Naturally, yes.

Jane elected to go to the College of Wooster in Wooster, Ohio, a Presbyterian school with very high credentials, to earn a B.A. in humanities, which she used to obtain elementary-grade teaching credentials. She came home after her 1950–51 freshman year full of enthusiasm, and it sounded good to me, so I applied there also and was accepted.

My course of study at college was pre-med, and the world should be very thankful that I never finished that course! I would have been the worst MD ever!

The courses at Wooster those first two years were all general liberal arts, including a history class taught by "Ma" Golder, the dean of women. When a test came up, I didn't have a clue what might be included, and I knew that I didn't have the knowledge required to pass the exam. This was a major test I didn't want to fail, so I decided that I better study something, *anything!* I hit upon the Stuart kings of England, and set about memorizing the succession. I realize now as I write this that it was God who gave me that idea, because the major question on the test was to write a short essay about the Stuart kings! I got a good grade on that test and wound up with a C for the course.

I also had an English class at Wooster with an emphasis on short stories. The final exam consisted of writing a short story and submitting it for a major grade. I didn't know what to do.

I had been reading a magazine called *Fantasy and Sci-Fi*, a monthly paperback printed on sub-standard paper and bound by a stapler, not at all in the same league as more literary books and magazines. (I like to read science fiction, because when you start out with the premise of "what if . . ." there is no limit to what you can write. You can make up any fantastical scenes you want. Nothing has to be based on anything which is normal in the present world.) In every issue, there was always a short short story, just two or three pages. I knew that such a publication was much too far beneath the instructor's standards, and that he would never stoop to reading such "trash."

So I plagiarized! Yes, I copied, word for word, two such short short stories and submitted them.

The teacher loved them! He was very cute about it: he wrote across the top of the paper, "Two short stories. Too short stories." He said if I had written three, I would have earned an A. As it was, he gave me a B+.

10

FUN in the Dorm

One of my two roommates in the freshman dormitory was Chuck Harper. Chuck was the son of missionaries in Sao Paulo, Brazil, and had the ability to swallow air and belch on demand. He used to walk around the room singing a song, and emphasize the beat with belches in the appropriate places.

Gordon French was the other roommate, and he came up with the idea of a "swear bottle," whereby one could drop in a dime and be allowed to utter a curse or an obscene word—all proceeds given to charity, of course. We decided that if someone put in a dollar bill, he could utter an unlimited stream of words. We were, at first, quite popular, with the door suddenly opening, one of the freshmen stepping in, depositing a dime, saying a "bad" word, and leaving. But the novelty soon wore off.

A lot of the students were always looking for a way to earn a few dollars for extra spending money. Many of them really didn't have much loose cash because they were there on scholarships or financed by a church, were children of missionaries, etc. I waited tables in the dining hall. One of the other guys ironed shirts for $0.25 a piece and others would do typing for papers due in class.

One of the more creative money-making characters that populated our freshman dorm was the "Sangee Man" (Sandwich Man). He hit upon the idea of selling sandwiches, which he made in his dorm room, and he got a welcome response from the guys. I often took a laundry basket loaded with ham-and-cheese ($0.50 each) or peanut-butter-and-jelly sandwiches ($0.25) and orange drink ($0.10) to one of the floors while he was on another floor. I took a cut of the proceeds, plus a bonus of left-over sandwiches.

We had picture ID cards at Syracuse, and used them mostly to get into sporting events, but also to gain admission to lectures or entertainment by outside groups. When my picture was taken, no one could recognize me, because the fluorescent lights in the picture booth reflected in my glasses, and it appeared like a huge band-aid was pasted across my eyes. Since my face was unrecognizable, I could "rent" my ID card to someone who might need it to go to a basketball or football game, and so forth, and avoid the admission charge.

Another way to save money was to buy a meal ticket to the cafeteria from one of the football players who was at Syracuse on an athletic scholarship. They always had more meals than they could use, so they sold the remaining punches on the card for half-price. We always found ways to do things cheaper, or earn a few extra dollars, at college.

11

$\mathcal{FUN}$ at the Burl-e-que

There is a subtle difference between the words "smart" and "intelligent." I'm sure you know some people who are very intelligent, but dumb as posts when it come to having "street smarts," which translates to "being aware of what is going on in the real world."

The dean of Wooster College was William Teusch. Very intelligent, but naive about real life. There was "chapel" every Wednesday at Wooster. Not an actual chapel service, as there was on Sundays, but simply a time when all the students could be informed of upcoming events and other pertinent information, plus a short program. It was the Dean's job to read the list of announcements. He was given a handful of 3x5 cards, and if you wanted to be included, you had to see he got your card before the chapel began.

One of the traditions at Wooster was the annual trek by the male student body to Canton, Ohio, to the burlesque show there. Dean Teusch was completely caught off guard when he announced that, "All students of modern dance are urged to attend a recital of modern dance, given in Canton this coming Saturday by Miss R. L. Rose." The titters started in the back of the chapel, and grew in volume until the whole building shook. Dean Teusch was bewildered, and turned to the college president sitting directly behind him and saw that he, too, was doubled up with laughter. "What is so funny?" he asked. "Why, R.L. Rose" was the reply, and even then he had to be told, "It's Rose LaRose, the stripper at the burlesque theater" before he understood that the joke was on him.

I was among that entourage to Canton. The entertainment was continuous, in that the theater was not emptied between the matinee and evening shows. So when the matinee ended, the college men moved down to the front rows. Rose LaRose asked for a volunteer from the audience, and we all pushed the senior class president up onto the stage. She did some funny flirtatious things with him while he got embarrassed, and sent him back to us with a huge red lipstick kiss on his forehead. Back at school, he covered it with transparent scotch tape for a week or more.

12

FUN at Midnight

The Freshman Mixer was an event where you got to know your fellow inductees better. The upperclassmen rousted us out of our beds at midnight and herded us off to the football field where we were "instructed" to do many silly things, really a "hazing" to embarrass us poor freshmen. The freshman girls were subjected to the same sort of experience, administered by the senior women students in another part of the campus. After an hour or so, we were finally ushered into the gymnasium, where the freshman girls were also, and were served refreshments by the football team, who were dressed in weird costumes. There were no chairs, so we had to sit on the floor, but there was also recorded music and dancing. We were not allowed to dance with the same girl twice, so we did "mix."

We were obliged to wear our "beanies" at all times. The beanie was a small cap with an almost non-existent bill, in bright yellow with a black "W" stitched to the crown—the school colors were yellow and black—and since they all were the same, we were advised to identify our caps with our names on the liner.

At Wooster, I went out for football my freshmen year. But I had a major drawback because my head was too big. Wooster didn't have a helmet that fit me. (I remember when I was ten, my mother took me to Amberg's in Niagara Falls for an Easter outfit, including a hat. The salesman measured my head and came out of the storeroom with a man's fedora, which certainly wasn't appropriate for a ten-year-old! My size was 7-1/8 long oval, and children's hats didn't come in that large a size.)

There was one other student on the team, first string, who also had a large head, but he brought his own helmet that he had used in high school. So any time I was put in scrimmage, he had to lend me his helmet, and he was not happy about that. Since I had no prior experience, there was a lot to learn. I never played in an actual game; the coach said that if I so desired I could suit up and remain on the bench, but I declined.

13

NOT *FUN* with Fraternities

There were no national fraternities or sororities at Wooster, but there were "sections," which had Greek letters and acted like the nationals. The dormitory for the freshmen was a long building three stories high, with each floor divided into sections separated by fire walls, for safety, with a center section, and then a wing on either side consisting of two sections. The dormitory for the upperclassmen was similar, but larger and with three sections in each wing. The center section of each building housed a lounge and the living quarters for the faculty resident and his family on the ground floor, with dormitories on the floors above. So there were seven "section" fraternities for the men, and due to the large number of students who attended Wooster, two more sections were added in individual houses.

During the first semester of our freshman year, we were all invited to "smokers," which were entertainments to induce us into wanting to join a particular section, and cigarette samples were given out (the dangers of cigarettes were not widely recognized in the 1950s). Then, during the first week of the second semester, ballots were distributed where we could indicate our first, second and third choices of the section we desired to join. During the second week, those who were voted in by the members of each section were notified, and a two-week hazing commenced, after which the new members were deemed to be full members.

I don't know the particulars about the sororities, because Jane never desired to join one, but I can tell you about one of the stunts they had the girl inductees do. Outside the chapel on campus there was a large rock, about ten feet wide, and as high. The girls were given a burlap feed sack to wear as a dress and had to climb onto the rock and sing silly songs. Bear in mind that this was the '50s, and mini-skirts were not in style. The feed sacks barely came to mid-thigh, so a great deal of embarrassment was evident.

The men were never so embarrassed—all they were required to do was to line the crotch of their pants with thumb tacks with the points protruding outward through the fabric so as to be visible!

34

That second week, when we were seeing if we had been accepted by one of the sections, was a nervous one, and I was just as nervous as anyone. But I ended up crying on my bed because I didn't get a bid. I had no idea that someone in each section I picked didn't want me and had voted "no" (the voting had to be unanimous).

So when I returned the next year, I found myself in Behoteguy House, where those who had not been chosen lived. That first week of the second school year proceeded like the first week of the second semester of the previous year, and again I was passed over. I stayed the course, bitterly disappointed, but I resolved to transfer away from Wooster for my next two years.

Why was I rejected? Well, maybe I was a bit out of the norm in some regards. I tried to get some of the students interested in folk dancing, and hosted a session every Saturday night for a while, but that was a flop. I was on the campus radio station for a while, with recordings of classical music, but my style of introducing the music was not well received and someone else took over. Also, I was the only one on campus with a bicycle; I took my English bike with me and rode it everywhere. Everyone else walked, so maybe they thought I was making a spectacle of myself. I don't know.

But I did have friends, and that sustained me. That group—we were eight in number—stayed together even after leaving Wooster. In the summer of 1952 six of us took a week-long bicycle hike in Vermont. Let's see if I can remember their names. Virginia Martin ("Ginny"), Mary Lee George, Mary Lou Cramer, John Cato, and . . . ? We had a marvelous time, and spent two days atop a small mountain in a log cabin. The owner raised goats, and delivered a quantity of fresh goat milk to us every day.

14

$\mathcal{FUN}$ with the Girls (Part 1)

In the summer in 1951, I was attracted to a young lady at church who I hadn't seen there before. I found out she was the daughter of the bass soloist in our choir, home from school. Her name was Laura Turner, and she was beautiful. So I asked her out, and took her to dinner in Buffalo. We had a good time, and I found out she was a dancer, attending a ballet school in New York City.

We were on our way home on the parkway along the upper Niagara River, still in Erie County, when I got pulled over for speeding. I was only a little over the limit, and not really paying attention to my speed (after all, I had my arm around a very attractive girl!). The officer said that since I was not in Niagara County, I would have to accompany him to the station. Then, because I didn't enough money to pay bail, they put me in a jail cell. First, however, they took. away my belt and my necktie "so you can't hang yourself." (For speeding?) But they did let me make one phone call.

Here it was, almost midnight, and I got my mother out of bed. She, in her wisdom, had some "mad money" stashed away, in the form of travelers checks. She found someone who would cash them for her, then made the long trip to the police station in Buffalo to bail me out.

You know your mother loves you when she is willing to go to all that trouble and drive all that way just to save your butt! Lewiston is seven miles from Niagara Falls, and Buffalo is another 30 miles, and it's after midnight, and not many businesses are open, and getting woken up from a sound sleep is not good—but it's your son, and you love him, so you do it.

Poor Laura! She just sat there in the police station until Mom arrived. Mom offered to drive her home, but Laura said no, she'd wait for me. Here again is an example of a person's integrity and trust. I got her home about two a.m. My mother asked Mrs. Turner if she had been worried when Laura didn't get home at a decent hour and Mrs. Turner said, "Oh, no. We knew she was with Ted." Wow!

So I had a date with a traffic judge in Buffalo. Just to insure that I would have a way home if he suspended my license, I asked Hal Babb, our assistant minister, to accompany me. We took some money along, not knowing how much the fine would be, but the arresting officer had said probably fifty dollars. I was fined $100, and my bail money was returned in the form of a check. We didn't have $100 cash with us, and they refused to take a check, even though the check was theirs! We went back and forth with this and finally got the bail returned as cash, so we could pay the fine.

I had one more date with Laura, at Prudhommes, a resort in Vineland, Ontario. They had a golf course, riding trails, a sand beach, and a hotel with all the usual ritzy amenities. They also had a ballroom with an orchestra, open to the public every Saturday night, with a midnight lunch included in the price. I said Laura was a dancer, and she was; I thought I was pretty good at making up steps as we danced, but with everything I threw into the mix, she never missed a beat, never stumbled but followed my lead perfectly. In the course of the evening, she kept adjusting her strapless gown, tugging it up a half-inch, and it would go down again. I finally told her, "Laura, you have a beautiful figure, and there is absolutely no way for that gown to fall down, so don't worry about it." That put her mind at ease, I guess, because she didn't tug the rest of the evening.

That evening I discovered that her school in New York wasn't a college, but a high school which was also a ballet school, and that Laura was only 15! I was very surprised, to say the least, but she talked so intelligently that I had no idea. She returned to school right after that date, and I never saw her again. I did ask about her a few years later, and learned from her mother that she had to quit dancing because of a leg injury that was not repairable enough for ballet.

15

FUN with the Girls (Parts 2 & 3)

Like all college students at a co-ed institution, we had dates for dances, walks, etc. One of the more frequent and casual dates at Wooster was a "lib date," which consisted of a study time at the library followed by refreshments, usually at the Student Union (the place for cokes, sodas, snacks and talk on the campus).

Mary Lou Logee was frequently my selection for such a date. As we studied, I would often just turn my head and look at her. At age 19, with a good figure and often wearing a sweater which showed it, she really caught my attention. She would feel my eyes upon her, and turn to say, "You're supposed to be studying," to which I would reply, "I am," with a wink. She would blush a little, and smile.

Sometime in 1956, I came home late from work to find a note that said to join Mom and Dad at the Buffalo Folk Dancers dance, and they gave me the address to find them. When I arrived, Mom told me to break into the line of a line dance they were doing, "right next to that little lady there," so I did, and that lady showed me the steps. I was concentrating on the dance, and didn't notice who was dancing with me on the other side. Imagine my surprise when it turned out to be Mary Lou! She was living and working in Hamburg, NY, about 15 miles southeast of Buffalo. We had a good talk, and agreed to dance again the following week. Well, I was there, but she didn't show up. The next day I called her. She was put out because she thought I was going to pick her up, and I thought that she was going to meet me there. So to her mind I had "stood her up," and that was the end of that.

Another of my dates at Wooster was one with Heather Munson. She was petite, red hair and freckles, a nice-looking gal, but nothing special. But she appealed to me, and I asked her for a date to one of the more formal dances on campus. I went to her dorm, with a corsage, and all, and didn't recognize the simply beautiful girl descending the stairs.

The girls in her dorm had done a make-over on her, and the result was nothing short of miraculous! That evening many of the boys said, "I thought you were bringing Heather. Who is that girl?"

"That is Heather," I replied, and they couldn't believe it.

That romance was just a friendly one, however, and I left it behind when I transferred to Syracuse. I later read in the Alumni News that she married John Eby, one of my freshman buddies, who thought it was cute to wear two different cuff links that spelled out his name: "E" and "B."

Once during the winter of 1951, I went tobogganing with some others down a hill near Wooster. I had a brand new pair of blue jeans, never washed, and wore them for this fun time. We were headed down the slope and straight for a drop-off into a creek, and couldn't steer away from it. I was the rear-most person on the toboggan, so I slipped off the end and dragged my posterior through the snow to slow us down.

Well, it worked, and we stopped just short of the drop-off. But we had a good laugh, because the dye in my pants ran, as I put on the brakes, and looking back we could see a long blue groove down the hill!

16

FUN with Music

I took voice lessons while at Wooster, and my instructor, Karl Trump, was also the director of the men's glee club. I sang tenor. We went on a tour in 1952 during spring break, giving concerts in Presbyterian churches practically every evening. We were housed in the homes of the parishioners, for the most part.

But one time we had to stay in a hotel. It was not a modern one, but what do you expect in a small town in 1952? The bathrooms on our floor were situated on either side of the main staircase. We had with us a female soloist; she made a wrong turn early in the morning and ended up taking a shower in the men's bathroom. The men discovered this and formed a double line from the men's bathroom to the women's bathroom and then got the chaperone (yes, we had one of those!) to roust our soloist out. We applauded her as she walked the gauntlet from one bath to the other. She was very blonde, and very red.

At one church, there was a grand piano on the raised portion at the front of the nave, where we would have to stand to perform. It needed to be moved over a short railing and down about two feet to a position on the floor of the sanctuary. How to get it there? We all lined up, on both sides of the piano, standing as close as we possibly could one behind the other, and put out our hands beneath the piano and lifted. With ease, we raised the piano high enough to clear the railing, then shuffled forward, in step, and slowly approached the edge. Then by twos as we could shuffle no further, the lead men went down to the lower level and extended their hands higher to accept the load. Thus repeated, the piano was lowered to the floor. Then when the concert was over, we reversed the method and restored the instrument to its original place.

Our tour took us a bit south, into Tennessee and Kentucky. At one place we were hosted by church members who had very young children, so they had hired a girl to babysit while they attended the concert. We asked her to say something with a real southern accent, and she blushed and said, "Oh, Ah cain't when Ah try," with an accent so broad you could walk on it!

In 1999 I traveled to Bellingham, WA, to visit my 99-year-old father on his birthday (Hallowe'en!). While there, the whole family attended a concert by the Bellingham Symphony. The featured work was Mozart's Concerto in C Major for Flute and Harp.

The harpist was a very ordinary-looking woman, who played her instrument well. But the flutist was a statuesque woman with a fantastic figure, wearing a form-fitting gown that elicited some gasps from the audience. But when she started to play, all thoughts on her appearance faded because the performance was so excellent.

The applause was unceasing. The artists came back for four curtain calls, and were not let go until the last movement of the concerto was repeated. What fantastic music, played to perfection!

17

FUN in the Kitchen

I waited tables at Wooster during my sophomore year to earn a little extra spending money. I would come to the men's dining hall early to set up my station, which consisted of two tables seating six each, with a serving table against the wall between them. Every place got two 8-ounce bottles of milk, silverware, and a salad. The milk was in glass bottles with a cardboard lid which extended over the edges of the mouth, so as to be clean if the drinker wanted to drink directly from the bottle. This wasn't allowed, of course, so each place setting also included two straws, packed double in a paper cover.

After the first seating, speed was of the essence to get my station cleaned up, dirty place settings and serving dishes removed, and the tables set for the second wave of diners. To do this, the waiters all would get a large oval tray and ring it with 24 bottles of milk and fill the space in the center with silverware, napkins and straws. Then a second tray was on top of that, containing 12 salads. The tops of the milk bottles were covered, as stated, and provided a some-what non-slip surface for the second tray. This double arrangement was kept in the cooler for quick access. As you may imagine, there was a real hustle and bustle through the kitchen in the interim between the first and second seating.

So here I came with my second setup, rounding a corner in the kitchen, and I slipped. There was some spilled water on the tile floor and my feet slid to the left while my double tray went to the right, and there was a terrible mess! Crockery, salads, milk, broken bottles and silverware falling into kitchen equipment and prepared food, all over the floor, and other waiters running an obstacle course to get their own stations set up.

Occasionally, a waiter would catch the kitchen door the wrong way or stumble for some other reason, while on his way out with a tray full of dirty dishes, and create a loud crash. Then all the remaining diners in the hall would stand up and cheer and clap, so the object of their jeering would have his moment of fame. But not so with me—no crash was heard in the dining room, so no cheers or applause. Alas, poor me!

The straws were in a paper wrapper, as I said above, and played a vital role in the traditions of Wooster. Every meal was a chance to see if you could stick your wrapper to the high ceiling. The wrapper was carefully torn at the end so that the naked straws were revealed, then the other closed end was dipped lightly into the gravy or other liquid and the resulting slightly soggy missile was shot up to the ceiling by a good puff of air. If successful, the wrapper would stick up there. The ceiling, by the end of the first semester, was festooned with thousands of paper straw wrappers. Then a scaffolding was erected in the dining hall, and all the pledges for the fraternities were required to climb up, lay on their backs and scrape the ceiling so it could be painted. A weird tradition, indeed!

18

FUN on Two Wheels

The purchase of a motorcycle was Mom's idea. Like so many of her ideas, I tried it, and found out I liked it. So we answered an ad in the newspaper, and asked Chucky Boos, a neighbor whose whole family rode, to come with us to evaluate it. He considered it a good deal, so we bought it. It was an Indian Scout, a US Army bike, with a gear shift lever about 30 inches long extending up from the engine. It had to be operated by hand, so only one hand was on the handlebars during that short time. It was dubbed the "suicide shift" by the Army. I was driving my motorcycle that summer of 1952, on my way to rendezvous with my Wooster friends in New England. I was still in New York state when all of a sudden the motor seized up. When I had last added oil to the crankcase, the plug had not been tightened securely, and the oil leaked out. Well, I was not going to let this stop me from meeting my friends, so I walked the bike to a nearby farm and asked the people there if I could leave my cycle there and I would return for it later. They said yes, we found a good out-of-the-way spot, parked it and I hitch-hiked on to Vermont. When the bike hike was over, I got a ride with Ginny Martin back to her home near Rochester, NY and Dad picked me up there.

I must say that my folks were generous, to bail me out after my dereliction of duty vis-a-vis the oil plug, but they did, sending the motorcycle repair guy out to the farm to rescue the motorcycle and then having it repaired.

It was 1953 at Syracuse University. I was there for summer school, and I was running around on my trusty WWII Indian Scout motorcycle. I had a spiffy light gray jacket to wear on cool days, and was wearing it the day I took one of my coed classmates for a ride.

We were tooling along a country road, when a groundhog decided to cross in front of us. I stomped on the brakes, and the girl riding behind me was thrown into my back. Now, the fashion then for women was to wear heavily applied lipstick, and my beautiful gray jacket was emblazoned with large red lips. I never washed that jacket!

In 1953, I rode the motorcycle home from Syracuse for Thanksgiving. It was a brisk day, so I bundled up in my warmest winter coat and my blue nylon ski parka. Stocking cap and gloves too, of course. I also had goggles to keep the wind from my eyes—I didn't have a windscreen.

In Rochester, at a traffic circle, I took a wrong turn and wound up on Rt. 104 East instead of Rt. 104 West, and went 30 miles before discovering I was headed in the wrong direction. So I turned around and drove back, all the while getting colder and colder. I was chilled to the bone, and stopped as often as I could to get some hot tea to warm me. Our house in Lewiston was on Ridge Road, which is 104, so I didn't get my directions mixed up again, but I was freezing to death! When I finally did turn into our driveway, I was so-o-o-o cold! Mom welcomed me home with a big bowl of oyster stew (basically a hot milk soup with oysters in it) and I never tasted anything so-o-o-o delicious!

During the winter of 1953 at Syracuse I lived in a rented room and the landlord gave me permission to use his garage. I took the bike all apart with the intention of painting the frame, but it never got done, and I finally sold it to the motorcycle repairman while still apart in bushel baskets!

19

$\mathcal{FUN}$ Outdoors

I transferred from Wooster College to Syracuse University. I was not accepted into a fraternity at Wooster, but at Syracuse I found the Outing Club, which only required a person to sign up. They did all sorts of outdoor recreation, and also did Folk Dancing! I was in my element, and enthusiastically jumped in with both feet. But when I arrived at one meeting, I overheard someone say, "Speak of the devil" in a less-than-enthusiastic voice, and wondered about that. Afterward, a friend took me aside and said they all were glad I liked the Outing Club, but to tone it down—I was too "gung-ho." So I calmed down, and everything was OK after that.

The Outing Club was a part of the Intercollegiate Outing Club Association, which had branches in many colleges and universities. Every year there was an intercollegiate weekend gathering of many of the clubs in the early fall on a island in Lake George, NY, and Syracuse was there with a busload of campers in 1952. It was great fun meeting the students from Cornell, Ithaca College, Yale, Wellesley and other schools.

The Syracuse people who planned our menu had everything done right, and included a large can of apple jelly for making peanut butter and jelly sandwiches on the tasty Old-World Bakery pumpernickel bread which we always used for our trips. But when the can was opened, we discovered "Mint Flavored" in small letters!

The planned activities included competitions such as fire-lighting and log-splitting, etc. Each club had a team, and the winning club received the "Raunch Trophy," which was handed down from the previous year's winner. What was the trophy? One-half of a fur-covered toilet seat!

There was an electric generator, and they strung up lights to have a square dance. But the generator couldn't support much more than the lights and a sound system, and the record player played so slow that we couldn't dance. Someone recalled that I played the harmonica, so I was recruited to supply the music. It was a plastic mouth organ and took a lot of wind, but I accomplished it and played into the microphone all evening, twenty minutes at a time. Puff! Puff! I felt like I had run a marathon.

On the way home we stopped for gas and piled out of the bus to stretch our legs. Someone suggested we do a hora (Israeli line dance); I was the designated musician, and we danced all around the gas pumps, to the amusement of several onlookers.

20

FUN in the Snow

The Outing Club also went mountain climbing in the winter, and the Adirondacks were the mountains of choice because of their proximity. I went on a climb up Mt. Marcy my first time. The club had a lot of gear, much of it US Army surplus, and among the stuff were several pairs of "shoe-pacs," which were leather boots with rubberized exteriors to make them absolutely waterproof. But there were none in my size, so I went to town and bought a pair of five-buckle rubber overshoes. When I wore my regular shoes encased in a pair of long woolen socks that came a good way up my leg, and added the galoshes, I was set for deep snow. How deep? A hike up that same trail earlier in the fall showed red trail markers nailed to the trees fifteen feet over our heads! We used snowshoes, of course.

One of our members who lived in town wanted to go on that winter climb, but her mother wouldn't permit it. She had heard that the guys and girls slept in the same lean-to (I don't believe she knew what a lean-to was). Good heavens! That would never do! When it's twenty below zero, nobody goes traipsing around in their underwear! Most of us—no, all of us—got into our sleeping bags fully clothed except for our very bulky outer jackets, and undressed inside the bag, if indeed we did.

Here's where my overshoes idea turned out to be good thinking. Everyone else took off their boots before getting into bed, and had to stow them in the rafters of the lean-to, along with the axes and snowshoes. (Otherwise, a wandering porcupine might gnaw on them, because of the oils on the leather and ax handles.) Then in the morning, they had to wear stiff, ice-cold shoes. But I could take my regular shoes inside my bag with me and have nice warm feet first thing in the morning. Other things that were a must to take into the sleeping bag were dishwashing liquid, bread and packaged food like cheese, ham, peanut butter and jam; these would be frozen solid if not "cuddled." But as necessary as that was, we forgot to "cuddle" the bread, and wound up with no way to make sandwiches for the trail. What to do? One of the climbers, who was a camping veteran, had a folding bow saw in his pack. He assembled it, and we sawed off slices of

48

bread! All fine and good, but the sandwiches were carried in a knapsack, which was not next to someone's body, so when we stopped for lunch, we had frozen sandwiches! We had to gnaw at them. My teeth hurt for days afterwards.

For Easter vacation, we climbed Mount Katahdin in Maine. It is about as high as Mount Marcy, but the trail is not as steep. With Marcy, we used ice axes and crampons, but with Katahdin we did a fair amount of climbing without snowshoes. We were six in number, myself, Dave Raney, Stella Roberts, Joanne Sedgewick and her fiancé, and "Ma" Sedgewick, our chaperone. What impressed me about this trip was the Easter dinner we had, prepared on an open campfire. "Ma," Joanne and Stella really knew how to do it. We had hot ham slices, scalloped potatoes and (get this!) pineapple upside-down cake, all prepared on an open fire!

Back at the campus, one of our members who also did rock climbing gave us a rappelling demonstration. There are no high cliffs near the Syracuse campus, and we would never be allowed to rappel down the side of one of the buildings. So we assembled in the science building, which had four floors and a basement, and a center stairwell for that full height. We took our places on the stairs, where we could watch and listen as he explained how the ropes and slings worked, then watched him rappel himself down the open stairwell.

I ate many of my meals in the cafeteria, often with other members of the Outing Club. At the entrance to the cafeteria, lay a large old dog, almost like a door mat. We had to step over or around him, and nothing seemed to bother him at all. He would move if nudged hard enough, then lay back down in a different place, but still in the doorway. All snacks cheerfully received, though. Another couple of pooches would eat with us at the table. We soon had them trained to sit quietly on a chair, with no paws on the table and a napkin tucked into their collars, and daintily eat from a plate whatever we put there.

My stay at Syracuse initiated me to some innovative ways of doing things, not only personally, but corporately as well. The city of Syracuse was, like Rome, built on seven hills. The driving in the winter can be treacherous, so snow removal is very important. The method used was new to me. The cars are all parked on the even-numbered side of the street, leaving the other side empty, and the plows come through at night and plow clear down to the curb on that side. The next day the cars are parked on the odd-numbered side, and the process is repeated. Very efficient! Cars parked on the wrong side are ticketed.

Also, when there is an emergency and the first responders must get through downtown traffic in a hurry, the traffic signal lights go to red in all directions so all traffic comes to a halt, and the ambulances, fire trucks, etc. can weave their way through quickly and safely. A center reserved traffic lane is added on the wider streets, too.

21

FUN with Honor

To earn some money and a free lunch and dinner, I worked as a waiter at a fraternity, the Nova Club. It was waiting for its charter from the national fraternity, Zeta Beta Tau, an all-Jewish fraternity. I got the job because I had classes with some of the members. I wasn't the only one in the kitchen; there was also an exchange student from Israel, and the cook, Nettie, who was illiterate but had hundreds of recipes in her head. It was there that I learned to dislike catsup. The men would put that stuff on everything, I even watched in horror as they put it on cherry pie!

But the guys liked me so well that they wanted me to become a member. I would have been the only Christian nationwide in that Jewish fraternity! Wow! What an honor! Take that, you snarky Sections at Wooster!

One other time I felt very honored was when I was home for the summer from college in 1952. The Holy Name Society at the only Catholic church in Niagara Falls which still held masses in the native tongue of the parishioners (Polish), wanted someone to teach their grandchildren a native Polish dance. I knew how to do the Krakowiak ("Dance of Krakow"), and I had the record and a record player.

The children, in the twelve to fourteen age range, didn't want to learn the dance, but their grandmothers were not to be denied! (The Krakowiak is a courtship dance, and the kids were all giggly about that.) So we practiced, their mothers made costumes (native Polish clothing is very colorful), and the kids performed beautifully. Just think—Ted Budrow, an American Protestant, teaching some Polish Catholics a dance from "the old country." Quite an honor!

22

$\mathcal{FUN}$ in College Classes (Part 2)

My most non-attended class at Syracuse was taxidermy. I was the only one signed up, and the instructor had to go out and shoot the animal to be stuffed. He didn't get around to it for quite a while so for several weeks there was no class. When he did shoot a specimen, it was a crow, and during molting season, so my bird was nearly naked because all the feathers were falling out. He also shot a squirrel, and when I finished stuffing it, it looked almost like a ferret—so long and skinny! But he gave me a B, anyway.

I went to my class in genetics early to be the first in the door, so I could sign the attendance sheet and leave before the professor came into the room. Somehow, there was no challenge with this course. I would learn which chapters in the text were going to be tested, read them once, and always got an A.

I had a class in organic chemistry with 200 students in it, and the seating for the lecture portion of the course was unusual—an amphitheater arrangement. The professor was on the stage, with a three-panel blackboard which was assembled like a double-hung window. The boards were twelve feet long and four feet high, and when the first one was filled with his "chalk talk," he would pull down another one and keep going. Half-way up the center aisle of the tiered seating was a stair which opened up to reveal a slide projector. This was manned by a graduate student, who manipulated it to project on a screen over the professor's head the exact things the prof was writing on the board.

The text we followed was not a bound book, but a spiral-bound syllabus the professor had written himself. The syllabus was printed on only one side of each page and, it also contained the exact information as on the slides and on the board. So when opened, the lecture was on the right with a blank page on the left for the student to write his/her own notes. A very efficient method of lecturing on a subject which was not subject to change.

The other half of the course was in the lab, where we did the actual experiments. The professor was a lover of classical music, and played records throughout the sessions. That was the first semester, and I got a B.

The second semester I found that I could take the course in night school, which I resolved to do since my days were already pretty full. Off to the side of the lab were some classrooms. They were about fifteen feet wide and forty feet long, with a blackboard running the full length of the room, and three tiers of benches facing the blackboard. The professor would come in, start on the left, and "chalk-talk" his way to the other end of the board. That was all there was to the lecture, and again, the syllabus was identical. The lab session followed immediately after, with a graduate student available to explain whatever you needed to know about the lecture. I always paid strict attention to the lecture and the explanations.

At the first lab session, I checked out all my equipment, then left. At the last lab session, I checked in all my pristine and unused equipment, and left. I never did even one experiment! I understood the lectures completely, and aced every test with a 95 or better, so I got an A for lecture and an F for lab, and ended up with a C. (I had much better things to do in the evenings than bum around in a lab—Outing Club things! Dating things! Fun things!)

Comparative Anatomy was a fun class—we got to dissect a cat. (Doesn't that sound nice?) The animals had been injected with dyes, so the arteries were red and the veins blue, which was a help. We were also given a box of bones to study, and we had to memorize the names of each one. Can't get to sleep? Just reach over and run your fingers over the identifying ridges and shapes of your bones and repeat the name of each one. It's better than counting sheep—hah!

Some of us had male cats and some had females. Among other parts of our specimen, we had to dissect the reproductive system. Now, there are times in any group of people, who are talking only occasionally to one another, when a moment of complete silence occurs. During one such moment, one of the girls asked the boy next to her, "Bob, can you show me your gonads?"

I had the same professor for three classes: Comparative Anatomy, History of Communicable Disease, and General Physiology. I failed that last one—the course involved calculus, and I had never studied that subject.

But the professor was a fun-loving guy, and in the midst of projecting slides of human tissue for us to identify, he inserted one of his daughter as an naked infant. (She was in the class, and what a shriek she let out!)

He might also impose a task on the persons who gave wrong answers, such as, "All right, you bring the napkins," or "All right, you bring the soda," etc., and we knew that the next class session would be a party.

After failing General Physiology, I took a different class the following semester: Human Physiology. It was a nursing course, and much easier—no math! In lab, one of the experiments was to stand on one leg with your other foot propped against your calf with your eyes closed, to see how long it took before you had to lower your foot to maintain your balance. For most of us, it was only a matter of seconds, but two guys in the class were gymnasts, and they could keep that pose for hours, if need be.

When I went to summer school in 1953, I took a course in physics. The class was lecture in the morning, and lab right after lunch. The first day, at the suggestion of the instructor, the class decided to start earlier, have lecture and lab together, and still have time to get to the cafeteria before it closed. That left us with the whole afternoon free.

To facilitate this, the instructor, who had a small farm nearby, would bring in fresh cream from that morning's milking (he had just one cow) for a coffee break between lecture and lab. Up to this time, I had always preferred tea, but one sip of properly sweetened coffee, with cream so rich and fresh that you could stand up a spoon in it, and I was hooked! I've preferred coffee ever since.

For the required gym credit at Syracuse, I elected handball. We played inside a box, really. The court was a room about twenty feet in every direction, and other than one line which marked the edge of the opening serve, there were no boundaries. Play could be made off any surface, including the ceiling. It was a fast-paced game—and a painful one, if the ball hit you! Its cousin is squash, which is the same thing only with a short-handled racket—which means the ball is traveling much faster when it collides with your body!

Syracuse University also had a ski school that qualified as a gym class, and as a credit course for athletic majors. The Outing Club sponsored a Hallowe'en maze at the ski lodge in the fall of 1953. It proved to very popular, but at first they were stumped when it came to finding the right kind of music to pipe through the blacked-out maze to give a feeling of ghoulishness to the participants.

Again, Ted to the rescue! I had a 78-rpm recording of a Jewish dance, played by a klezmer (Jewish folk music) band with wheedling clarinets. We played it at 27 rpm, and it really did the trick. People came out of the maze asking, "Where did you get that awful, frightening music?"

23

$\mathcal{FUN}$ in a Canoe (Part 1)

I rented a room in the summer of 1953 from Toni Spano—well, really from her uncle, Alvin Soule. (Toni lived with the Soules; they were her guardians, since both her parents were deceased.) She invited me to go on a weekend canoe trip with her and some others, and I of course replied affirmatively. Imagine my surprise to find myself the lone boy among five girls!

I can't recall all their names, but I can describe them. Toni, like me, was an experienced canoeist and camper and knew how to swim. One girl, a blonde, could handle a canoe and swim, but had never been camping. Another girl had camped a few times and knew how to swim, but had never paddled a canoe. The other two were completely new to everything—but only one of them could swim!

We went up to Tupper Lake in the Adirondacks in Toni's old car, packed in like sardines, three in the front seat and three in the back. There wasn't enough room in the trunk for all the food, etc., as well as six sleeping bags, so we unrolled the bags, laid them out on the back seat, and sat on them. We left as early as we could on Friday, after summer school classes, and arrived that afternoon at the canoe rental. Three canoes were used, with Toni, myself, and the blonde paddling in the rear where we could steer, and the other three up front to do the grunt-work paddling.

The day was beautiful, with the breeze light and in the right direction, so it did not affect the steering of the canoes. We traveled along the shore for about a mile, to an inlet off to the right, then another half mile or so to its end, where we were greeted by a small sandy beach and a lean-to. (The Adirondack Mountain Club, an all-volunteer group, maintained about a hundred lean-tos throughout the Adirondacks, free to anyone to use while camping.)

We unloaded, got a fire started, and began to think about supper. But before that, Toni said, "Ted, why don't you show these girls how to dig a latrine (toilet)?" She was grinning from ear to ear, and the girls were embarrassed, but I was eager to demonstrate. So I led them into the woods a ways and showed them just how to dig, how to assume the position so that you didn't fall, and explained the hygiene involved to leave the woods as clean when we left it as when we got here. Four giggling, embarrassed girls became critically informed. Yes, it isn't something to brag about, but it's a camping necessity.

We had supper, talked around the campfire, ate some toasted marshmallows, and so forth, and I asked Toni if she would like a back rub.

"Sure," she said. She prepared to lay face-down on her sleeping bag. But first, to the horror of the other girls, she unbuttoned her shirt. Then she lay prone and folded her hands beneath her head. Kneeling behind her, I placed my hands on her back beneath her shirt and undid her bra. More gasps from the assembled crowd! I massaged Toni's shoulders and lower back, then refastened her bra, and she sat up to button her shirt. I offered to rub some more backs, but the rest of the girls were too squeamish and shy.

Saturday was a fun day, and we spent most of it clad in swimsuits. How to change, and where, so no one sees you? Toni led the girls behind the lean-to, with the promise that I would do my changing inside. So I got into my suit in record time, and quickly found a crack in the back wall to watch. I'm sure Toni knew I would do this, but she didn't say a word!

The water in our little pond was warm, not too deep, and afforded ample room for canoe jousting and swimming. We noticed that some other folks were camped at the end of our inlet, where it joined the lake. So we went to introduce ourselves, and found a Boy Scout Explorer Post. There were about a dozen boys, housed in tents. We chatted with them for a while before retiring to our little oasis, s'mores and sleep.

The next day was Sunday, and we had to get back to Syracuse. So after a leisurely breakfast, we did a final cleanup of our area, then packed up to go. We got as far as the lake, to find the Scouts all gone and a brisk wind on the lake. Now, when I said that three of the girls had never paddled a canoe, I didn't mean they were incompetent. Two of those girls were in pretty good physical shape, but the gal who was in the bow of my canoe was a marshmallow. She sure looked good in a swimsuit, but I don't think she had ever really used any of her muscles.

The wind was directly against us as we retraced our way up the shoreline towards the canoe rental, and it was tough keeping the canoe headed into the wind to avoid the waves hitting us broadside and swamping us. The girls in the bow of the other canoes paddled strongly and helped to keep their canoes in line, and they made it to the dock okay, without too much trouble. But the girl in the bow of my canoe, being the only one of our group who couldn't swim, was scared to death. I hollered to her to paddle on the side to keep the bow of the canoe forward, and then on the other side when necessary. She switched as I told her, but had a hard time of it when she had to do it left-handed.

She had never worked so hard in her life, and when we did finally make it back to the dock she was literally exhausted! She crawled onto the dock and immediately fell asleep. We took care of packing the car and paid the rental fees—and she still lay there, completely out. We lifted her into the car and propped her up against the window, and she slept the entire way home.

24

$\mathcal{FUN}$ in a Canoe (Part 2)

Valerie Smith was a 1952 freshman at Syracuse, and a trifle crazy. I met her at one of the Outing Club square dances, and dated her a few times. She was always interesting, but there was no real romance in sight. I remember walking with her in the winter, and we passed a house with a small but pristine front yard where the snow had not been disturbed. She suddenly hopped over the short hedge which separated the yard from the sidewalk, stomped "s--t" in the snow, hopped back, and ran down the sidewalk, all giggles.

That summer of 1953, Valerie called me. She wasn't coming back to Syracuse, but one thing she had always wanted to do, and never got the chance, was to go on a canoe trip. She had heard the others in the Outing Club talk about it, and it sounded like a lot of fun, but since she lived in New York City, she figured she would never get to go on one.

So she was planning a last-ditch effort. If she took the bus to Raquette Lake (in the Adirondacks), could I get some people together and meet her there for a canoe trip on Labor Day weekend? "Sure," I said, and got Edmund Moser, a German exchange student, to go with me. Jean Boutillier, one of the folk dancers who lived in town, asked if she could come, too.

I didn't have a car, so the three of us took the bus to the city limits and hitch-hiked to Raquette Lake. We arrived in a light drizzle, and slept under some trees with a tarp across our three sleeping bags. The next morning dawned bright, but became overcast by the time Valerie's bus arrived from NYC.

Valerie brought a friend, Michelle, with her, so we were five instead of four. Still, we made do with two canoes. Ed and I were in the stern, Val and Michelle were in the bow, and Jean was just a passenger.

We started out, following a topographical map published by the state forestry service which showed a stream emptying into the lake and a lean-to up the stream a ways. Either we didn't read the map right or it was wrong to begin with, but we didn't find what we were looking for. It started to rain in earnest, so we beached the canoes, unloaded them and sat with them inverted over us for shelter.

So that their shirts wouldn't get wet, Valerie and Michelle removed them and sat there in their bras. Jean didn't say a word, but I could see she disapproved. She had a poncho, and wrapped it around herself.

After a while the rain stopped, and we found what we thought was the stream on the map. It proved to be wrong, but as we canoed up we came to a large building in the middle of the woods. Since there was no lean-to, and it was getting to be late afternoon, we resolved to break in to the building for shelter.

We successfully did this without having to actually break anything, and found two light airplanes inside. A cursory inspection showed them to be foreign, and the script on the instrument panel and elsewhere made us suspect they were Russian. (With the Cold War in progress, we were a little scared!) The floor was concrete, but over in one corner there was a second level constructed of wood, which was a little softer. We ate cold food and went to sleep.

The next morning, stiff, cold and sore, we retraced or steps back to the lake. As we came out onto the lake, the early morning mist was rising, the sun was just making itself known, and Michelle, who by this time had had all the rotten experiences she needed for a lifetime, laid her paddle across the gunwales, looked with awe at the beautiful scene, and said, "Now I see what camping is all about. This makes the whole trip worthwhile."

There was a small island with a lean-to on it, owned by one of the hotels. We asked the hotel if we could use the lean-to, and they said okay, but they apologized, saying that it was in disrepair and might have a leaky roof. So things were looking up! We built a fire, cooked our food, and started having some fun.

In order to keep the rain from putting the fire out, we rigged a tarp high over it. We found a spot where the leaky roof didn't drip, and settled in for a decent night's sleep. But during the night the wind came up, and threatened to blow down our tarp. Someone had to fix it, and that job fell to me. Now, I always slept naked in my sleeping bag, so I told the others, "I'm getting up to fix the tarp. I sleep naked, and I'm not going to dress and get my clothes wet just for the sake of modesty in the middle of the night. So if you want to watch, be my guest." I don't know if anyone watched or not, but I pegged the tarp down and the fire didn't go out.

The next day was bright and sunny, so we swam and generally had a good time. As I stated, Valerie was a trifle crazy, and while swimming she and Michelle decided to skinny-dip, and removed their swimsuits while submerged. I did likewise, but on the other side of the island.

Monday came too soon, and we said goodbye to Valerie and Michelle, who said she had been ready to throttle Valerie for talking her into coming on this adventure, but was taking it all back now. Jean, Ed and I hitch-hiked back to civilization. Ed wrote me a letter when he returned to Germany, and his first words were, "How is the naked man?"

25

FUN with the Girls (Parts 4 & 5)

The men's athletic building at Syracuse University was quite complete. The basketball arena could hold a thousand screaming fans, but there were also other venues: handball courts, weight-lifting rooms, an Olympic-sized swimming pool, and a rifle range. The Outing Club would commandeer the very large lobby on Saturdays, push the overstuffed lounge furniture out of the way, and have a square dance (I often did the calling) and a folk dance.

Marlene LeGault was only five-foot-two, but she could dance! She also happened to be my "main squeeze." One Saturday, taking a break from the dancing, we explored some of the facilities of the building, and happened upon the rifle range observation booth, where a man was studying five shooters taking target practice. We watched for a while, then Marlene opined that the shooters had it easy, lying prone or sitting with their arms braced on their thighs, so how come they didn't hit the bullseye every time?

The man turned out to be the coach of the NROTC rifle team, and he challenged her to try it out, since she derided his team. So she went with him and put ten rounds through the bullseye while standing. He was amazed! She said that if she had her own rifle from home, she could do better. So a couple weeks later she did have her weapon, challenged him to a match of a hundred rounds, and beat him, 100 to 98.

The upshot was that upon studying the requirements for being on the team, you had to be a student, but it did not say the member must be in the NROTC program. So she went with the team, and won all her matches! An only child, she was her father's "son," and an avid hunter, so she honed her skill with a rifle very well.

I attended a swim party in that Olympic-sized pool one evening, at the invitation of one of my friends. Among the bathers was a pretty blonde, one I hadn't met. She became quite distraught towards the end of the party, because she lost a ring in the pool. It was very valuable to her for sentimental reasons, and she was quite upset. Then someone found it—they could see it at the bottom, resting on the division between two openings of a drain. Either opening was larger than the ring. Just a nudge, or a little flow of water, and the ring would be down the drain and irretrievable. This was an Olympic-sized pool with regulation diving boards and platforms, and was eighteen feet deep where the ring was located. Who would go down to the bottom to retrieve it? You guessed it—me! Down I went, having never been that deep before. I carefully picked up the ring, placing it upon my little finger so as to not drop it, and was the hero of the day. Later, at the home of the faculty member who chaperoned the event, I developed a splitting headache due to the water pressure at eighteen feet down in the pool. I was allowed to lay down, with warm compresses on my brow to relieve the pain, and that blonde sat on the bed with my head in her lap and stroked my face. Ah-h-h-h! Subsequently, I dated her a few times, but the spark was gone.

26

$\mathcal{FUN}$ with Dancing (Part 2)

In my senior year, I was elected to be Folk Dance Chairman of the Outing Club. My main duty was to organize the annual folk dance festival. I had a list of all the ethnic groups that had participated before, and some new ones, but the biggest challenge of all was to select two folk dances to be performed by us.

Don Miller was a local man, not a student, but he was accepted as a member of the club. He arranged a simple Israeli dance to be an exhibition piece, and it was easily the better of our two offerings. His dance had a minimum of costume making, and was a dance we all knew well. It was also one we could easily do when we did one of the many exhibitions for different groups around Syracuse. It was lively, lots of movement, and went over with the festival audience very well.

My selection was a new dance we had never done, so we had to practice, make costumes and some props, and then record the music. The dancers reviewed my selection and approved it, but we should have done something else! I'm sure their approval was just because they liked me, not because they thought the dance was so great.

The dance was French, entitled La Jardinier—"The Gardener." The girls all sewed, and we didn't look too bad. But the music was recorded twice, and one side of the phonograph record was flawed. So which side was played? You guessed it! We had to just stand there looking dumb while an extra eight bars were played. I was embarrassed, but the dancers were very kind about it.

Years later, after we were married, my wife Lou and I heard about a square dance club in our area of Camp Hill, so we looked it up and found Ranchland. Tom Hoffman was the caller, and the owner of the facility where the dances were held. It was a nice setup, with a large dance floor, commercial kitchen, and dining area, suitable for weddings and other parties, as well as square dancing.

We joined, and stayed with that club until we moved to Rochester, NY, in 1963, and rejoined when we were forced to return to Pennsylvania in

1965. One of the highlights of that time was a square dance convention in Washington, DC, at one of the largest hotels there. Three ballrooms were going all the time, with thousands of dancers. We had a blast!

When our children, Calista and Alfred, were 14 and 18, respectively, we decided to introduce them to western-style square dancing. For several weeks we attended dances in Spry, PA, as "angels" (people who were introducing newcomers to square dancing). Calista was a very pretty girl, and danced well, and attracted the notice of a young man who was also learning the more intricate steps of club-level dancing. He wanted to date her, but she told him that he had to wait until she turned 16. He noted the date of her birthday, and was very patient. The day after her sixteenth birthday he called, only to find out she was already engaged to be married! That poor boy – my heart always goes out to him whenever I recall that situation. To be so patient, and to receive such news! Tsk-tsk!

27

FUN with College Pranks

At Wooster, there was a "student resident," an upper classman, assigned to each section of the freshmen's dorm. He was there to help out with any problems that we freshmen might have. He was often the target of a practical joke as well. George Kusmijian was one the recipients of such an action. The men in his section jimmied the lock on his door and woke him up in the middle of the night. They stripped him naked and rolled him up in the rug he had on his floor and delivered him, gagged and helpless, to the freshman girl's dorm. This was a former mansion, with a central atrium. There, an accomplice opened the front door and he was deposited in the center of the atrium. Then the fire alarm was set off, so all the girls fled their rooms to find this hostage. "Ma" Golder, dean of women, was the faculty resident. She was not surprised to find George gracing her hallway, having experienced student high jinks for several years, but now she had to figure out a way to get him unwrapped (he was naked, remember) with the least embarrassment. Every college has its share of high jinks and practical jokes played on the college by the fraternities. Perhaps the sororities also played some pranks, but I never knew of any at Wooster or Syracuse.

The one that I'm sure will go down as a classic at Syracuse is this one:

A new specialized library was built, the gift of some very rich alumnus, and a bronze statue was commissioned to grace the entrance. The statue was by Ivan Mestrovic, a leading artist of the time (1953), who was an art professor at Syracuse. It was titled "Supplicant Persephone," and was a ten-foot-tall nude with her hands raised in supplication to some unknown deity.

When the day of dedication arrived, all the big-wigs from the university were there, along with dignitaries from the city. The statue was cloaked from prying eyes until the grand moment of unveiling. The emcee of the event pulled the cord and the enshrouding cover fell away to reveal . . . WHAT? Someone had painted an orange bra and panties on Persephone! (Orange and blue are the school colors of Syracuse.) Everyone was shocked! The festivities went on, but a bit subdued.

The maintenance crew was called in to take the paint off, and they tried everything, but to no avail. Finally, in response to the University's desperate plea, along with a pledge of no recriminations, the frats disclosed that all they had to do was give Persephone a bath—they had used water-based poster paint for the dirty deed!

28

FUN with the Young Adults

During the late 1950s, my girlfriend Lou (later my wife) and I belonged to a group of young folks known as "Saint Paul's Young Adults," based at St. Paul's Methodist Church in Niagara Falls. I was one of the founders of the group, having been raised in that church from the Cradle Roll on through my college years. We always met on Sunday evenings for Bible study, fellowship, singing and, of course, eating. During the winter months we had an attendance of twenty or so. But in the summer, we met in the afternoons and went to the beach or picnics or band concerts or hiking, etc., and increased the attendance to thirty-five or forty, because the young adults from the other churches joined us, especially when it was a beach party.

Lois Nelson was a big, rather clumsy farm girl, a nice girl but a bit homely and very unsophisticated. But she could play the piano, and we often ended up our evenings at St. Paul's around the piano singing. Ed Weiss was short, a little pudgy, also unsophisticated, and his one passion was his red car, kept in A-1 polished condition at all times.

The occasion was a beach party at the summer cottage of one of our member's relatives, in Canada on Lake Erie. We were given maps to get there, and the cars all left St. Paul's in a caravan. But somewhere along the way we all got separated. We ended up at the location, but Ed's car wasn't there—and his passenger was Lois. They finally arrived an hour late. It seems that they couldn't read the map, and got lost. But we all ribbed them mercilessly, saying they got lost on purpose, just to have time together. Well, maybe that was the reason, because they started dating and were married a few months later. We all felt good about it, a sort of "getting the two ugly ducklings together" kind of feeling.

Kenny Nelson was Lois's younger brother, a good ol' farm boy, handsome, soft-spoken and shy. When Peggy Loushner showed up one Sunday night, it was literally "love at first sight." They were married the following summer, and all the Young Adults attended the ceremony. It was held in a small Methodist church out in the country, and our gang took up the three front pews on the groom's side. About half-way into the vows, Kenny went white and almost fainted. The pastor and the best man grabbed hold of his arms and held him firmly until he recovered, then proceeded with the service.

At the reception afterward, we all teased him, but with affection.

As you can see, our group was a matrimonial bureau, and quite a few marriages came about because of the natural tendencies of young men and women, and we were no different. Lou and I were one of the fortunate couples who were included. It is always a blessing when young people find a partner within a Christian environment.

One of our best events was the Hawaiian Luau at Hatch's Swamp. Jerry Hatch was one of our guys, and his family owned a cottage on Lake Ontario. It wasn't right on the beach, which is a rocky shore there, but along a small creek which fed into the lake. We called it a swamp because before it reached the lake the stream widened into a nice-sized pond.

We made a table from a three-foot wide paper roll laid four layers thick on the gravely beach, cut coconuts in half for drinking cups, had a watermelon with a short curly stem for a "pig" centerpiece (with an apple in its mouth, of course), and the usual picnic fare, only we labeled it "fish and poi."

We had a pearl diving contest, having dropped handfuls of marbles into the stream. Ron Swick and Dick Dahlstrom arrived via canoe with a head-hunting "witch doctor" (David Wright), who proceeded to "capture" the "missionary" (David Hopwood), who protested, "You can't boil me; I'm a friar!" We swam and ate s'mores, and sang until the sun went down on one more delightful St. Paul's Young Adult experience.

Alma Hughart had grown up at St. Paul's, as I had, and also came to our Young Adult affairs. She and I were very good friends, but there was no romantic interest there. However, being so well acquainted for so long, and such good friends, we could flirt with abandon. I always greeted her with a big hug, which she returned, and sometimes I would put my hand on her back, squeeze, and unhook her bra. That always earned me a glare at first, then a laugh, as she retreated to the lady's room.

The Methodist churches in our Episcopal Area maintained a retreat center and youth camp at one of the smaller Finger Lakes. Silver Lake was at one time a resort hotel, now restored to house campers. There were houses there, too, for the clergy and other personnel. Alma and I, among many, were recruited to carry a car full of junior high kids to Silver Lake for a work week-end to help clean and get ready for the camps later on.

On Sunday evening, time to pack up and go home, we were waiting in my car for the girls to bring their stuff out to the car, and Alma was putting on her lipstick, using my rear-view mirror to do so. "Hey, Alma," I said, "Would you like to blot that lipstick?" She looked at me impishly and said, "Sure!," and we clamped on a good lip-lock. There was lipstick all over my face! Just then the junior high girls came out, and they were shocked! Alma and I had a good laugh at their astonished expressions.

29

FUN on New Year's Eve

When I square-danced those alternate Saturdays in Lewiston and Youngstown in my teen years, the caller usually was Ernie Wensley, and I had run into him quite a few times after that. He knew that I had done a lot of calling in college, so he contacted me to see if I thought I was good enough to call a regular square dance in his place. Back then he was calling at a fire hall in North Tonawanda (just north of Buffalo, NY) every Saturday. They wanted him to call also on New Year's Eve, but family matters prevented him from doing so.

I said yes, I could do it, and for three Saturdays prior to New Year's I took a date to the dance in North Tonawanda and would call one set every night so the dancers could accustom them selves to my voice and my style.

I persuaded six of my fellow Young Adults to accompany me and my date to the fire hall for the occasion of my first "commercial" calling debut. So we had one square of all my friends (I asked one of the regular attendees to partner my date) among the other eleven or twelve squares on the floor.

Everything went very well. No slip-ups, everyone understanding the calls, the sound system worked OK, the orchestra (a small combo) was OK, and at midnight everyone went downstairs for a very nice feed. After that, it was upstairs again for another set of squares.

30

FUN at Our Wedding

I lived with my parents until I married Maralou on January 14, 1961, whereupon we moved to Pennsylvania, PA, and my new job as a salesman for Moore Business Forms

Our wedding was held at St. Paul's Methodist Church, and had over 400 guests. I had been a member there starting with the Cradle Roll, my parents were very active there, and Maralou was very well known and liked at her church, St. James Methodist.

St. Paul's was a large cathedral-type building, and boasted a large community hall and kitchen, so the facility was ideal. My grandfather, Noah Garwick, a retired preacher, gave the closing prayer at the ceremony. He had a booming bass voice, and was heard clearly all the way in the rear of the sacutuary without amplification.

The reception line was very long, and we were glad to get away to Lou's home for a late meal. Then we headed off in my new Ford Falcon to our new life together.

31

FUN with Housing

Our first residence was on North Fourth Street in Harrisburg, PA, an upstairs apartment in the home of Mabel Steitz. She was an old lady of indeterminate age, who was very nice, but a less-than-perfect housekeeper. Everything was neat and surface-clean, but she couldn't see the big dark water-beetles against the dark wood floors and the dark baseboards. We started looking for other "digs" as soon as spring arrived.

That first apartment was not too attractive, and I was in there for two weeks before Lou and I married. I tried to spruce it up by painting all the dark woodwork white, and that helped a little. I was taken in by that nice old Mabel Steitz, I guess, and overlooked the things that would naturally be of concern to Lou.

I had arranged for Lou's furniture to be shipped, so that was there, but we needed curtains on the windows in the bedroom—there were large windows which opened to let in lots of light and stares from nosy neighbors just outside. Lou had curtains in her dresser drawers, but the federal gold flowers didn't go well with the red rose-flowered wallpaper and were a trifle short. To put it bluntly, my attempt at decorating was just plain bad, and poor Lou was stunned. But she gamely carried on, because she loved me.

The first Sunday in our snazzy pad, she made us a beautiful ham dinner with scalloped potatoes. She had spent all week scraping the baked-on grease from the old gas stove (the kind which is up off the floor on long legs, with a small oven on the left and four burners on the right, and a shelf above the burners to hold salt, pepper and matches). She had never cooked with gas before. She had a cookbook which told her how to do everything, and when dinner time came, the table (card table) looked beautiful. The small ham was glazed, with pineapple rings, maraschino cherries, cloves and scored just right. Then when I carved the slices, we found they were stone cold inside! She saw the directions for 150 degrees and set the oven for that, but that temperature was for a meat thermometer—it was supposed to be 150 degrees inside! Well, no matter, because it was a precooked ham, but for the rest of our married life I always would always tease her with a questioning look whenever she served ham!

We found a house in Camp Hill, across the Susquehanna River, a one-story rancher, and in our price range, since we found out we could assume the mortgage instead of negotiating a new one. We were in a subdivision of similar dwellings, on Neponsit Lane. I was a not-so-successful salesman for Moore, and we had to scramble for the $95 mortgage payment (Really? That low?) each month. But we managed, and Alfred was born while we lived there.

I did some research and went for counseling to John Goodyear, a Christian counselor, to determine what career course I should try for, since my sales job was not going well. He gave me a book, *What Color is Your Balloon?*, which had a unique approach to finding a job, whereby you interview the human resources manager, rather than the other way around. Shortly thereafter, Lou and I took a week's vacation up to Lou's parents home in Rochester, NY. After some discussion, we decided to move to there and look for employment using the procedure outlined in the book. I ended up working for Bausch & Lomb in an eyeglass frame factory!

My father-in-law, Alfred Griggs, my son's namesake, bought a new car every year, a Ford Crown Victoria, and kept it in showroom condition. No food or drink in that car ever, and although he was a smoker, he never lit up in that car!

As a treat, one summer day in 1964 in Rochester, NY, he drove us all to the zoo. It not only had animals on display, there were also a few kiddy rides for Alfred, who was two years old then. No sooner had Maralou stepped closer, to read the small sign on the rhinoceros cage which said, "Beware of Animal Spray," than the beast in question let loose with a garden-hose-sized stream, and Lou was bathed head-to-toe with rhinoceros piss!

We solicited some plastic trash bags from the grounds-keeper to wrap around Lou and cover—completely!—her Dad's pristine car seats, and so got her home. He never took us to the zoo again!

We had tried to sell our house in Camp Hill, but were under a time deadline to find a new job, since we had no savings to fall back on, so we delegated the whole business to Naftsinger Realty in Harrisburg, who found us a renter. After close to a year in Rochester, we were notified by our tenants that they would be sending the rent monies to us directly instead of to the property manager, because Naftsinger was suddenly out of business.

(It seems that old Mr. Naftsinger, the owner, had wiped out the business bank account and fled to South America with one of his secretaries!) Then the tenants decided to move, so we headed back to Pennsylvania. I got a job with the Commonwealth (PA is not a state, technically), and we were again at number 11 Neponsit Lane, Camp Hill.

A lovely addition to our family arrived shortly thereafter. Calista was always a joy to us, our whole lives. Lou used to hold her infant daughter to look out the front picture window, and tell her, "See the pretty day?" Calista's very first words were not "Mama" or "Dada," but "See pretty day."

32

FUN as a "Privy-Sniffer"

The title for my job with the state was "Sanitarian," and consisted of inspection of schools, nursing homes, eating-and-drinking establishments, public swimming pools, landfills and sewage disposal sites to enforce the state Health Department laws and regulations.

The town of Royalton, south of Harrisburg, did not have a central sewage disposal system. The homes there all had either cesspools or septic tanks, and many had outdoor privies instead of indoor toilets. My job there was to survey and report and list all the residences which had such sewage problems, and issue citations, enforced by the sheriff, to the privy owners. Hence, the origin of the term "privy-sniffer"!

As part of my training, I was sent to Pittsburgh where I joined other trainees from around the state, to attend a week of instructional lectures and field trips.

While I was there, my father was also in Pittsburgh to attend a meeting of the board of trustees for a national Christian ministry, and we got together to watch the Pittsburgh Pirates lose three games in a row.

Being a sanitarian was a responsible job, one where I felt that I was doing something for the good of all, but the pay was low. Oh, I got twelve or more days of paid holidays and a week of vacation time each year, but not enough money to go anywhere, so I started looking around for better-paying employment.

33

FUN with Computers (Part 1)

In the course of my travels as a Sanitarian for the state, I ran across an ad for a free aptitude test for data processing. I had read that computer programmers were well paid, so I took the test and was assured of my superior (?) intellect and wouldn't I like to enroll in their data processing class for just a modest fee? Shortly thereafter I saw an ad for programmers at Caterpillar in York, PA. I applied, and was given an aptitude test. As providence would have it, it was the same test! I aced it, of course, and Caterpillar was then anxious to have me start.

They were just getting into computers in a big way, and all the programmers started out by "going back to school" to learn the brand new data processing language—COBOL (COmmon Business Oriented Language). The technique used to self-teach was a process known as Distributive Practice, whereby the small bit of information learned each moment was used immediately to process the next small bit of information. It was a very effective way to learn a lot in a short time, but it was like force-feeding your brain, and I went home exhausted every day.

Later, when we wrote programs to handle the thousands of parts that York stocked for the many Caterpillar machines around the world, we had to take the raw programs to Philadelphia to have them "compiled," or proven to be correctly programmed; sort of like having your English teacher checking something you wrote for spelling, grammar and logic. The turn-around for the necessary compilation was usually two days, because companies other than ours were also going through the same COBOL growing pains.

To further understand how a computer operated, we were sent to IBM in Philadelphia for classes twice, for a week each time. There were four of us: Ilsa, Rae, Bruce, and me. When the Caterpillar folks in York reserved our rooms in the hotel, they only gave our names, not identifying us by gender, so that when we got there we found that "Ted" and "Ray" were in one room, and "Ilza" and "Ruth" (Bruce) were in the other!

In the course of our studies, we were told that a file (essentially a list of data items) probably wouldn't ever be more than a thousand items, and the instructor was taken aback when we informed him our smallest file contained over 20,000 entries! The warehouse of parts was a half-mile long, and the girl who delivered the mail used an electric scooter to get around. One day Bob Shinn, one of our programmers, commandeered it and came barreling through the office.

The second week we were in Philadelphia, the hotel put us up in a suite, consisting of two bedrooms and a separate bath. The rooms were similar, but one was slightly larger and contained a TV. Remember—this was the 1960's, and having a TV (only black and white, of course) in a hotel room was considered a new thing. The hotel had the genders right this time, and assigned the smaller room to Bruce and me. We were all gathered in the larger room watching TV when the phone rang in the other room. Ilsa was nearest the door, so she went next door to answer it. She came back to say the call was for me.

When I said "Hello?" the first words out of Lou's mouth were, "What were you doing with a girl in your room?!" I explained the situation to her, and we laughed about it afterward.

My colleagues were content to sit in front of a TV every evening, but I elected to do some sight-seeing in this historic city. I saw the Liberty Bell and walked in Independence Mall, etc. One afternoon after class I attended a concert given by the Polish-American String Band, one of the famous Mummers groups, playing that evening in Independence Mall. They were playing one polka after another.

There was a small paved area immediately in front of the orchestra, and I went to the conductor and asked if they could play an Obetech (o-beh-tik), a Polish country waltz. He said yes, and I turned to the audience and asked a young lady there if she would dance with me. She accepted, and we "tripped the light fantastic." (An Obetech has a distinct rhythm of 1-2-3, 1-2-3, 1-2-3, stomp-stomp!) When we ended, I twirled her around and sat her on my knee with a flourish, and all the people applauded.

I also found some folk dancing one evening, at the Museum, on the paved courtyard in front of the building, and did the "Family Waltz," among others. So I had a good time in Philly.

I had a daily stipend, but wanted to bring something home with me for Lou, so I skimped on my meals, eating as cheaply as possible. With the money left over, I bought her a teacup-and-saucer for her collection.

34

FUN with Female Fashions

My major contribution to Caterpillar's corporate welfare was a program that handled the methods of payment for orders. Since Caterpillar did business with both private companies and with governments worldwide, there were a number of hoops to jump through for every sale. This was a program which ran weekly, and extensive testing was done to make sure it ran right.

But for six weeks straight it ran wrong. My neck was being measured for a noose each time. But no, it was the systems analyst, who failed to figure out the "Murphy's Law" (if anything can go wrong, it will) aspect of data processing, and the weird conditions which any particular order might have attached to it. So I fixed the program six times, and came up smelling like a rose every week!

The computer at Caterpillar was as big as a small SUV, and we had only 30,000 bytes of data manipulation to work with. Compare that to the age which is in effect when you are reading these memoirs! We had a computer operator who fed the programs, on punched cards, into the machine, and then pressed certain buttons on the machine to start and run the program, and produce a printed output. When one program was finished, the computer halted until the operator manually started the next one.

The read-punch machine could read what was punched into a card and also punch a "raw" card with some of the data input for the next program in the series.

To facilitate input, the programs were stacked one behind the other in a long (about five feet) chute positioned on the right. A similar chute full of unpunched cards was on the left. Between them were four receptacles for the cards which were generated by the program, and one for the program cards after each was read. As these receptacles filled up, the operator would take the stack of cards and put them into one of twelve other receptacles which were behind the card read-punch machine.

Certain programs were run in more then one way, depending on the date or calendar: daily, weekly, monthly, etc. There was one such program, but every time a certain operator ran it, it went haywire. The operator was quizzed extensively, and proved to all that she knew what she was doing, but nevertheless every time she was the operator, the program ran amok, but never the same way twice. The way the program worked was that a trio of sense switches had to be set to tell the program which way to run. These were very sensitive, about an inch square, and positioned just below the five center receptacles. The figure style for women then (the 1960s) was to have pointed breasts.

Our subject operator, Loretta, was short, about 5-5, and had a very solid figure, and every time she leaned over to put the cards in one of the twelve proper receptacles, her breast would touch one of the sense switches, thus causing the program to act in an irrational way. She was so embarrassed! How to fix it? They built a platform, put rubber matting on it for comfort and safety, and increased Loretta's height by three inches, and all was fine after that.

I smoked a pipe at work in those days. The other programmers didn't complain, but it was a well-known scent in the air. I had a stash of tobacco in my desk drawer. One day, after lighting up, I smelled a foreign odor. When I tracked it down, I found that someone had cut up pieces of brown-colored rubber bands and mixed them in with my tobacco!

The union went on strike for higher wages, and when that was settled, we non-union folks in the office got raises, too. So an additional $400 per year was happily received, and I thought that now I had found a job for life. But such was not the case.

For the July Fourth week of 1971, we camped near the Atlantic Ocean. It rained, and our 8x8 army surplus wall tent kept us dry while the campground became a muddy mess. We brought our folding cots close together, and played Parcheesi that night with the children. Our only light was a toy kerosene lamp, which we placed in the center of the board. Calista won.

It was during my time at Caterpillar that I witnessed one of the most humorous incidents of my life. Market Street, the major street through town, was one-way east, and I traveled it every day to get from our house on the west side of town to Caterpillar, which was on the east side of York. This particular summer day I was stopped at a traffic light, right behind a cattle truck. Beside the truck was a convertible, top down, with six well-dressed passengers. Before the light changed, one of the cows decided to relieve herself, and right through slats in the side of the trailer ahead of me went the liquid defecation, right on to those poor commuters! What an awful thing to begin the day with!

Caterpillar decided to move their data processing to the company headquarters in Peoria, IL. Lou and I didn't want to relocate, and I looked about for another position. One of our systems analysts was now the data processing manager at Borg-Warner, so I called him and he hired me.

35

FUN with Computers (Part 2)

Borg-Warner was another international company, making mostly air conditioning equipment. My big contribution there was a program which tied together employee attendance with speed and cost of production. The employees were given ID badges which were punched with holes like those in a data processing card, and they used that badge to log in at the beginning and end of their shift, and also at the beginning and end of each batch of piece-work they did during their shift. It was a major program, and worked perfectly from the beginning. But after three years there, I foundered, ran into a programming problem I couldn't find my way out of, and was asked to resign.

This was the first of nine times that I had to come home to tell my beloved Maralou that I had lost my job. But did she become angry? Did she complain? Not once! What a wonderful wife!

I went on in data processing, working at Schraff's Candy in Reading, a small programming outfit in York, Read's Drugs in Baltimore (since bought out by Rite-Aid), Anaconda in York, Pentamation in Shiloh, Teledyne-McKay in York and Blue Cross in Harrisburg. In the in-between times, while pestering employment agencies for new jobs, I helped a friend install aluminum siding, held traffic signs for road and electric crews, studied to become an investment salesman, worked as a head-hunter, and did a lot of indoor painting and paper-hanging.

Then one of the employment agencies found me a job teaching data processing at a vo-tech school in Perry County. I was there three years (1987-88-89), and it was not a good job. I had thirty students (I use the term loosely) from six different schools each morning, and thirty more from five different schools each afternoon. The pupils treated me with no respect, did not behave, and generally made life miserable. I stuck it out for those three years, and quit.

36

FUN with Preacher Brown

When I was working at Read's Drug Stores in Baltimore, the fifty-seven miles going home was a dangerous drive. I was tired after a full day's work, so I listened to the radio. But music put me to sleep, and the only talk shows were either sports games or preachers. I couldn't get a picture of a basketball, football, or hockey game in my head, but only a baseball game--and the Orioles didn't play every day, so I ended up with the religious broadcasts out of necessity. At this time also, Lou had some surgery done at Holy Spirit Hospital in Harrisburg.

One evening I was driving home from visiting her there, late at night and after a full day's work, and tuned in to Preacher Brown to stay awake.

I didn't know this man, having only heard his voice on the radio. As usual, he was preaching salvation, but it seemed to me that he could some-how see me because the message was aimed directly at me.

I was raised by Christian parents, always went to church and Sunday school, always attended youth fellowship meetings and activities, went to a church-related college, sang in church choirs, met and married my wife through a church-affiliated young adult group, was baptized as an adult and re-baptized with my wife to further cement our marriage, BUT—it occurred to me that I had never said "the sinner's prayer," nor formally accepted Jesus as my personal Savior! I must have acquired my Christianity by just absorbing it like a sponge from my Christian surroundings.

So Preacher Brown talked directly to me:

"Pull over to the side of the road and say this prayer with me."

So I did.

"Go to your pastor and tell him what you have just done, and ask for prayer."

So I did.

I rang Dick Benner's front doorbell at 11:30 at night. He came to the door in his bathrobe and slippers --- I had roused him from sleep.

"Hi, Ted --- what's wrong?"

"Dick, I just now received Christ as my Savior."

You could have knocked him over with a feather! Here I was, a choir member and a counselor to the senior-high youth and I had just now received Christ?? We sat and prayed and I told him what had just occurred, and all was well.

37

$\mathcal{FUN}$ with Alfred

When Alfred was about 19, I was making a living by doing indoor painting and paper-hanging. I enlisted his help to paper a ceiling, which is a tricky job because the wet paper tends to fall down as quickly as it is put up, and you can't stop in the middle of everything to rest, but have to keep going until the end. Al wanted to rest, but I said to him, "You can take a break when I take a break."

Several years later, when he was living in Ohio with his wife and one child, Lou and I went out there for a visit, and he enlisted my aid to help paint some rooms in his church. We had been at it for quite a while, and I suggested a rest. Quick as a wink, he came back at me with my own words: "You can take a break when I take a break." Payback!

Lou and I visited Alfred and Teresa in Ohio in the spring of 1989. Their daughter Micah was two, and Lou and I took her for a shopping trip to pick out a new dress for Easter. At the clothing store, we set her in the shopping cart and reversed the direction when we pushed it, so that she would see where she was headed. We asked her advice on every outfit we saw, and watched her reactions. At two, she wasn't talking, but we could see she was very intelligent, and so was interested and understood what was happening. We ended up with two dresses, and laid them out for her to choose. She eyed them both carefully and made a choice. We took her home and told her parents how she picked out her own clothes. They marveled, and Micah was a very happy child.

Micah married and became the mother of four. That intelligence is quite evident in the way she raised her children. She married an Air Force soldier, Jedidiah Coover, and took the opportunity to earn a degree in Early Childhood Education. She home-schooled, and also taught them how to be good Christians.

38

NOT *FUN* with Lou

Later in 1989, Maralou sued for divorce. We had not seen eye-to-eye for quite a long time. She really loved me, but was not at all happy in our relationship. I loved her, too, and didn't want to comply, and pointed out that in the Bible God said He hated divorce. But she went on a one-person retreat for a week-end, spent all her time in prayer, and came back to say that God told her to get the divorce. She contacted a lawyer, moved out of the house to an apartment, and so left me.

I was alone in our Bairs Road house, not able to afford the mortgage each month, facing foreclosure and teaching data processing at a vo-tech school where the discipline problem was forcing me to resign. I finally signed the divorce papers with reluctance, but did so because I didn't want a "messy" divorce, since I still loved Lou.

I got the call while I was at the vo-tech school, that the divorce was final and I was, I think, at the lowest ebb in my life. I was losing my job, my home and my wife at the same time. In my classroom at the vo-tech school, there was a locker next to the wall, and if I opened the door so it shielded me on one side while the wall blocked the other side, I could thrust my head between the two and cry unobserved. I did so.

39

$\mathcal{FUN}$ with a Fork-Lift

I continued to live at the Bairs Road address while my school term expired, then I worked for PFC, a Temporary Employment agency at various places: a manufacturer of electronic components, a large-scale book-printing plant, and at an office supply company.

At the book-printing company, my job was operating a fork-lift to collect the large baskets of trimmed-off paper scraps and then bind the waste paper into bales and load them into a trailer-truck to be taken for recycling. In loading the trailer, the procedure was to first load one bale, then to load a two-high stack above the first, thus making a three-high stack, which reached the top. Some skill was required, since the two-tier load on the fork-lift might tend to fall backward. This happened to me, and I automatically raised the forks to catch the top bale, and thrust the mast of the fork-lift right through the top of the trailer! The driver of the truck didn't raise a fuss—said he always did like a sky-lights in his trailers.

I always called in to the temp agency before my shift at the printing plant was over, to check where I would be working the next day. That daily check-in earned me employee-of-the-month award, and I even earned a week's paid vacation.

I next was sent to work for an office-supply company in Harrisburg, installing cubicle dividers in offices. I did well, and the company ended up hiring me full-time. About this time the real-estate dealer for our house found a buyer, and I moved out of the Bairs Road garage apartment and into a trailer in Highspire, a small town south of Harrisburg. I was given the assignment of installing a complete office area with new cubicles, including the electric wiring and light fixtures. I discovered that the original layout was measured wrong, and the area was actually three feet shorter than shown on the specifications. So I had a problem, but worked it out to everyone's satisfaction.

When that project was completed, I was switched to delivering supplies. I drove a panel truck, and the radio was on most of the time. Every time I would hear a love song, my heart would hurt, because I loved Lou, and she was gone.

While I was still divorced and living alone on Bairs Road, I returned home one day to find a sheriff's sale in progress! Luckily, since Lou had taken almost all of the furniture when she moved out, I had moved the remaining pieces to the garage apartment. The Sheriff's Sale was confined to the house, so the furniture in the garage apartment was still mine. I didn't know how these sales worked, and was surprised to find that the pictures on the wall were considered attached to the structure, and were not included in the confiscation.

40

FUN with Family (Part 2)

My mother's father was Noah Garwick, who was born Amish, left that culture to obtain a law degree from Drake University, and gave up that potential career to become a minister of the gospel. His mother was Anna Zook, whose roots were in Lancaster County, PA. Jacob Zook, one of her distant cousins (there are several pages of Zooks in the Lancaster telephone book) dealt in Amish hex signs, and I struck a deal for a discount on a case of coffee mugs with his logo on them.

The other unique item in Lancaster's Amish community is their famous Lebanon Bologna.

In Exton Pa, at the Exton Mall, at the time of this writing, is a large stone farmhouse, "The Zook Haus," built by my Amish forefather in 1750.

I was contacted by my cousins in Minneapolis to tell me of the "Great Garwick Get-Together" reunion to take place in Minnesota in June, 1989. I resolved to go since I only had myself to consider. I got to meet and know a plethora of kinfolk I had completely lost touch with. My Uncle Kenneth had five children, and they all had a bunch of kids, and I didn't know any of them. I was quite a hit with all those relatives because of the coffee mugs with Amish hex signs on them, and a big Lebanon Bologna sausage which was served at lunch. The following year, they had another "Get Together" and this time my father and sister showed up, coming in from Bellingham, WA.

I was "into" these reunions, so when Phyllis Rae Odekoeven, my mother's cousin, who I met at the "Get Together," wrote me about an Eddy Family reunion in Massachusetts that same summer, I was eager to go. There is a direct bloodline, according to the Mormon genealogical charts and published books by the Eddy Historical Society, from Samuel Eddy, who arrived in Massachusetts from England in 1630, to my mother.

I was entertained and offered a place to sleep by my thirteenth cousin, Rosalie (that means we had a common ancestor, our great-great-great-great-great-great-great-great-great-great-great-great-great-grandfather!). Rosalie and I got along very well. She was a singer, also, with a fairly renowned group which had even had a European tour.

I invited her to meet me in White Plains, NY for the upcoming 1990 barbershop Middle-Atlantic District Convention. She accepted, and was blown away by the singing, having never heard that wonderful sound before. So she invited me to come back to her neck of the woods for the New Year's festivities, which would include her chorus and the local barbershop chorus. I went, and subsequently she came to visit me in Lancaster and attend our annual barbershop show.

Things were getting pretty friendly between us, but that spark of love was not there for me. Rosalie wanted me to move to Massachusetts to be with her, but I refused. I couldn't imagine being hundreds of miles away from my family in Pennsylvania, so I wrote to Rosalie that what she wanted was very nice, but my heart really was not there, but longed to reconcile with my wife.

41

$\mathcal{FUN}$ with Reconciliation

Imagine my surprise and delight when Lou called me to say she wanted to go to Ohio to visit Al and Teresa, but didn't want to go alone; would I go with her? YES!! We found out that as long as we didn't talk about "us," that we could converse just fine.

Not long after we returned from Ohio in 1992, I asked Lou to accompany me to the Edgar Allen Poe weekend at the Mt. Hope winery. I knew Calista and Bob would be there, too. We arrived, and Calista just about had a heart attack when she saw us together.

Lou then invited me to accompany her to a Christmas dance that Intermedia Marketing was having for their employees, and since it would go on until the wee hours, to spend the night in the apartment she shared with Linda Greene in Lancaster. We went, we danced, had a wonderful time, and wound up in bed together.

That was the beginning of the new beginning for Lou and me. She visited me in my trailer apartment in Highspire and I burned up the roads between there and her "digs." Linda got married, then Lou's landlord wanted the apartment for another use, so we rented a townhouse apartment in Lancaster, and were there for two years. Then the rent went up, and we bought a house in Landisville. We knew it was the right place for us, because of the price, of course, and the area, of course, but the deciding factor was the bush at the end of the driveway, yellow roses! Lou's favorite!

Lou and I remarried Sept. 9, 2000. The wedding was outdoors in Lancaster Central Park in the gazebo there. Our five grandchildren were the attendants, and our sixth grandchild was the wedding present, born the day before the ceremony.

42

FUN on Bairs Road

When I was hired in 1968 by Caterpillar in York, Lou and I started to look for a house in York, to avoid a 25-mile commute each day on US15 to and from Camp Hill. We found a nice house near a stream in the Shiloh area on the north side of York, and thought that this was the place. But when we tried to get a mortgage, we were turned down. In the meantime, our house in Camp Hill was sold, and we had nowhere to go.

So the real-estate dealer we were working with found a house west of York on Kevin Drive that was available, but the, owner, a divorcee, still had furniture, etc. in the house. We moved our furnishings into the basement of that house, and temporarily lived in a trailer park rental until we could complete the real estate transaction and move in. Meanwhile, the house in Shiloh turned out to be a very bad choice, because during a severe rainstorm, the abutting stream flooded, and the entire first floor was under water.

While we were living in that trailer, a vandal broke into the Kevin Drive house and turned on the water in the basement, flooding all our possessions stored there. All our clothing, drapes, etc. had to go to the cleaners, and almost all of Lou's shoes (she had some forty pairs!) had to be thrown away. Somehow, the mattresses and bedding had been placed on top of everything else, and were not damaged. It took several rolls of paper towels to place between the pages of picture albums, etc., to keep them from spoiling. The neighbors from across the street saw our plight, and came over with sandwiches and coffee, and helped us salvage what we could.

We were devastated, but to show how God makes a good thing out of such situations, we got to know our new neighbors, the Slonakers. Bob Slonaker was the tenor for a barbershop quartet, The Ultimates, and introduced me to this style of singing, the start of over forty years of pleasure and fun for me.

We lived in the house on Kevin Drive for a few years, but it wasn't, for me, the ideal place. I had always dreamt of a house like the one I grew up in, in Lewiston.

One Friday in 1974, driving around, we turned up Bairs Road, through the woods adjacent to Wolf's Church, and saw a sign: "Lot for Sale." We wrote down the number, and called, and ended up buying the lot. I sealed that deal with John Sipe with a handshake and fifty dollars cash, and went to a stock broker right away to sell the Caterpillar stock which I had acquired. The broker said it was too late to sell my shares on Friday, but he would do it first thing on Monday.

That Saturday, an agent of the biggest real estate developer in the area went to the lot owner with an offer that was twice the asking price, but was told that the lot was under contract, due to a handshake.

The stock broker said that the price of my Caterpillar shares went up drastically at Monday's opening bell, and then as soon as my transaction was complete, it fell back to Friday's closing price. So now I had the rest of the money for the building lot. Now, there were two lots for sale, and we bought the larger one. The real estate firm bought the other one, again at twice the asking price, so the value of our lot was immediately doubled! We then set about designing and contracting for a house to be built for us. My amateur plans were taken to an architect to make a set that a contractor could read, then we hired the Hoffman brothers to built it for us.

We needed to get a construction mortgage for the new house, so we went to a finance company for a second mortgage on our Kevin Drive property. The manager there gave us the second mortgage, and when our house was complete, he transferred the lien to the new property, leaving the Kevin Drive property free and clear so it could be sold. When that happened, we took the proceeds to pay off the second mortgage on our new Bairs Road home, so were left with only one affordable mortgage payment.

The upshot of all this real estate palaver is this: God blesses us in wonderful, mysterious and unexpected ways. Consider these things:

- We couldn't get a mortgage on the house we originally wanted.

- When we had no place to go, we were offered a place to store our furnishings until we could move in.

- We found a For Sale sign which had just been placed there.

- We only needed fifty dollars and a handshake to assure us of buying the lot.

- The money to buy the lot was furnished in excess by the stock price sudden rise.

- The mortgage arrangements were handled in an unusual way, to our advantage.

- I became a barbershopper.

We lived in that house many years, raised Alfred and Calista there, had a young adult group meet there, and generally "lived the good life." We dedicated that house to the service of God, because of the miraculous way it was acquired.

43

FUN with Beans and a Steer

The farm which was behind the house, beyond the edge of our woods, belonged to John Shearer, who turned out to be a very good neighbor. The field directly at our rear was planted in green beans, and the mechanical harvester would miss a few feet at the end of a row as it turned around.

So we asked John's permission to glean, were given the OK, and picked the dust-covered beans left on the vines. To wash the beans before canning or freezing them, we dumped then into the kiddie pool and swirled them around. Calista, then 10, called them "fishy beans," and when we ate them later, we would often remark that there was "something fishy" about supper, or that "they don't look like fish, but they taste like fish," or something like that.

In one of the small towns nearby, Jefferson, the volunteer fire company held a fund-raising carnival each year. We attended, and won a few prizes. We were astonished to find Alfred with a handful of cigars!

He had been watching as the men tried to ring the bell at the top of a pole by hitting a levering board at the bottom with a heavy mallet. The participants swung the hammer as hard as they could, but seldom won a cigar. After carefully watching, and noting exactly where the "sweet spot" was, Alfred stepped up and won a cigar with every stroke. The men were amazed that a 14-year-old was showing them up!

We also bought some chances, for Calista, on winning some baby livestock: a piglet, a bunny, a colt and a calf. We were surprised to learn, a few days later, that Calista had won the calf! What were we going to do with a calf? A member of the fire company called to say that he had the means to transport the animal, and where did we want to take it?

We called John Shearer, since he raised steers, to see how to handle the situation. He referred us to one of the men who worked for him, and we hired that man to raise our beef-on-the-hoof.

So we went to get the beast, and found that the "calf" was in fact a half-Hereford, half-Brahman bull! The man with the cow trailer said, "Before we transport him, I think we better castrate him, because that will make him docile and easier to handle while you raise him."

So he told Alfred to hold the "calf's" head, while he and I worked the "pinchers" to pinch the tissue above the scrotum so that it would atrophy and fall off.

We accomplished that, and asked Alfred how the animal took it, since there was no kicking or stomping . Al said, "He didn't make a sound, but his eyes rolled way-y-y-y back!"

That steer was put into a stall, and never moved. He was fed a mixture of oats and molasses called "chop," was mucked out and bedded with new straw every day, and grew to over 1000 pounds. The "pay" to the farmer was a quarter of the beef.

When it became time to butcher him, I took Alfred with me to witness the procedure, as a sort of rite-of-passage. I had witnessed the same, in a larger scale, when I visited a meat-packing plant in Pittsburgh during my days with the state as a sanitarian.

Since the steer was never moved, never had any exercise, but just stood there day after day, the meat was exceedingly tender, and even the so-called tougher portions were able to be cut with a fork!

44

$\mathcal{FUN}$ in the Bakery

While we lived in that house, for a few years Lou worked in an office at Bowen-McLaughlin-York, a manufacturer of army tanks a few miles away. There was a woman in the office whose job included answering the telephone, and this person often would swear when it rang and say, "Jesus Christ! That damn phone again!"

So Lou would get all excited and cry out, "Oh! Oh! Is that Jesus on the phone? Let me talk to Him, please?" It wasn't long before all the swearing stopped. That was my Lou. She didn't preach, she didn't appear offended, etc., but she witnessed effectively.

Later, we baked a banana birthday cake for that woman. She almost always had a banana in her lunch, so we baked a three-dimensional banana cake, about two feet long, with the peels folded back to reveal the fruit and a huge pair of red lips taking a bite. It was received with wonder. No one had ever seen a cake like that one before.

We proceeded to bake some other "wondrous" cakes, always in 3-D. A duck, a four-poster bed, a grand piano complete with candelabra, a "Spirit of St. Louis" airplane and hanger, a church, a tugboat with smoke coming from the smokestack, root beer barrels cargo, Life Savers (candy), a train with several different cars, a bowling alley showing a four-inch-tall bowler crying while he watched his ball create a 7-10 split,—these were a few of our cake creations.

So to my son, who is very imaginative, and his reaction to all this? One day, coming home from work at Bowen-McLaughlin, Lou walked in to find a cake on the dining room table that looked like a three-dimensional IBM electric typewriter! It was colored gray, with white dabs of frosting denoting the keys, a black licorice space bar, a platen made from the inner tube from a roll of paper towels, knobs on the platen made of marshmallows, and a paper being typed which was sprinkled with toasted coconut to resemble letters.

Al had the very willing help of Calista to create this masterpiece, and as it was Lou's birthday, you can just imagine the many hugs and kisses that followed. What is more, the children mixed and baked the cake according to the recipe on the box, then mixed the color for the frosting and applied it, and did all this, and cleaned up, so there was absolutely no mess; the kitchen was pristine!

45

FUN when the Dog Died

"Ma" and "Bampa" (my in-laws) were with us at our home on Bairs Road, when their 50th wedding anniversary occurred. Lou planned a surprise party for them, and it was a huge success. Bampa was the oldest of nine siblings, and they were all invited and all of them came to the party. We had a hard time keeping the secret and still make all the preparations.

Alfred and I were the custodians of Wolf's Church picnic grove, in the trees just to the south of us a quarter mile away, so we commandeered the refrigerators there to hold trays of goodies for the party. But all that food prep had to be done at night while the anniversary couple slept. We also made an elaborate two-tier wedding cake, and had to store it in our freezer chest because of its height (after moving all the other stuff out of there --- we had to store that food in picnic freezer chests). There was a lock on that chest, and Ma wanted to know why, because she couldn't get in to get stuff out for dinner, etc.

Came the day of the party, and Ma noticed her brother-in-law's car turning up our driveway, and got all excited, "Al, Al! Your brother Tommy is here, and there's no food in the house!" Then the rest arrived, and Ma and Bampa were properly surprised. Food appeared like magic, and we all had a good time.

The two-tier elaborate wedding cake was a big hit. However, it was a sunny summer day, and that frozen cake started to melt. The frosting became quite soft, but held up long enough for pictures and to be served reasonably well.

Fifty years prior to the party, Ma, as a new bride, wanted to please her new husband by cooking things the "right" way, which meant "the way his mother did it." So she asked her mother-in-law how to make bread. Well, Laura Griggs had the recipe in her head, not written down, so Ma had to remember what was said. She did her best, but the loaf she produced didn't rise.

Now, Bampa had a kennel of hunting dogs, none of them named, none of them considered as a pet. Ma tossed the unleavened loaf to them and one of the dogs ate most of it and died. Ma was very sad about it, but she never told anyone. At this party, however, someone remarked on the sorry occasion fifty years before, and the story came out for the first time!

46

FUN at Dutch Oaks Worm Farm

With Lou working in the office at Bowen-McLaughlin, and me keeping busy painting and paper-hanging, we were doing all right, financially. But we never seem to get really ahead of the normal monthly bills. We read about people who were making money raising earthworms. Some research showed that it was a fairly easy setup, and could be lucrative. So we decided to give it a try.

We first had to build "worm beds." These were boxes, about three by six feet, and some eight inches deep, filled with earth. They had to be made with exterior-grade plywood because the earth had to kept moist. We fed the worms a slurry of water and manure, applied daily, and covered the beds with opaque black plastic so the worms would surface and eat the "food" provided. A light bulb over each bed kept the worms from escaping during the night, since they stay away from all light.

I was papering and painting a room at a horse farm at the time, so I had plenty of raw material for the slurry, filling five-gallon buckets with "road apples" daily. I also had a pickup truck, which I used to relieve a local farmer of some of his drier bovine waste. This was piled in a heap in the woods behind our house, and we injected it with water to start it fermenting. We had to turn it over daily to keep it from burning, and Lou would remark often, "I got married to be a housewife and homemaker, and look where I am—shoveling shit!"

This scheme (we thought that Dutch Oaks Worm Farm might make a good title) lasted for about a year, and we found that we couldn't separate the saleable large worms from the undersized ones easily enough, so sold the entire operation back to the guy from whom we purchased our initial start-up of worms.

We wanted to keep expenses down, so we looked for an inexpensive source for the exterior-grade plywood needed for the beds. We found it in the collapse of the roof of a furniture outlet in Lancaster which had succumbed to the weight of accumulated snow and ice. The construction was proven to be shoddy: the roof trusses were four feet apart, and the four-foot wide plywood was nailed to them only in the outer 7/8 inches, which was not good enough.

So I wrote the company, offering to remove the damaged roof for free, if they would allow me to salvage the wood. They accepted, and we did so. Alfred assembled a crew of his friends and had them arm themselves with chain saws and crow bars, and we tackled the damaged roof. We hired a "cherry-picker" crane to lift off the roof trusses, and the boys would take them apart with the saws to pile the 2x4s and 2x6s in piles to be sold, and the 4x8 sheets of plywood to be taken home to be cut up for worm beds.

Every day we would gather in a circle and join hands in prayer for a safe day on the roof. But one day the cherry-picker arrived before we were ready for him, and since we hired the machine by the hour, we omitted the prayer and got right to work. The crane had a wire rope sling which was put around the main beam of a roof truss to lift it off its supports and lower it to the ground. The sling slipped, and I stepped out on a portion of unsupported plywood to re-hitch the sling, and fell forty feet to the cement floor atop that sheet of plywood!

I fell face-down, and fractured my face on the right side, cracked four ribs and chipped a bone in my right wrist. Lou rushed to my side, and the Lord told her, "Put your hand in his mouth." She did so, and immediately large clots of blood came forth. The EMTs which arrived on the scene told her that if she hadn't done that, I could have choked to death.

I was completely knocked out, and didn't wake until I was in the ICU at St. Joseph's Hospital. Lou jumped into our car to follow the ambulance, but when the ambulance ran a red light, horns and sirens blaring, of course, she stopped. As she waited for the light to change, a man, carrying a Bible, opened the *locked* passenger-side door and poked his head in to say, "Your husband is going to be OK, Mrs. Budrow," closed the door and walked away.

I awoke in the ICU, all hooked up to tubes, etc., and heard Lou and Alfred singing "Kumbaya," and I chimed in on the bass for harmony, and immediately fainted again. Then Richard Benner, the pastor of our Wolf's Church in York, was there, and I told him, "Dick, my own stupidity got me into this mess. If I had paused a moment to think, I never would have stepped onto that unsupported roof. But if this can be used to glorify God, that's what I want. Here I am, and you can tell the folks at Wolf's to Praise the Lord!" "I'll tell them," he said. The doctors warned that there was a chance of death.

Lou and Alfred were shown the x-rays of my skull and chest, and laid their hands on the pictures and prayed individually for every broken bone. My face was puffed up like a basketball on the right side, all purple, and filled with a massive hematoma (collection of blood). The doctors said that the first thing to do was to stabilize me, then lift the bones of my face. Lou and Alfred left to get some supper, and when they returned an hour later, the hematoma was GONE, and the side of my face was all caved in. The doctors couldn't figure out where all that blood went!

Lou and Alfred went to a friend's house for the night, and returned first thing early in the morning. I was not in the ICU! Instead, I was in a wheel chair, going to a room. "We need the area in ICU for someone else," they were told. X-rays taken that morning showed ALL broken bones healed, and the shape of my face was fully restored!

I was admitted to the hospital on a Tuesday. On Thursday, I was transported to the York Hospital, where an examination showed the chip of a bone in my right wrist. So when I returned to work, after a week at home, with my arm in a sling, people asked me what happened, and I told them. If I hadn't had that sling, there might not have been an opening to proclaim God's mercy to them, but He arranged it so that His love could be shown!

The Sunday following my week at home, I went as usual to Wolf's Church, and the people couldn't believe my story. But they had heard from Pastor Benner, and his testimony of my broken state at St. Joseph's, and here I was, all hale and hearty and singing God's praises! How great is our God! Psalm 103, verse 3 says He heals all our diseases. I can attest to that!

47

FUN at Fish Camp

My father-in-law was referred by all as "Bampa," and was an avid fisherman. My in-laws lived on a small lake in Florida, which was nice for them. But during the summer he and "Ma," as she was referred to by all, spent their time at their fish camp in upper New York state, near Ogdensburg, on the Oswegatchie river, which connected to Black Lake, famous for its bass fishing.

Lou and I and the children went up to Black Lake for our vacation in 1968. Lou told me that I didn't know how to fish. I said that sure, I knew, but she insisted that I didn't. Bampa's formal education only went through the sixth grade, and here I was, a "college man" stealing his "son" (he sired three daughters, but the oldest left home to live with relatives when she was thirteen, the youngest never got along with her parents, so Lou was the one who learned how to fix cars and swing a hammer). There was a feeling of coolness towards me, so I was told that I was to be a rank beginner, absolutely clueless about anything to do with fishing. I listened to her good advice, and my "education" while in Bampa's boat earned me some brownie points.

Lou, Alfred and Calista all caught fish when we were at the fish camp with Ma and Bampa, but I never did. Well, almost never. We were out in the Oswewgatchie one day, and I, as usual, cast into the water and got hung up on weeds. Imagine my surprise when the weed clump which I pulled up revealed a Northern Pike inside! He had given me no fight whatsoever; I had no clue. Lou said to throw him back, that northern pikes were very bony and not a good food fish, but I was adamant—I finally had caught a fish, and I was gonna eat 'im, by golly! So Bampa skinned him and Ma cooked him and I ate him, but Lou was right, there were an awful lot of bones.

On their trips back and forth from Florida, Ma and Bampa would always stop to stay with us for a few days in York Pa.

Bampa's right arm began to bother him, his shoulder mostly, and it became painful for him to cast when fishing. So they cut their time in

Ogdensburg short, one summer. While they were staying with us on their way back south, I came downstairs to go to work one morning, and found Bampa sitting in front of the rear picture window rubbing his arm. I asked him how he was doing, and followed up with "Would you like me to pray for you?" and he answered "Yes." I raced to Lou and shook her. "Wake up! Your Dad wants us to pray for him!." This was big news because Bampa didn't put much stock in prayer. So we laid our hands on him, prayed for a healing, and Lou's folks left for home.

All the way back to Florida, Bampa used his right arm more and more to hold the steering wheel, and by the time they arrived home, he had complete mobility, and no more pain! God is so good!

The Griggs' next door neighbors in Ogsdenburg were a couple who lived in their fish camp all year long. We would hear them at night, when they would go out with a powerful flashlight and a 0.22 rifle to hunt frogs. The man worked for Ogdensburg, operating a bulldozer at the city dump. He found two old 20-gallon milk cans with the name of the dairy stamped on the lids. Since they might be valuable as antiques, he gave them to Bampa, who gave them in turn to Lou and me. Today, a thousand-gallon milk truck goes to a dairy farm and picks up the milk from the farmer's refrigerated holding tank, but in the past, the milk was brought to the dairy by the individual farmers in these aluminum cans.

With the addition of antique blue glass quart canning jars, I converted them into floor lamps. Lou painted the body of the lamps and they are still in use today.

48

$\mathcal{FUN}$ with Randy

Alfred started to attend York College, and met there a group of guys who, like him, were interested in playing "Dungeons And Dragons" video game. There he met, among others, Randy Schiller and Bob Strausser. These three became very close friends for the rest of their lives.

They were a mixed group, in that some were Christians and some were not. They all went to Randy's house one very snowy and blusterous winter night for a party, and the only ones who showed up were the Christians, and they all brought Christian albums with them (this was before DVDs, you know, the dark ages?) Randy lived at the end of a long twisty drive way through a sizable wood lot, and there were those who chose not to venture out in such weather. So Randy, one of the unsaved, got a dose of Jesus that night.

Al and Calista invited Randy to go with him and others to a Christian coffee house in downtown York. Between sets, the band would talk about salvation, etc., and while the others talked and joked about other things, Randy listened to the Jesus-talk.

Al and Calista took Randy with them when they attended a Happening weekend in Canton, PA (a "Happening" is a retreat for young adults, similar to a "Cursio" retreat for adults, both sponsored by the Episcopal denomination. We worshiped at the Church of the Holy Spirit at the time.) Randy received Christ while there, and when they returned, before Randy left to go home, he asked us to pray for his father Brad, who was definitely not saved, and an alcoholic, to boot. So we sat him down, told him to be a proxy for his dad, laid hands on him and commenced praying. The result was that the Baptism of the Holy Spirit fell on Randy, and he began to speak in tongues. Later on, he asked Lou and I to be his Godparents at his water baptism. He did street ministry, taught church school, preached on occasion, and became a true evangelist for God.

49

FUN with Bob

Lou and I were, as I said, Episcopalians at that time, and we hosted a group of adults in our home for praise, worship and Bible study on Saturday nights. Al was interested in attending, too, and asked if he could include some friends. Well, so many came that the group soon evolved into a young adult meeting, too boisterous for the "old folks."

We averaged about 20 interested parties every Saturday night. Everyone who played an instrument brought it with them, so there was a lively song each session, along with Bible study, teaching, socializing and, of course, food! Lou and I were the main suppliers, but often there were additional contributions.

I told you about Randy, and one of the memorable occasions was when the rest of us were in the living room, Randy was in the family room with Andrea. He came booming into the living room with, "Hallelujah, everybody! We have a brand new sister!" because Andrea had just received Jesus as her savior.

Calista was four years her brother's junior, but since we lived so far out and she didn't have people her own age to pal with, she became a sort of "mascot" for the group. She fell in love with Bob Strausser and later married him, but at this time she was only in 11th grade. The other girls at school were quite snooty to her because she always wore slacks (Lou wouldn't let her wear jeans) and wasn't vain like they were. When it came time for Homecoming, they mockingly asked her, "Who are you going to the dance with?"

"My boyfriend," she replied.

"Who is that? You're not dating anyone."

"He's in college," said my daughter.

"O-o-o! A college man! Aren't you the fancy one!"

Calista was very beautiful (in my completely objective opinion, of course) in her dress for the dance. She came home in a joyful happy mood, eyes shining, and to her parents said, "Yes-s-s-s!" The girls at school were awed and put to shame when Calista showed up with a six-foot-one handsome man with the physique of an athlete (he played football in high school), dressed impeccably, with an air of competence and experience.

Calista and Bob were married at Wolf's Church that summer, and when she came to school for her senior year wearing an engagement and a wedding ring, those girls couldn't believe it.

"Why are you married? You're not pregnant?"

"Of course not!"

"Then why get married?"

"Because I'm in love." They were shocked!

Calista had enough credits, and so graduated in January and left for Bellfonte, PA to set up housekeeping while Bob finished his education at Penn State. Their first child didn't arrive until six years later.

50

$\mathcal{FUN}$ with Kraig

As a by-product of the young adult fellowship we had at our Bairs Road home, when our daughter Calista fell in love with Bob Strausser, they couldn't wait. So they married that summer of 1983, and we remodeled our two-car garage into an apartment for them. We had to run electric, heat, water and sewage lines, of course. Not too hard to do for the electric and water, and we had made provision for the heat (ours was a baseboard hot water system) with the idea of a future heated workspace in the garage.

But the sewage hookup to the septic system was another matter entirely, involving digging, and laying pipe. The men of the group were very willing to do this grunt work for their friends. So there we were, down in a hole, having cut the cast iron pipe in two places and ready to connect a Y-intersection, when we heard from the bathroom window just above: "I'M SOR-R-Y!!!" and we jumped out of the way just in time!

It was earlier that same day, while we were starting to dig that hole, that Lou called from the front yard to introduce us all to Kraig Helberg. He was six-four, with a smile that could light up a dark room. He had been out walking, when a car pulled up and the people inside told him that they had a call to pick him up. That was surprising, and he didn't know these folks, but somehow he felt this was right, so he got in. They didn't explain, but drove in silence, and when they got to our driveway, told him to get out. They drove off, and he never saw them again. So he started to walk up the driveway and met Lou at the top. He explained the unusual way he arrived, so Lou took both of his hands in hers and said, "Let's pray."

Kraig was having some spiritual issues, so God sent him to us. He became one of our regulars, and often brought his sister Kecia with him. Later he married and lived with his new bride in our garage apartment for a while. He went to school to become a prosthetist, making artificial limbs, and donating all his vacation time to Stand Up With Hope, a Christian organization which served God in Africa, making legs and arms for destitute people there.

Twenty years later, there was a follow-up to all this. Lou and I planned a birthday party for Bob Strausser (graduate of Penn State and happily married to our darling Calista), but something always seemed to come up for the Straussers, and they "couldn't make it, so put it off a couple weeks, O.K.?"

This went on and on for a while, but finally a date was set. Bob and Calista came in through our front door, and the conversation was naturally moved into the kitchen. Meanwhile, people were going around to the back, and arriving through the patio doors into the living room, *silently.* When we finally adjourned there, it was a real surprise. A dozen or so of the former "kids" were there with instruments and song sheets, and we had a wonderful reunion. We found out that almost 100% of those young people who had honored our Bairs Road home with their presence were still very active in various ways and venues, to be God's ambassadors. What a blessing!

51

FUN in Arizona

In 1971, we took a trip to Arizona to visit my parents. They had sold their home in Lewiston and bought a house in Mesa, AZ. It was in a retirement community, one floor, two bedrooms, living room, dining area, compact kitchen, patio, very attractive. Since it is a desert state, most of the homes in this community had no lawns, but instead filled the "lawn" area with gravel, white or colored green. A few had blue or pink stones, too. These were enhanced, like my folk's, by islands of soil where flowers and trees were grown. These islands were watered by an underground sprinkler system which automatically came on for a couple hours every night.

The real estate deal my folks entered into when they bought their house included a membership in the club connected with the retirement community, and the use of the club's facilities, including a hot tub and swimming pool. We went there to take the children swimming in the pool, and had a good time. On the way out, we were walking along the edge of the pool, and Calista grabbed my swim trunks (Lou and I had changed into our street clothes, but the children still wore their swimsuits) and threatened to toss them into the pool. I told her that if she did, I would toss her in to retrieve them. She looked at me with a devilish look in her eyes, and flung my trunks out about twenty feet into the deepest part. So I picked her up and "shot-putted" her out into the water.

Some older ladies, lounging in the hot tub, were aghast that a six-year-old was being thrown into such deep water, and watched with apprehension as she disappeared beneath the surface. But Lou and I had taken Calista for swimming lessons at the Jewish Community Center in York, and had no fears. Soon, a little red bottom appeared, then a face with a huge grin, and Calista gripped my swimsuit in her teeth and dog-paddled her way back to us. I hauled her up and greeted her with a big hug and kiss. We laughed all the way home.

52

FUN in Scotland

In 1954, my friend and fellow folk dancer Bob Macdonald had planned a trip to Europe, primarily to visit his relatives in Scotland. He had never met these folks before, but was interested to see where his forefathers had come from. So he researched his genealogy and contacted many of the Macdonalds, and received a lot of positive replies. My mother (she always was looking for ways for Jane and I to have fun and new experiences, and since Jane had taken her junior college year in Austria, thought that here was a golden opportunity for me to have a similar experience) suggested that I join Bob and go to Europe. I did, and planned to visit some of the people who had graced our home in Lewiston.

The plan was to sail from New York in July, but Mom insisted that I get a clean bill of health from the dentist before the embarkation date. Well, we couldn't get an appointment in time, so Bob sailed alone, and I had to sail later, from Quebec, Canada.

I met up with Bob in England and we made the rounds of his relatives. I won't go into details of all the places we visited or saw. There is a daily journal which I kept, in the form of letters to my parents, and that is available to tell of my complete adventures those five months of traveling on a BSA "Bantam"125cc motorcycle. But I will mention a few of the more memorable experiences.

We went to Elgin, Scotland to visit the Grierson family. I don't recall the exact relationship, but Bob had written to them and they were expecting us. Their oldest daughter was Susan, about fifteen, and she entertained us while we waited for supper. She brought out the family picture album to show us various photos. One batch of pictures was of a family outing at a park with a small stream running through. Susan, then 13, was in charge of the small children who were playing in the water.

The children were all naked, and she was, too. Showing such pictures was entirely natural, and she was not the least embarrassed to show them to us. Throughout Europe, nudity at a beach or park, especially for children less than six or seven years old, is quite normal. Elgin is right on the coast of the North Sea, and Susan related how, after a dance the young folks she was with decided to have a swim before coming home. So they all doffed their clothes and dove in. There was a huge rock between the boys and the girls, and they made sure they were submerged whenever the lighthouse light shone down. A bit "naughty," but normal fun.

Since the ancestral home of the Macdonalds was Duntulm on the Isle of Skye, we took "The Road to the Isles" as the words to that song laid out, and ended up getting to Skye by boat, a small vessel which carried the mail. Landing ashore there was treacherous because the quay was a sloping pier of stone with thick slippery wet moss on it, and we had to muscle the bikes up it, nearly losing them into the water.

I already said that Jane and I were taught how to read a map when we were 13 and 14, and my mother drove across country, in that new Mercury in 1946. Well Bob never was so taught, and because his motorcycle was 150cc and he was lighter than I by 40lbs he could travel faster than I, and got lost on our way to London. He was five miles down the road before he stopped to let me catch up, and when he did I asked him if he noticed the route signs a ways back that pointed the way to London, and he admitted he didn't know how to read them.

Later in Milan, Italy, he couldn't read a street map. The Youth Hostel in Milan was in a large house surrounded by a high wall and a locked gate. Bob and I were advised to not ride our bikes into town to see the sights, but to walk; as a parked motorcycle was an invitation to thievery. Although the bikes might not be taken, they would be found minus everything but the bare bones if left unattended. Unless, of course, you paid someone to guard it in your absence. So we walked.

After visiting the cathedral, buying some hot roasted chestnuts (yum!) and a couple slices of pizza (yuck!), Bob tired out and wanted to go back to the hostel. I agreed but said "Just another few blocks in this direction." But that wouldn't do, so I gave him the city map we were using. "I can't read that thing!" he said. Now, Milan was a fairly large city, 200,000 or so population, and the map we had was only about twelve inches square. So I persuaded him to go "just two more blocks"—and there we were, right at the hostel gate!

In Malakoff, a small town near Paris, the youth hostel was in the field house of the town stadium. There were the usual dormitories for the men and women, but the bathrooms need explaining. The toilets there were "squat johns," a rectangular porcelain floor insert, about three feet square, with two raised areas where you placed your feet. A hole in the center took away the waste, and a flange around the extremities flushed water to facilitate this. You activated this by a pull-chain to a tank on the wall. Don't lose your balance!

In Paris was the famous Folies Bergere. We had heard of it, and that it was quite risqué with a lot of nudity. We wanted to go, of course, but were told that it was sold out for months to come. But we were informed that the Casino de Paris was very similar and much less pricey, as well as being available. So we went.

The show was a burlesque and a revue. Yes, there were a lot of beautiful females strutting around wearing little or nothing, but also some funny skits and some truly artistic offerings. The one which took my rapt attention was of two statues which "came to life." The statues were well-muscled men (wearing, like the women, the minimum) who proceeded to do stylized gymnastics in slow motion with each other. It was an amazing display of strength and grace, and to my mind, not the least bit lewd.

53

FUN at Oktoberfest

One of the places we visited was Munich, Germany, where we went to the famous Oktoberfest beer festival.

A word here about Bavarian traditional clothing:.

The "dirndle" is a full skirt which is tubular, gathered at one end for a waist. When whirling, the skirt flares out for a short distance, then drops straight down. The dirndle costume is completed with a tight bodice over a short-sleeved blouse which is always white and low-cut to accentuate the wearer's breasts. The costume always includes a solid-color apron, usually white or black, and a scarf or large kerchief worn over the shoulders and tucked into the bodice. The entire costume is often referred to as a "dirndle," and is also often used as a term for a young woman.

"Lederhosen" (literally "leather pants"), are either shorts, or knickers gathered just below the knee with a strap, always made of gray, black or brown suede. They are always worn with leather suspenders which often are decorated with embroidery.

The Oktoberfest is a beer festival, and every brand of beer has its own large tent, where food and beer are served to the patrons, seated at tables very much like American picnic tables, and most wear traditional German clothing: dirndls and lederhosen. When we talked to them, they all claimed that their brand of beer was the best, the others all weak and not worth anything. Bob and I both said we didn't like beer, and were met with much disbelief and laughter, but no disdain.

The Oktoberfest is also a carnival, with traditional carnival rides, such as the Ferris wheel, but there were three rides that neither Bob nor I had ever seen before.

The "Teufelrad," or "devil wheel," is a 20-foot rotating circular disc on the floor, highly polished and raised in the center. About ten or so people sit on the disc as close to center as possible. As the disc spins and accelerates, centrifugal force causes the people to slide off the disc, to land in embarrassing positions around the padded circumference.

People who were watching from the sidelines cheered the participants on—especially the girls, knowing that they are going to expose their underwear (the women never wore trousers, especially in 1954!).

Some American girls who were there (in Europe) thought it very cute to wear lederhosen shorts, but the Germans were insulted by that behavior.

The Rotor is a vertical cylinder about 12 feet in diameter and 18 feet tall, with a floor which can be raised and lowered. Spectators are admitted to climb stairs to a circular ramp which winds downward in an ever decreasing spiral until they are at a door which opens into the Rotor, and those who choose to ride are admitted to stand against the wall. The Rotor spins on it's vertical axis, creating centrifugal force which plasters the people, about 10 to 12 in number, to the wall. As they spin around, the floor is lowered. After a few minutes, the Rotor slows, and the people begin to slide down the wall. The walls are made of narrow vertical strips of wood, and the clothes of the riders tend to stick to the wall while the wearers slide down. Again, the girls, in skirts, are in danger of exposing their undies. When the Rotor stops, a lower door leads to the outside.

The Swings are just that, like those on almost any playground, but the flexible chains or ropes are replaced with rigid metal bars about fifteen feet long. These are fixed to a platform about four feet by 18 inches, with places for the riders, one or two, to stand. While riding, the riders' feet are securely bound to the platform to prevent falls. The riders pump to get the swing to go higher and higher, until eventually they can go completely around, 360 degrees. Of course, approaching the apex, the riders are upside down, and, again, the skirts are falling down about the girls' heads and the undies are on display.

In the city of Munich, just the same as on the fairgrounds, each brewery has it's own restaurant and beer hall. Bob and I wanted to find somewhere where we could observe some Bavarian folk dances, and our inquiries led us to the Eisinger beer hall. Because of our clothing, we were immediately recognized as Americans, and were ushered to two chairs at a table of friendly Bavarians. Again, our preference for no beer was met with laughter, but not with disdain. We were offered cold "apfelsaft" (apple juice) which was elegantly served in a small earthenware pitcher on a matching tray with a glass.

The Eisinger beer hall had a stage which projected out into the restaurant, so that it was surrounded by the patrons. The dancers did indeed perform some folk dances, including a "schuhplattler" (literally "shoe slaps"). That is a dance where the men slap their thighs, hips and shoes in a fast rhythm, while their partners pirouette around them in a circle. The men, feigning ignorance, cannot remember their partners' faces, but they can remember the color of the garter each one was wearing. So as the girls whirl around, the guys flip up each skirt until the right girl is found.

54

$\mathcal{FUN}$ with Toilet Paper

Bob Macdonald left for home because he had to report for active army duty, but I stayed on to do some more visiting with people who had visited our home in Lewiston. I retraced some of my steps, and in Switzerland I stayed at a youth hostel located quite a ways off the main road. I had directions, so followed a sign pointing to a path through a meadow and came upon a cottage built into the side of a hill.

There were two floors, the upper one like an open-air deck, with deep seats all around which I supposed could be used as beds when the weather was warm. The main floor was built into the hill, with stone walls, and contained a welcome wood stove (the weather, with fall coming on, was a bit chilly) and two rooms for sleeping. The other occupants were two Polish men who spoke very little German and no English, and a girl who spoke very good English with an Australian accent. She was actually a Hungarian, but her family had settled in Australia when she was a young teenager.

We had a good conversation, then she excused herself to use the toilet facilities. I warned her that there was only an outhouse, and that the only toilet paper available was slick pages torn from a catalog. But I offered some of my hoarded toilet paper stash for her comfort.

When she returned, she thanked me profusely, and I explained that when Bob and I, after experiencing the toilet paper in Britain (glazed on one side and like sandpaper on the other), found soft toilet paper on the ferry to France, we stole several rolls each. So I gifted her with the remains of my next-to-last roll.

The up-shot of this story is that in the hostel in Rotterdam, waiting for my ship to USA to sail, I ran into this same girl. She greeted me and confided that I was a life-saver—she had used the roll I gave her very sparingly, and was down to her last three sheets. So I again gave her the rest that I had. How's that for improving international relations?

I visited the Haymans in Darlington, England, during my European tour in 1954. In many English homes the toilet is not in the bathroom,

117

but in a separate small room called a "water closet." At the Haymans', the user was offered two choices: awful English paper on a nondescript holder, or a rustic decorated holder with soft American paper. Which to use? No contest!

But when I pulled the soft tissues, the holder rotated to wind up a music box. The Haymans were directly below me in the kitchen, and were just waiting to hear the tinkle-tinkle of the music box, and I heard their laughter. They knew exactly what I was doing!

55

$\mathcal{FUN}$ with Russians

In Austria, in 1954, there were only two roads to get to Vienna. This was during the Cold War, remember, and Austria was split up into three zones, the American, the British and the Russian. Vienna was in the Russian zone, but was accessible by only two roads, one from the north and one from the south. As long as I traveled on the road itself, I was O.K. But if I wandered onto a side road or even walked a few feet off the pavement, I could be picked up by Russian troops. Now, the road was paved with "rund steins" (literally "round stones") which were granite, about a foot long, square body and a round top, which were packed in vertically to make a solid pebbly surface which was slippery when wet.

Well, it was raining and I was following a Russian troop transport truck up a grade, very slowly because the truck was in low gear to make this assent, and my bike just slipped sideways out from under me. Immediately the truck stopped, and the soldiers jumped out to help me up. "Amerikanski OK? OK?" I was scared! But I finally assured them that I was not hurt, and they climbed back into the truck and continued. I let them get far-r-r-r ahead of me before I continued on!

In Vienna, Bob and I were the guests of Walter Michalitsch, who had been a guest in our Lewiston home. While in that city, we attended the Sudatenlander's Ball. Sudatenland is an area of Austria which was the first place the Nazis invaded in 1938.

I was intrigued by one of the dancers, an old gentleman dressed in full Sudatenland costume. He wore black knee-breeches, white stockings, black square-toed shoes with two-inch heels and big silver buckles, a white blousy shirt and string tie, a cut-away coat with square tails and yellow accents, and a low-brimmed black hat with a large feather tucked into the hat band. He danced the Viennese waltzes with abandon, and with a different beautiful girl every time he came around the dance floor.

The hall was large, with a full orchestra on stage, and a centerpiece of flowers, easily ten feet by twenty feet in the center, and the dancers went around and around it. With a Strauss waltz, you don't stand still, you move, and always in a counter-clockwise direction.

Vienna was a three-sectioned city, just as Berlin was, and beyond the city was the Russian zone, as I mentioned. The Austrians went through the checkpoints with ease, and they were very rarely stopped, due to the many students at the university having homes outside the city. So we stripped our bikes of anything extra, like mirrors, leg shields, windscreens, luggage racks, lights, etc. and muddied up the remaining result to look dirty (especially the license plates), and we went, behind the "Iron Curtain" to visit Walt's home village. We were the first Americans they had seen for sixteen years.

Walt's parents ran a farm, and it was in an old river bed and very fertile. The main house was at the front of the property, and formed a corner of an enclosed farmyard. The yard was behind a wall, about fifteen feet high, and was about forty feet wide and a hundred feet long, entered by a large gate at the front, and a barn at the back through which you could drive a tractor to the fields beyond. The sides of the yard were taken up by equipment sheds and livestock sheds on both sides. And right in the middle was a square enclosure, about four feet high, made of concrete, which was the manure pile. There were flies everywhere!

We were served a delicious lunch inside the house, and I noticed that even with the windows open, and a welcome breeze coming through, and that the house, being an integral part of the farm yard and only about thirty feet from the manure pile, there were NO flies in the house. How come? There were no screens on the windows either. Have you ever smelled a geranium leaf? There is an odor which to human noses is not offensive, but it turns flies away. So at this farmhouse there were geraniums in flower boxes at every window. The windows were opened just to the tops of the plants, and the air could get through, but not the flies.

56

$\mathcal{FUN}$ in Kalrsruhe and Stuttgart

One of the towns we visited in Germany was Karsruhe, the home of Herbert Zerr. He was one of the many visitors we entertained at Lewiston. He and his friend Jurgand took Bob and me on a two-day journey through the Schwartzwald (Black Forest). We ended up for supper the first day at he home of Herbert's uncle. He served home made apple wine, which I didn't drink. One of the guests was a man who had been a P.O.W. In the U.S. during the war, and understood English pretty well. I told Herbert that the wine tasted like vinegar, and this fellow understood my comment. He laughed uproariously and told everyone the joke. I was quite humiliated.

But we got to talking, and he wondered how it was that we Americans could belong to different political parties and still be friends, because in Europe it seemed as though your party was the only party, and you couldn't be sociable to someone from a different point of view.

I was in Stuttgart, Germany, and was wandering around town after checking in at the local Youth Hostel, and I saw a poster in a store window advertising "Tibor Varga Spielt Bach in der Kleine Goldene Salle am Sieben Uhr" ("Tibor Varga plays Bach in the Small Gold Room at seven o'clock"). I went inside and bought the last ticket. I went back to the hostel and, since I was the only one staying there, thought that perhaps I could come back late after the concert, but was told that no, I could not—the doors were locked precisely at ten, no exceptions!

The Small Gold Room was a small concert hall over the top of a movie house, and it was entirely baroque, with fake columns on the walls interspersed with scenes of nymphs and Grecian landscapes. The ceiling was likewise decorated, with frescoes framed by plaster moldings. There was no tiered seating or theater seats, but all were upright chairs, in white with gold accents. About a hundred seats on a flat floor, and a small balcony with only four rows. My seat was the last one available, in the balcony.

Tibor came in with his violin, taking his place on a small stage with five or so other instruments, and the music was superb. I was thrilled to hear such fantastic baroque music in the perfect baroque setting! Alas, I had to leave before the concert was over, to meet my ten o'clock curfew. But the memory will last a lifetime.

57

FUN Going Home

I returned from Europe in the fall of 1954, bringing my motorcycle with me. I had to realign the shape of the bike by removing handle bars, leg shields, windscreen, luggage carrier, etc., in order to ship it as a bicycle rather than a motorcycle, and so to save money. There was no limit to the number of pieces of "luggage" I could have. When I arrived back in New York, I had to reassemble the bike so I could ride it home.

On my way to Lewiston, I stopped off in Syracuse to visit Liz Macomber, one of my girlfriends from college. She was a folk dancer, too, and was interested in seeing the costumes I had acquired on my travels. She tried on the kilt which I purchased in Edinburgh and then told me that now I could experience one of the joys of being a woman—standing over a hot air register on a cold winter's day!

In Europe, I had with me a dark blue nylon parka, and had also acquired a lot of embroidered patches where ever I traveled. On the voyage home, I spent a lot of time sewing them onto the parka. Later, on a ski trip, I was at the top of the ski run at the end of the day, and a member of the Ski Patrol asked if I would take the main trail down to the bottom, checking to see that all skiers were off the hill. I said, "Sure," and did so. It must have been my outfit which impressed him, with all my patches, and my Austrian hat with the ski badges pinned on it, that made me out to be an experienced skier. If he had watched me ski, he would have known I had just a so-so ability. But I certainly could cut a good figure as long as I was standing still!

58

FUN with Ping-Pong (Don't Mess With Alfred!)

This is a story about my son Alfred when he was in high school. We raised him to always be respectful of his elders, and behave as a Christian should, so you might say we were very surprised to be called into school on a discipline problem concerning a new teacher.

In the school entry lobby, a ping-pong table had been set up, and was in constant use during the lunch hour, and before and after school. The ping-pong balls, being highly destructible, had to be furnished by the students themselves, and the usual neighborhood candy, etc., store stocked them in a variety of colors.

On the occasion of "The Ping-Pong Incident," the new teacher was proctoring a study hall, with about 50 or so students present, and one other teacher. All was quiet. Alfred reached into his pocket for a pencil, and when he did so, his ping-pong ball fell out and bounced on the floor, making a noise and instigating a scramble to retrieve it.

The teacher said to bring the ball forward, and accused Alfred of deliberately causing a disturbance. He protested his innocence, but she would not listen. She instructed him to place the ball on the floor, whereupon she stomped it. Alfred indignantly retaliated with some less-than-complementary remarks about the destruction of his personal property, and was sent to the principal's office.

At home, Alfred ver-r-r-y carefully opened the red ping-pong ball which he bought, and filled it with ketchup. Then he ver-r-r-y carefully re-glued and restored it to its original appearance and took it to school. The next time Alfred was in study hall with that proctor, it just so happened that fate (?) decreed that this very blonde teacher was wearing a white pant suit. Fifty or so students waited in anticipation, for the word was out that something might happen. Alfred brought out the ping-pong booby trap and rolled it around on his desktop. The teacher made him bring it to the front of the room, and accused him of deliberately disturbing the class, which he admitted.

"Put the ball on the floor!" she said.

"You won't like it," he said.

Stomp!

Ketchup everywhere, and especially all over her white shoes and pantsuit!

Fifty-plus students standing, shouting, clapping, cheering!!

The other teacher suffused with laughter!

The victim teacher, beet red, having a bout of apoplexy!

Alfred was suspended from school for three days, and returned to tell his classmates that what he did was not the right thing to do. But an A-1 status with the student body? You betcha!

When Al started senior high school, he was approached by one of the older boys who offered him some "weed" (marijuana). Al grabbed him by the throat and slammed him against the lockers, holding him off the floor, and told him that if he ever offered that awful stuff again, he would have to look up his rectum to find his teeth! Don't mess with Al!

59

$\mathcal{FUN}$ at the Fair

In 1972, we found that our house had been invaded by an insect: Old Wood Borers. We built the house with a wood box next to the fireplace, with a small access door to the outside, so we didn't have to go outside for fuel. We loaded it with logs that first winter and enjoyed the comfort of an open fire while it snowed outside. But we didn't know that the wood, which we gleaned from our own woodlot, was infested with these insects, and they got into our woodwork. They are like termites, except they don't require water, as termites do. The result was that we were forced out of our home for a week while the pests were destroyed.

So we went on vacation. We went to a campground in Lycoming County which we had noticed in our previous travels up route US15 to and from Niagara Falls. While there, we went to the Lycoming County Fair. We walked around to see the sights, went on a few rides, had some fair food, etc. We watched with interest the greased pig event, where a dozen or so boys were trying to catch a small pig which had been thoroughly oiled to make it slippery to hold. That pig found a hole in the fenced-in area and escaped.

As providence would have it, Alfred noticed where that pig was hiding underneath the bleachers surrounding the greased-pig arena, and went under the bleachers and caught it. He returned the pig to the men in charge, and the chase continued. They thanked him for the recovery, but since he wasn't an official participant, no prize!

60

Why I Don't Fist-Fight

Throughout my life, I have never instigated nor participated in a fist-fight, like so many people do. As a grade-school student, I used to get beat-up often, but when the others picked on me, I would never hit back. I didn't understand this, and then made up scenarios in my head when alone in my room, showing me victorious.

I did have some retaliatory moves. When Jane and I, then in second grade, walked the mile or so to Hickory College, Alfred Meyer, an older boy, would throw horse chestnuts at us as we walked past his farm to the one-room school we all attended. I stopped by his house on our way home one day, and reported the incidents to his mother. He never taunted us again.

I learned from this situation. When, in fourth grade, my chief tormentor was the principal's son, I went to his father, and that put a stop to that right quick!

But I wasn't entirely blameless. On one occasion, in fifth grade, I was rightly beat up because I flippantly teased Billy Rose about his (very!) buck teeth. I was showing off in front of a girl, and when Billy attacked me a few days later I was apologetic, but to no avail.

In North Junior High School, pea shooters showed up in the hands of some of the boys and there was, naturally, some disturbing incidents. Emma Hulan, the principal, was an acquaintance of my mother. She knew how I had been raised, to always play by the rules and respect those in authority. So even though she knew that I was not one of the culprits, she knew that I knew who they were, and called me to her office. She quizzed me for their names, and when I said I didn't want to tell, she said: "Teddy, you MUST tell me!" Well, she was "authority," so I did. The boys really took it out on me after school! When I related the events to my mother, she said that in some situations you don't tell, and don't "squeal" on others. BUT Mom had some heated words with Miss Hulan, and I never even spoke to her after that.

When I was about four, in kindergarten, at the advice of a teenager helper (older than I, and therefore "authority"), I hit another toddler who wanted the same toy as I did. He cried, and I felt so bad that I cried, too. I had no idea, at that age, that I could hurt another person with my fist. This fear of actually intentionally inflicting pain on someone has stayed with me all these years, so I don't fist-fight.

61

FUN with My Darling Maralou

I used to smoke a pipe. I quit after many years, and it was Lou who convinced me to stop.

She said, "Stop smoking in the house—everything has that smoke odor."

So I stopped smoking in the house.

Then she said, "Stop smoking in the car when you are going to work because you burnt a hole in the upholstery from an ash from your pipe, and the car smells bad."

So I stopped smoking in the car.

Then she said, "Stop smoking while you're working at Caterpillar— your clothes all smell of smoke."

So I stopped smoking at work.

Then she said, "Stop smoking while you're out in the yard. All you do out there is to relight that pipe over and over and not getting anything done."

So I stopped smoking altogether.

All this while, I was singing with the York barbershop chorus. We went to the district competition in Ocean City, MD in 1967, and our small chorus decided to go by bus. It was a magical time for me, and I thoroughly enjoyed myself there.

Now, almost every chorus which competed had a hospitality room where there were snacks, etc., for any barbershoppers who cared to drop in after the contest was over. Using my "miraculous powers of deduction" (?), I went to the Bryn Mawr chapter's room because I thought that they would have a better afterglow (a continuation of barbershop festivities, which most chapters host after a show), due to being such a large chorus, and probably more money to spend. I was correct in my assumption—their room was quite big, with a l-o-o-ong table filled with beverages and snacks, and a raised platform in one corner with a microphone.

I bought myself a corn-cob pipe and a package of tobacco, filled my plate with a lot of food, and sat back to enjoy two hours of barbershop harmony. Every quartet which competed, and many which hadn't, came to get up on that dais and sing a couple songs. It was heavenly! As luck would have it, the very last quartet to appear was the "Ultimates" from our chapter, and I rode with them back to our hotel.

When I got back home the next day and greeted Lou with a kiss, she immediately accused me of smoking. I replied that since I (1) wasn't in the house and (2) wasn't in our car and (3) wasn't at work and (4) wasn't in our yard and (5) wasn't wearing my own clothes because I was in our barbershop uniform, I figured it was all right to smoke. So I had her boxed into a corner, but she loved me anyway.

Lou didn't like food that was noisy. She was the only one I've known who liked pretzels, but would hold one in her mouth and gum it to death until it was soft enough to chew without crunching.

At one of the young adult meetings that Lou and I hosted at our home on Bairs Road, Lou was seated at the dining room table when two of the guys (I think it was Tom Medill and Ed Levalee), each with a large potato chip at the ready, silently came up behind her and CRUNCHed! into her ears. She literally jumped to her feet in alarm!

Lou had a chronic condition, which often caused her pain in her back. I had read about Chiropractic, and suggested she try it for relief. After some deliberation, we decided to go to a Dr. Sigafoose, who was written up in various magazine articles as being a leader in that field, and his office was not far away. That started many years of us both going to a chiropractor for treatments.

When we moved to Landisville, I became a member of the Red Rose Chorus (barbershop) in Lancaster, and one of the songs we sang for contest was from My Fair Lady, "I'm Getting Married In The Morning." So I arose one morning, planning my day, which included a chiropractic visit to Tyler Mandel. A song came into my head, and to the tune of the above-mentioned song, I sang to Tyler:

"I'm going to Mandel in the morning,
He's gonna straighten out my spine,
He's gonna shove it,
And I'm gonna love it,
When my bones are all in line.

"The subluxation ain't got a chance.
When he is finished, you are gonna dance!

"'Cause when you go to Tyler in the morning,
Or afternoon or evening—any time,
He'll straighten out your back-bone,
From your tail-bone to your neck-bone,
And when he's done, you're feeling fine!"

He just looked at me, shook his head and said, "Ted, you are a treasure!" I gave him a printout, and he hung it up on the bulletin board in his waiting room.

Lou always prayed for what she wanted. She opened her heart to Jesus as a young girl, and her strong faith enabled her to hear God's voice her whole life. One evening shortly before she began at Moore Business Forms, she was at her bedroom window and prayed that she would find a blond blue-eyed man for a husband. God said, "He's right now at the ice cream stand in Sanborn" (a small village nearby). Comparing notes some years later, we determined that yes, I had been there that evening.

She told me that when she saw me for the first time at Moore, she knew that I was the answer to her prayers, a blonde-haired blue-eyed man. Well, I know that although I had danced with a lot of girls, and dated quite a few, there was never a romantic interest until her, and since then I have concluded that our marriage was foreordained from the very first.

Later, when we were married and I was making a living painting and paper-hanging, I was working in Shrewsbury, a town 15 miles southeast of our house. Lou opened the mail to find something that needed my immediate attention. She had never been to Shrewsbury before, but knew approximately where it was. She got in her car and started out, asking God to show her the way. When she found Shrewsbury, she listened, and God told her,

"Turn right" and
"Turn left" and
"Go two blocks" and then,
"Look to your right—there's Ted's grey pick-up."

Lou and I met before we met. That sounds like an impossibility, but it's true. We both attended Methodist churches, and the Methodists had a retreat center er at Silver Lake, one of the smaller Finger Lakes. I had gone there a couple times in my youth, and so had she (keep in mind, I was eight years older than Lou).

So here I was, out of college and experienced in folk and square dancing and had my own sound system, and I got a call to see if I would go to Silver Lake to teach and call square dancing to the teenage campers. So I did, and I also taught a few simple folk dances. Well, for the folk dances, to demonstrate the steps, I needed a partner, so I selected a pretty girl from among the campers for that task.

After we had been married for about a year, Lou and I were reminiscing, and she brought out a group picture of the campers at Silver Lake when she was there. We noted several people we both knew, and I remarked that I had revisited Silver Lake as an adult, to entertain with a square dance and teach a folk dance or two.

"And you needed a partner to demonstrate, didn't you?"

"Yes . . ."

"That was me!!"

So you see, God knew that we would meet again at Moore Business Forms and St. Paul's Young Adults—all a part of His Plan.

Within our young adult group at St. Paul's, I often had a load of passengers in my car. Somehow, it was always Maralou Griggs who was the last one to be ferried home. Now, how come . . . ??

One snowy Niagara County Saturday night, we ended up, as usual, at her place at the end of the evening. A few miles earlier I had negotiated a large drift spanning the road, (with my BOSS two-toned V-8 Ford with hooded headlights and tail fins!), so I wasn't surprised to find one spanning her driveway. Ever the macho and chivalrous guy, I came around to her side of the car, picked her up and carried her in my arms to her front door, wading through that shoulder-high drift to get there.

The next morning I was there again to give her a ride to church, and discovered that if I had only walked a few steps to the right the night before, I could have gone around the drift instead of through it. Did I regret doing it the hard way? No, Sir!!

One memorable evening, Lou and I were in my car in her driveway, saying good night with the usual hugs and kisses. I looked into her eyes and saw the love that was so evident to me, then gave her the most intense kiss of all and said, "Oh, Lou, will you marry me?' I hadn't planned to say that, it just popped out of my mouth! But there was no hesitation in her answer: "Yes!"

I didn't have an engagement ring handy, because the proposal was as much a surprise to me as it was to her. So that night I selected a violet-colored agate in a tear drop shape, glued a clasp to it, and gave it to her as a substitute until I bought the ring. She wore it around her neck for a long time, even after she got her ring. Over the years it was always a prized possession, and now resides on the urn containing her ashes.

In March of 2017, Lou suffered a stroke, and her left side was paralyzed. I became her caregiver, getting out of bed every two hours to check on her and see to her needs. This regimen was very hard on me, and interfered with our notary business.

I had planned to retire from notary work in June of 2017, when my license expired, so it all worked out. Leslie Spohr, Lou's nephew, had moved here from Colorado, and now took over the business from me at a time when he really needed the income.

Alfred noticed my distress, and determined to quit his contracting work to become our full-time live-in caregiver. He negotiated the various hoops that he was required to jump through because of being a blood relative, and accomplished that, ending up by getting hired by a caregiving company, giving him a weekly paycheck.

A word here in praise of Cindy, our beloved daughter-in-law, who gave up her husband so he could live-in with us 30 miles away in Landisville for quite a long while, until things were settled for us to live with her and Al in York.

Al used his construction skills and contacts to build an apartment onto his house for Lou and me, all built specifically for invalid care. There were flat entrances lined up with the driveway so there were no steps, all overhead lighting so there were no electric cords on the floor, a wheelchair-accessible bathroom, commercial low-pile carpeting to avoid tripping falls, together with living, dining and kitchen areas. A large overhang outside double French doors sheltered the area behind the entrance to the wheelchair van Al purchased, or to an ambulance. Lou's hospital bed was separated from the living area by a curtain, which afforded privacy when needed, but allowed family and friends full access for visiting.

We sold our house in Landisville and moved into the apartment. The equity allowed us to fully pay for the new apartment and every other bill we owed, so we were completely out of debt, 100%, and had a sizable bank account left over.

Praise the Lord, for He was the one who whispered in Lou's ear to become notaries, and He sent us all the business, making it possible to have a full, worry-free retirement.

To illustrate how God turns tragedy into triumph, Lou's affliction allowed Al to quit worrying about deadlines, employees, payrolls, materials and late-paying clients, to devote himself to his parents' needs, and to give him time to pursue other interests while staying at home. Since I stopped notarizing, and was available during the day, Al's check-ins every 20 minutes were sufficient, and he could raise sprouts for sale, plant vegetable and flower gardens and repair his 165-year-old house.

Al came into Lou one day with a beautiful vase filled with flowers for her. I'll never forget the look on his face. He was just beaming, because *he* planted the seeds in *his* garden and brought *his* flowers to *his* mother! Lou may have noticed, or not, but it brought tears to my eyes to see the love in his eyes.

Although Lou knew she was nearing the date of her "Graduation" to the ultimate level in heaven, she never lost her sense of humor. Just a week or so before passing, as Alfred was changing her, she said that although she didn't like it, she knew she must "go" in her diaper. "Where I'd rather like to be going," she quipped, "is Bermuda!" And when I would tease her by asking if she would love me forever, she would often say "maybe" or "I'm working on it." What a gal!

Our daughter-in-law spoke with her just three days before her death, and Lou told Cindy that she was "ready to go home to Jesus"; that when Billy Graham asked if she died tonight, would she be ready (she had been watching repeats of his Crusades), she could answer "Yes!" without a doubt.

Lou went to meet her Lord January 23, 2021.

These memoirs end with a tribute to Maralou, the most Christian person I ever knew.

And a sincere heart-felt "Thank You" to God for allowing me to have a life of LOVE and

FUN!

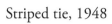

Striped tie, 1948

High School Grad
yearbook picture, 1950

Two young men in the snow,
1951: Ted Budrow and college
roommate Chuck Harper

Kilts, 1955: Ted Budrow and fellow
European traveler Bob Macdonald.

Me and my Ford Falcon (first new car), 1958

Wedding, 1961

Square Dance / Western shirt 1964

Palm Sunday, 1979, outside after church. holding palm leaves.
Above, me and Lou; below, Alfred and Calista.

Me holding our first grandchild, Micah, at nine months, 1987.

Part 2

Budrow European Journal

(June 17–December 6, 1954)

Five Months on a BSA 125cc Bantam Motorcycle

England, showing our route.

SCOTLAND

Duntulm

Elgin

Dunvegan
Portree

Monymusk

Glenelg

Dundee

Ballachulish

Tyndrum

Edinburgh

Carlisle

To Darlington, England

Scotland, showing our route from beginning to end.

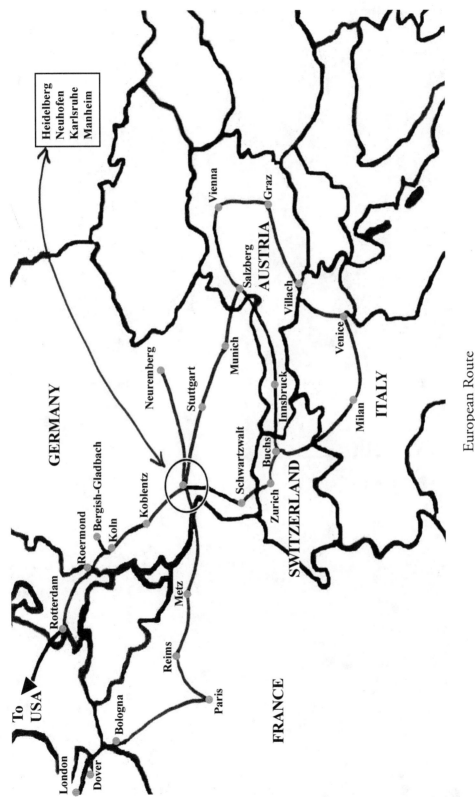

European Route

Introduction

This is a journal of my trip to Europe in 1954, after my graduation from Syracuse University. My very good friend and fellow folk dancer, Bob Macdonald, accompanied me.

We lived at that time in Niagara Falls, NY, a place well known throughout the world, and both Bob and I had many foreign visitors after the Second World War, mainly university students. The idea was to visit many of the people who had been in our homes. Bob had researched his family ties in England and Scotland, so we visited them, as well.

Each day I sent a letter home, detailing the day's activities. Interspersed among the entries are a few additional letters, as a sort of postscript, to inform my parents of additional plans and personal requests.

We traveled by motorcycle. The hostels in England would not accept anyone who arrived by motorized vehicle, but everywhere else in Europe we were welcome.

The Journal

Thursday, June 17, 1954

Came down to New York City by train. I met a most interesting girl when I got off the subway. She, out of a clear blue sky, asked me what kind of sleeping bag I had, It turned out she had just come from the American Youth Hostel office, and was interested in folk dancing and hosteling, and had been abroad. She had had a little longer preparation time, three weeks, when she had gone over, but hadn't known until the last moment whether she was going or not. I guess I'm not the only one. Well, here's hoping.

Friday, June 18, 1954

Today was a hectic one. Up at 7:45 a.m. and off tout de suite to the passport office. Everything was in order except my birth certificate, which didn't have a seal on it. So an affidavit was wired from home. If I had skipped my dentist appointment and come down to New York City Wednesday morning, I probably could have picked up the passport Saturday morning. Now the passport won't get here until Monday. All the ships are full up, and my only chance of getting aboard one is to be standing by as the passengers board. This I will do on Tuesday, Wednesday, Thursday, and Friday. There's another one leaving the following Tuesday, but unless I can get a passage assured before Saturday noon, I'll leave for home.

At the Home Lines office (Holland America) this morning I was offered a berth on the *Atlantic*, sailing July 1st from Quebec. I hesitated, and he who hesitates is lost. I told him "maybe," and when I came back a short time later he had sent it to Boston, where an agent said he had an interested customer. The same man told me he had been offered the job of booking passengers for the *Seven Seas*, and that he knew I could get on if I could stand by, but the passport is not here, so what can I do? Well, I'll wish Bob bon voyage and see what turns up.

All other things have been taken care of, though, or are about to: Toiletries have been bought, and my vaccination record certified. Tomorrow

I will buy a money bag and pass at the American Youth Hostel and a pair of Boy Scout shorts at the Boy Scouts of America's retail store, and move from the Van Dusen's to Sloane Place (the YMCA). Who knows? I may be going on the *United States* or the *Queen Mary*!

Saturday, June 19, 1954

Well, Bob Macdonald got off on the *Seven Seas* all right. We really made a funny sight, I'll bet, walking down the street with packs and all. And all the streamers were flying and the pictures were taken and they they got off to a good start.

Then I betook myself to the Sloan House (YMCA) and got a room, after waiting in line for about an hour. It's a really nice place. The price is $1.85 a night, and there's a gym, showers, dances, guided tours, billiards, lounges, good cafeteria and generally pleasant surroundings included. There are quite a few foreign students and travelers, too.

I'm too tired tonight to go to Folk Dance House, what with getting only four hours' sleep last night. Bob and I repacked all his stuff. Boy, he sure did have a lot of little stuff. I gave him two of my plastic bags to put it all in. So I'll shoot a game of pool and hit the sack. And so to sleep again. . . .

Sunday, June 20, 1954

Well, I went to the Bible Breakfast this morning after a good night's sleep and I heard a talk on how to take Christ into the plants and factories.

Then I went with a group to Christ Church and heard Sockman. He was very good, as I expected. He talked on "Learn and Live," transposing that title from the old adage "Live and Learn." The church is beautiful, and the choir (four sopranos, four altos, three bases, and three tenors) is terrific, and it was a very impressive service. Some parts of the service are almost Anglican in nature. Then after grabbing a quick bite, I went on one of the guided tours to the Statue of Liberty. Well, I climbed all the way up and back and didn't need my ice axe, either! It really is a terrific view.

Then supper, and afterwards a variety show by some kids from a dance studio somewhere New York City. Tap dancing, all that sort of stuff. It was something to do and a few numbers were really good. Then there was a dance, but all the hostesses look like something the cat dragged in, so I walked down to Times Square. I saw the film *Beauties of the Night* (1952) at a cut-rate theater, and it's really good. Like so many foreign films, the publicity builds up the sexy bits and doesn't mention the real story. It's a French farce and is a real side-splitter from the very beginning.

Home again, and to bed. But I'm reminding myself that this is Father's Day and poor Dad is probably still taking his meals standing up after his hemorrhoid surgery. I didn't get him a card or anything, either. Tonight I thought about getting one of those 97-cent loving cups and inscribing it "To the Man Whose Money I Love to Spend," or something like that.

Well, here's a Father's Day greeting, Dad:

> *I heard from a bird of your terrible plight,*
> *You stand all the day, sleep face down every night;*
> *But cheer up, me bucko—all things you can master,*
> *And you will survive this awful dis-ass-ter!*

Love, your son

Monday, June 21, 1954

Today was a good day. I slept late and went to the passport office. Everything was waiting for me except my birth certificate; they kept that. Across the street at the Home Lines office they had a birth for me on the July 1st sailing of the *Atlantic* from Quebec, and I took it. Then I went around town to the to America Youth Hostel headquarters and picked up a pass, international handbook, patches, decals, moneybag and silverware.

After supper (the meals in the Sloane House cafeteria are excellent), I went to the folk and square dance upstairs. I met a bunch of very nice people, the crowd necessarily limited because of the small number of girls, and they did most of the standard dances in a way entirely different from all that I've done or seen done. I met a nice little German girl, Anni Fittler, who has been in the US for just eleven months and has worked all that time, not getting out of New York City at all. So I gave her my folks' address and phone number and I hope I talked her into going there for a couple days in August. I suggested she go to Chautauqua for the remainder of her week's vacation.

Earlier in the day I met a fellow from England, Keith Blackburn, who was traveling around the country visiting steelworks. He's a metallurgist and wants to look into American methods of steel manufacturing. I gave him my folks' address too, since he planned to stay in Hamilton, Ontario, for a month.

Then I hit the sack. It was a long and very hot day. Tomorrow: Albany and Quebec.

Tuesday, June 22, 1954

I spent all day traveling today. I checked out about noon after enjoying a late sleep and ate lunch with Jim Carr, one of my friends from Syracuse University, before I left. At 1:15 p.m. I hopped the bus for Albany, and arrived there around 5:30 p.m. I had something to eat and called the Troy Youth Hostel. Then I had to get there. My bus connections were perfect. I waited five minutes for a bus to Troy, then another five for a bus that went right past the hostel. A couple of nice old ladies ran the place, sisters, one a widow and the other a spinster. A nice lake afforded a refreshing swim about a half-mile down the road. A rip-roaring thunderstorm cooled things off a bit. I slept very well, let me tell you!

Wednesday, June 23, 1954

Just six days to sailing time! As the time grows nearer, I get more excited. I was awakened at 7:30 in the morning by the houseparents in order to catch an 8:20 a.m. bus to Troy. Once again the connections were good. A half-hour wait in Troy was just time enough for a leisurely breakfast before the bus to Schenectady pulled in. I took that bus out to where it crossed Route 9, and there bought a black marking crayon and made a sign with "Montreal" on one side and "Quebec" on the other. A ten-minute wait brought me a ride with a salesman selling Reynolds Aluminum to wholesale distributors, and he took me all the way to Burlington, Vermont. I arrived there at 2:30, and from there on the going got rough. It took me another four hours to get from Burlington to the Border. Those Vermonters must be awfully suspicious or something.

Anyway, I got three more rides, with interminable waits in between, and a mile walk (that was a killer) before I got to the Customs House. Everything was in order, and the first out-of-state car that came through took me all the way to the YMCA in Montreal.

So here I am. A hot supper and a swim in the pool got me set for a short game of pool or billiards and a walk around town.

What a town! Trying to get directions is like pulling hen's teeth. The intercity bus lines don't know a thing about the city routes, and vice-versa. I walked my feet off trying to find something about the city routes or someone who could tell me how to get to the edge of town so I can hitchhike. But I finally managed it, after going to two bus stations, the fire hall and the police station. I got a map of the city, finally, and got back to the "Y" again.

It's now almost 1 a.m. I want to get a traveler's check cashed in US money, so I'll sleep late tomorrow and catch the banks when they are open, then on to Quebec. I have the address of the YMCA and the hostel in Quebec, and it's only 173 miles. So I should be there by tomorrow night. After a few letters, I'll hit the hay.

Thursday, June 24, 1954

I got up late again. Checked out of the "Y." The Montreal YMCA is very nice place, much better furnished rooms and sixty-five cents per night more expensive.

I went to the bank first thing and cashed a traveler's check. Then I took two trolleys and a bus to get out to the far eastern edge of town. I left my sign on one of the trolleys, so I had to make a new one. It was amusing— the storekeeper at the little grocery store spoke no English and my poor French doesn't go very far, but we managed, and after this brief interlude I finally got down to the serious business of hitchhiking.

I waited no more than fifteen minutes before getting my one and only ride, which took me straight to the YMCA in Quebec City. The fellow who picked me up lived in Quebec and worked as a sales supervisor for the Swift Company, could speak better French than English, but he didn't do too badly in the latter, and told me many interesting things about Quebec in particular and Canada in general. We followed the Saint Lawrence all the way. He was continually saying,"Look at that view! Isn't it wonderful?" I, of course, agreed. The sky was cloudless and the water a very deep blue. We passed the Greek liner *Columbia* as she sailed from Montreal.

We stopped first at the youth hostel, but I couldn't stay there because repairs were being done on the building. So I stopped at the YMCA. It's a small but complete building and quite new, only two years old.

I have a roommate. He just immigrated to Canada from England. He landed here just today and is going on to Montreal tomorrow. Tonight we took a walk up to the big city park near here, the "Plains of Abraham," to see the fireworks which are usually set off on Saint John the Baptist Day, which is today. He's the patron saint of the city. Then we turned in. Our room is very nice with new beds. We'll sleep well.

Friday, June 25, 1954

George Simpson, the Englishmen, left for Montreal this morning. I slept late. I really like this kind of life.

I took a bus to the Chateau Frontenac, the large hotel and landmark which occupies the principal point of land overlooking the harbor. From there I could look far down the river and see all the shipping. I went to the main post office just next door to mail all the letters that should have been mailed the day before from Montreal, and met a man from St Matthew's Anglican Church. He told me about his church and a few others in the city, some right near the Chateau and post office. Since there was yet an hour or so before the sight-seeing bus left, I looked into them. I saw the Anglican Cathedral (the first Anglican church in Canada) and the Catholic Church, "Notre Dame Des Victoires." Then I took the bus tour.

We saw more monuments, convents, churches, fortifications, statues, schools, and seminaries than you can shake a stick at. We also saw the Natural History Museum, the Parliament buildings, St. Laurent's home, the Protestant high school, the main shopping districts, and gleaned quite a bit of historical knowledge.

The city of Quebec is divided, both geographically and historically. There is the "upper town," which contains the "old city," with it's thick walls and massive gates, complete with fortifications, and there is a "lower town," built around and below the high ground on which the "old city" stands. The "new city" is built around and away from the "old city" and "lower town" on all landward sides. The streets in the oldest section are extremely narrow, and many of the buildings, some dating back 200 years, are still in use.

The main industry is paper, mainly newsprint. Next is tourism, and next to that, shoes. Two of the three newspapers are French (one is controlled or owned by the Catholic Church), two of the three radio stations are French too. But oddly enough, only three of the 14 or so movie theaters are French. So much for the town.

When I got back to the "Y," I found that I had a new roommate: Lawrence ("Lawrie"), an Australian who was working his way around the world. He started from Australia in April, and arrived in England via the Suez Canal in May, the voyage taking five weeks. Then he worked in England for a month or two and came to Canada. He didn't see any of the European continent, though. He is going to get a job here, then ship on to the west coast. He'll see the states, then stop off at Hawaii and New Zealand on the way home, arriving there in the fall of 1955, he thinks.

The interesting story about Lawrie is that while he was traveling from Australia to England, he spent almost all of his time acquiring a tan. He was the only passenger on a tramp steamer, with an all-male crew, and the weather was sunny most of the time. So he stripped to the skin and laid out a lot, until he was, as he put it, "brown as a nut." If it wasn't for his blond hair, he said, he could have passed as an African!

Being a member of the British Commonwealth, he easily found a job in England as a lifeguard at an indoor swimming pool. He complained that his fantastic tan disappeared entirely in a month. He hated English weather!

Saturday, June 26, 1954

Today was a nothing day. I didn't go or do much of anything. I decided not to go out to Sainte-Anne-de-Beaupré shrine, since it was probably just like the Catholic shrine at Montreal, which I've seen, and cost $3.00. The city itself is not too big, and yesterday's sightseeing tour was very complete.

So Lawrie and I just stayed around the "Y" here, playing pool, basketball, ping-pong, jumping on the trampoline and swimming twice.

In the evening we walked down to the terrace of the Chateau Frontenac and saw the live production of "Soirée a Quebec." I danced with them and got the low-down on a couple of the dances. The orchestra is a local affair, all non-union, and the choir is the same. The dancers, "The Villagers," are non-professional and most of them are students. They are hired by the CBC to to instruct the populace on these Saturday night parties. I introduced myself to the announcer and later on during the rehearsal the producer, who also announced, told the crowd about me. I didn't understand a word (it was all in French), but I was with one of the dancers and she told me. There was a rehearsal for the forty minutes prior to the broadcast time, then the actual show. It was a lot of fun, and I swapped notes afterwards with the producer and dancers ("Voice St. John de Baptiste"), and some good French Canadian musicians (Omar Dumas and Joseph Bouchard).

Sunday, June 27, 1954

We got up around 10 a.m. and went to the Quebec Baptist Church. It was a very pretty, small church There were maybe fifty at the service; the place was about one-third full. It's a struggling Protestant church in this

Catholic-dominated city. Of course, many of the Anglican churches have good attendance, likewise the United Church, but I'm afraid the Baptists are very few in number. In the afternoon I was taught how to play English Billiards and Snooker. Then the balance of the afternoon and evening has been taken up with the writing of these notes. I neglected to write any for Friday, so I had to do an hour's worth tonight.

Monday, June 28, 1954

Well, we all make mistakes now and then, and I'm no exception. I made the mistake of confusing Tuesday with Thursday, and although I knew perfectly well I was sailing July 1st at 1 a.m., I was confident (no need for me to check!) that July 1st was Tuesday. So I packed everything, got ready to go, and went around town to do some last-minute shopping, for some French Canadian folk records and Canadian stickers for my suit-case. I got back in time for an early dinner and bidding everyone at the "Y" goodbye. I took the bus to the pier. I had an uneasy feeling all the way down, and this turned to complete disgust for myself when I checked the calendar in my wallet. I was two days early! Stupid ! Then I looked around the pier, talked to some of the watchmen and others there, kicked myself in the pants a few times and went back to the "Y." They were surprised, need-less to say, and I was chagrined. Oh, well, it was better than being too late!

Tuesday, June 29, 1954

A do-nothing day. I got up at noon, took a very long hot shower, and resolved to save money by not eating until suppertime. I played a long game of pool, gabbed with the gal behind the desk, and let the ol' stomach growl away. Well, about three or four, I broke down and indulged in a very large malted at the drugstore. Just a little snitching couldn't hurt, surely? Knowing me and my hollow legs, feet, and toes, it didn't, and I managed to eat my way through a fair-sized dinner check later on. Then, since the ship had landed this morning, I decided to go down and take a look-see. The *Atlantic* was there all right, and a pretty good-sized ship she seemed, quite a bit bigger than Bob's ship, the *Seven Seas*. I talked some with the customs officer at the end of the gangway, and saw people going aboard. So I fol-lowed suit and toured the ship. I found my cabin and had a look inside. However, I was told I couldn't bring my baggage aboard until tomorrow night. I walked all over, saw the swimming pool (an over-sized bathtub), the outdoor bar, snack bar, dining rooms, lounges, library, and so forth. This place has all the luxuries of home except that it's not so comfortable. Then further gab with a customs man and back to bed around midnight. I sure am getting my sleep these days.

Wednesday, June 30, 1954

TODAY IS THE DAY!!

Up around 11:30 or so, and a good hot shower, then we were invaded. It seems the Army comes in every Wednesday afternoon for gym and a swim. The Canadian Officers Training Corps it was, about a hundred of them. I nearly got trampled to death in the locker room.

Then I went back to the room and finally met my new roommate, who was in bed when I got in last night and up before me this morning. He is immigrating from England to join the Royal Canadian Air Force, and is quite a likable fellow. He got out his atlas and showed me where he lives, in the Scilly Isles, Cornwall. Just look off the tip of Lands End in the furthest southwest corner of England and you will find them them, right in the middle of the Gulf Stream. The climate is quite balmy, with blue skies and sandy beaches, and warm enough to grow tropical fruits. Maybe I'll drop down there.

So another long pool game (I'm improving) and another leisurely dinner, and off again to the boat, this time knowing I was there on the right night!

There certainly is a lot to be said for getting to a sailing early. In any case, you have to wait, but if you're early you can do your waiting at your ease. There was only one ahead of me at the embarkation window, and it took me about 10 minutes to get on board. Of course, with this being a night sailing, and all, there weren't too many people at a time, But still, when the special trains arrived there was a jam. There was a lot of hustle and bustle, but none of the streamer-throwing that usually accompanies a sailing and the crowd on board easily outnumbered those on the pier. Coffee and cake were served in the lounge and we received our meal tickets there. The Englishman from the "Y" came over on the Atlantic, and set me wise to a few things. One of them was that the menus were different each day with a beautiful picture of an early ship on each, so I intend to save them, as he did. We got underway about two minutes late, with the aid of two tugs, and I went to the cabin. My roommates are an assorted bunch.

One is from Shreveport, Louisiana, one from Virginia and one from Pennsylvania. The latter is colored. I wonder how the other two are going to like that. They haven't seen him yet, and he's already in the sack.

Well, I guess I'll hit the sack, too. It was nice to get a letter and telegram from the folks. I got a card off in answer before we embarked; this portion will go ashore with a pilot in the morning.

Thursday, July 1, 1954

After getting a short night's sleep I'm still a little late for breakfast so I'll eat with the second shift. Then I begin one of my many days on shipboard.

It's a pretty big ship, just teeming with people. Everyone's pretty friendly; they're all imbued with the "one big happy family" idea. Tonight there was a dance, as there is every night, and because it was the first one, everyone was there. What a mob! I got it on the q.t. from the head waiter in the dining room that the women in tourist class outnumber the men by a ratio of 500 to 300, and everything I've seen today sure bears it out. In the lounge tonight there were all sorts of unattached females, and in our small corner of the dining room there are three tables with only one man apiece, the rest of the seats occupied by women. Yes I'm one of the three. I'm at a table with four teachers, all in their twenties. It seems like everyone here is on one of those planned tours, especially the young people. There aren't really any foreign-speaking people on board. Most are U.S. and Canadian. There's a symphony orchestra, too. The Montreal Junior Symphony is going to tour Britain,and they have open practices every morning. I'll have to get to hear them.

Friday, July 2, 1954

We're still in the Gulf of the Saint Lawrence River and the going is smooth.

After two days, I've come to the conclusion that the food would be better if they didn't try to be fancy with it. We get served individually from big silver platters which the waiter brings around. The deserts, though, are the worst; just tasteless blobs for puddings and so forth. Why don't you come on board, Mom? They need you!

Saturday, July 3, 1954

Well, these shipboard days are all just about the same. Breakfast at 8, luncheon at 11, dinner at 6. We get a different printed menu every luncheon and dinner with lovely pictures of ancient ships on them, and I'm saving them all.

Every night there's a movie in English or French and dancing with the four-man combo in the lounge. Every night now for a few nights we lose an hour, so it's always later than you think when you get to bed. Every night there is an elimination dance of some sort. They award some silly little prizes.

What gets me is, there are three or four places on board to get liquid refreshment of one sort or another, all alcoholic, but I can't get a strawberry milkshake anywhere!

I went down to the lounge this afternoon and ran into a good song session around the piano and met some more young people.

Sunday, July 4, 1954

Today is Sunday, and they've managed to dig up a Protestant minister from somewhere to lead the service. With the chaplain a Roman Catholic and a lot of Roman Catholic clergy on the boat, you couldn't tell for sure if there was even was a Protestant on board. The service was sort of a so-so affair; there weren't enough hymnals to go around, and the place was jammed; people were standing everywhere.

Earlier, the Montreal Junior Symphony Orchestra had a full orchestra rehearsal and I listened in. They were quite good. They practiced a von Suppé trombone concerto, a Mozart piano concerto, and a short modern beguine.

Tonight there was a masquerade ball. I was an Austrian, of course. A group of can-can dancers got first prize, Uncle Sammy and his sidekick, a red-hot firecracker, got second prize and an Indian Swami carried on a litter by four slaves, got third. Then in the singles class, Carmen Miranda (my cabin-mate) got second prize and an Indian snake charmer got first prize.

Monday, July 5, 1954

Today was the first really good day we've had, weather-wise. They say it was the best in the morning, but I wouldn't know. I stayed in the sack until (of all hours!) 1:30 p.m.! But then I put on my shorts and toted the harmonica along and had a good singsong on the afterdeck with a bunch of kids. I went up to the sun deck (I crashed the first-class area), and saw the folks swimming in the salt water pool. It's just a small pool, and the water was sloshing madly back and forth. I didn't stand too close to it for fear of getting drenched. And boy, to judge by the shouts from the pool, the water was cold!

In the evening there was a farewell party, and a few variety acts were included. My cabin mate, "Carmen Miranda," sang a few numbers; I and a cute little teacher, Deborah Plunkett from Ottawa, did the Austrian Zillertaler Ländler. A trio of girls sang, and a combo made up of members of the Junior Symphony played for dancing. They passed out streamers, balloons and paper hats, and we had a real gay time.

Tuesday, July 6, 1954

This morning we got our passports back, and our embarkation cards. I also went to the photographers and picked up a picture of me and my table mates at dinner.

I sat in the sun all afternoon. The deck was hard, but the sun divine.

Before the dance tonight there was a bingo game, during which I wasn't spending my money, but was, like quite a few others, out on deck, watching the lights on shore as we passed between the mainland of Lands End and the Scilly Isles.

Wednesday, July 7, 1954

We are behind time. It seems that this ship isn't as new as it used to be and some engine or turbine trouble has delayed us for about four hours. So arrival is a bit late. I don't know whether we can get off the boat tonight, or to wait until tomorrow morning. The ship's rails were all lined this morning as we pulled into Le Havre, France.

The part of the city nearest the waterfront is quite new, and a NATO radar post occupies a prominent spot. There are a few disintegrating piers around, but whether this is war damage or not is hard to determine. Most of the shipping sheds look fairly new, though, and there are facilities for a great number of ships.

The day is another bright and shiny one. Those getting off here will have a wonderful start on their European adventures.

I spent so much time and was so interested in the landing procedures that I missed the first sitting at dinner. So I had to get a meal in the other tourist class dining room at second sitting.

This afternoon I packed and then lounged in the sun. Just as we went into the first sitting for dinner we could see the barest outlines of the coast of England. After supper I went on deck and watched the English towns slip by on the starboard side. We docked at Southampton at 8 p.m., but we didn't know if we could disembark then or the next morning. They finally said we could say on the ship if we wanted to overnight, and I plan to do so. Then they changed their minds and said we would have to get off. So I hurriedly prepared. I got off all right at 10 p.m. and went through a very cursory customs inspection.

Then the inspector kindly direted me to the nearest bus stop, and got me started off to the Southampton Youth Hostel. But when I got there, and rang the bell, I was informed that the place closed at 10 p.m., and no more were allowed to enter after that time. I finally talked the warden into letting me leave my baggage there, and I left. It was a pretty poor welcome, if you ask me. There I was, miles away from Southampton, at the end of the bus line, and nowhere to go.

But the police are more cooperative. A cruiser came along and I told them my tale of woe. So they found me a room, not the cheapest, in a nearby hotel. I guess they really roll up the sidewalks around here early because only the night desk clerk was up, and all the lights were off at the hotel. But he gave me the only remaining room, a double with a private bath for one pound and one shilling. (That's two dollars eighty cents, plus fourteen cents), and that included a steam heated towel rack in the spacious bathroom, and breakfast the next morning. So it really wasn't bad at all.

Thursday, July 8, 1954

Today was a real busy and adventurous one. To begin with, I had a really hearty breakfast, then went back for my bags. I was told the hostel closed during the day after 10 a.m., and I should have come before that. "Phooey!," says I, and arrived at 10:30. What could he do? I took the stuff and left. I went into town to the railroad station, where I cashed a check and sent my suitcase on to Darlington. Then I sent telegrams to Darlington and to Bob's uncle in London to say that I had arrived.

Next stop was the cycle shop. I spent the rest of the morning there, picking out the machine and filling out papers. I got a driver's license, joined the Automobile Association and various other legal things, also. Then some lunch—and what a lunch! I realized that it was probably a high price by British standards, but only paid sixty cents for a meal that would have cost at least a dollar and a half in the US or Canada.

I went to the American Express office and sent a wire home.

Back to the cycle shop. They had the bike all ready to go by now with a thorough oiling, greasing, gassing, and a specially big carrier for my knapsack. So it took a little driving lesson and then was on my way. I found that although the country highways had no speed limit, most cars and trucks don't usually go over 50 mph. I was clocking about 45 mph most of the time, and had to use second gear on a lot of the hills because of the large amount of weight that the single-cylinder engine was pulling along (about 300 pounds, when you include me, a heavy pack, and the cycle). So I didn't make as good time as I thought I would. I'm afraid that Bob and I will have to revamp our notions of speed, distance, and time for traveling quite a lot.

So about 7 p.m. I was getting near Newberry, just 35 miles north of Southampton, and decided to head for the Marlborough Youth Hostel for the night, but when I was almost there I made the mistake of asking some fellows along the road where I can put up the machine, in order to walk on to the Youth Hostel, and they convinced me that this hostel accepted motorcycles. Unfortunately, this wasn't the case, but the warden there directed me to a bed and breakfast just up the road from him. Sodden (it was misting), I started out, and here comes the adventure:

I signaled for a right turn and heard a car honk behind me. Then, thinking the car wanted to pass on the right, I went to the left, and found the car right behind me. It bumped me from behind, and the machine skidded from under me. I fell, and the machine fell on my left foot. I got up, and my foot was cut up and felt broken. Darn! So after a little palaver, I got into the car and they drove me to Savernake Hospital. A doctor there put in a couple stitches in the worst gash and bound the foot up. Then a tetanus shot and a bed, and I was ready for the police officer. He questioned me and got a statement as to how the accident happened, and then left.

Well, it could be worse. Three puncture wounds and a bad bruise! This is certainly no way to start a vacation, is it? I guess this means that I won't get to Llangollen. Well, we'll see.

Friday, July 9, 1954

Up at 6, and my temperature and pulse taken. I tossed around during the night and didn't sleep very well; the sheets were all pulled out and bloody this morning. I keep kicking myself for being here. The nurses are very nice; quite a few are young girls in training. This is a nice ward, two walls are all glass with hinged walls that open onto a patio. There are only six beds in the ward; It's small and cozy. One young fellow here has a broken leg, all strung up with pulleys and weights and traction. He's the life of the party. He and the nurses get along wonderfully; they tease each other unmercifully.

The food could be better but I really shouldn't complain; I don't pay a cent for the treatment here. Breakfast at 8, lunch at noon, tea at 4 and dinner at 6. There's a lot of bread, tea and potatoes at every meal.

There are plenty of magazines in the ward, and papers arrive daily. There's plenty else for me to do, too. I've seen my clothes, and the one shoe was torn up pretty badly. There's a tear in my jeans and a rip in my raincoat, but I can mend them during my stay. Over each bed is a headset and a couple of dials. We can tune in the two radio stations of the BBC, the Home Service and the Light Program. There is a wealth of good music on both. Tonight at 8:30 to 9:15 I listened to the Llangollen Festival for 45 minutes. Well, that's something at least. Lights out promptly at 10!

Saturday, July 10, 1954

I don't know how long I'll have to stay in this place. It's nice enough and all but, it isn't getting to Llangollen. Today has been a warm and sunny one, and all were sitting out on the terrace. My foot is still messing up the sheets quite a bit.

Sunday, July 11, 1954

I got a good bandaging today, with a big wad of cotton over the wound that was bleeding,and then a good tight bandage all the way to the knee, in order to collapse the vein. It really feels good, and I can even get around, in a fashion, by using a cane and taking mostly hops on the good foot. So I went to a short service—the local Church of England "Passion" held in the neighboring ward.

I made some phone calls today. The doctor said I should stay for at least four or five days, and by that time the festival will be over, and I'll not have met Bob. So I'll call the Haymans in Darlington to tell them what has happened, and telegraph Bob's uncle in London (no phone there).

Monday, July 12, 1954

Another fine day. I'll bet that it rains all the rest of the time, after I get out of here.

They moved me into a larger ward next door today, to make room for some new patients. So now all the six patients in that ward are under the care of the same doctor. There are 12 beds in this one, and only seven filled. But they expect five more admittances, three for this ward.

Ada and Harry Hayman were not home yesterday, so I called them again today. They were glad to hear me and perturbed at my accident. They'll probably write to the folks; I hope they don't build it up too much. Odd, the phone's in Ada's name, not Harry's. I suppose because she is a professional singer.

My foot has stopped bleeding so much, although it still leaks a little. I can get around without a cane now, and the doctor is encouraged.

Tuesday, July 13, 1954

I borrowed a couple of books from the hospital librarian yesterday, one about mountain climbing and the other about jungle exploration. The mountain one is very good.

The nurses are interested in the American and Canadian coins I have with me, especially the bus and subway tokens. I had a hard time trying to convince them of the value of the metric monetary system, and I don't think I succeeded.

None of the new arrivals missed their cue; there was another emergency admittance, and another one was transferred to this ward. We'd be overcrowded, but one of the old men died this morning, so there are just enough beds to go around.

The doctor said today that the sutures could probably come out Thursday, and that perhaps I wouldn't be here for another Sunday service.

A letter arrived from Bob's uncle in London which said that he had sent Bob word of my arrival just as soon as he had received my telegram from Southampton. So now that he has my address, he'll probably direct Bob to contact me here.

Wednesday, July 14, 1954

A letter arrived from Darlington today enclosing the registration for the motorcycle which was sent from Southampton, and a letter from the folks. They still didn't include Liz McComber's summer address, though.

I finished both of the books the librarian lent me. I've read everything here that there is to read. There's nothing else to do except sit or lie, and listen to the radio, or read. I heard a program this evening that told about the Llangollen Festival, and I almost cried—darn the luck, anyway!!!

Thursday, July 15, 1954

Another letter from Bob's uncle in London arrived today, and a telegram from Bob himself! Things are looking up! I'm to call him at 5:30 tonight. All my American and Canadian money is going to the nursing staff for souvenirs.

Well, Bob and I didn't make connections tonight, so I'll try again tomorrow.

Friday, July 16, 1954

I called Bob first thing this morning. He was at his aunt's in Edinburgh. He plans to tour the highlands and meet me in Darlington on the 23rd. I was planning to go to London on my way up there, but we will be hitting London again on our way to Dover. Bob claimed the four days he spent there before were filled with business and he didn't get much of a chance to look around, so we'll look at it together.

I called the police, and found out that no one laid charges, so I guess my insurance company will take care of it all. I've written them a letter giving them all the pertinent details, and enclosing the name and address of the people in the car. I also called the cycle shop here in Marlborough and made arrangements to get the cycle. The doc says I can leave Sunday and high-tail it up to Darlington.

I've been wearing my shoe on the bad foot for the past two days, and I'm surely glad I didn't send it out to be stitched. If it wasn't split in a couple places, I never would be able to get it on over this swollen foot. The nurse, a few days ago, said cheerily that it was, "beautiful, just like a squashed grapefruit." How complimentary can you get? Anyhow, it's less black and blue than it was.

Saturday, July 17, 1954

Bob called again today. He had just received the letter I wrote right after our conversation, and he didn't understand my plans. So we have revamped the route. I'll meet him at Edinburgh Wednesday or Thursday, depending on how soon I can leave the hospital and how long it takes to finish my business in Birmingham. We'll stop overnight at Nottingham and Darlington on the way back to Dover.

I made arrangements with the owner of the cycle shop to get the machine out of hock on Sunday, when he was normally closed. Then I mapped my route to Birmingham.

Sunday, July 18, 1954

Well, it's Sunday again, the tenth day (and I hope the last day) in this sick bay. I've told the staff nurse that I want to see the first doctor who comes in this morning, and I'll leave as soon as possible after lunch.

The ambulance was leaving for town just as lunch began so I got a ride and went hungry. My motorcycle was dented in a couple places and a bolt was torn out of the rear fender but otherwise nothing else was hurt. It cost me ten shillings ($1.40). Then I had to get a new bracket for my Road Fund Tax sticker because the old one had been torn off and lost at the time of the mishap, and that cost a half-crown, or two and a half shillings ($0.35).

I got underway at 2 p.m. and reached Stratford-<u>upon</u>-Avon (not Stratford-<u>on</u>-Avon!) at 5 in the afternoon. I parked the bike and went for a walk. Ouch! My foot rebelled and hurt. Oh well, not too much. So I had some tea to warm me up, because I had bucked a wind all the way up—and me with no windscreen! I paid a shilling and six pence (twenty cents) to go through Shakespeare's house. It was quite interesting, and of course I got some postcards, seeing as how I don't have a camera yet.

I hobbled back to the car park (that's "parking lot" to you Americans), and took off for Birmingham. I took a wrong turn and ended up in Warwick, but I only went a few miles out of my way. I arrived at Birmingham about 6:30 and immediately thought about a bed-and-breakfast, since I made the mistake of looking for hostels after I got to Warwick, and not when I started out. There are two hostels, both on the west side of the city, and Warwick is on the east. So I inquired at a truck stop, and they directed me to a fine place where I got supper, bed and breakfast for nine shillings, or a dollar twenty-six. Not bad at all!

Now you'll wonder if I've seen anything of England at all so far, besides the inside of a hospital and the road going out before me. Well, the maximum speed in town is 30 miles per hour, and although there is technically no speed limit on the open road, they are so winding and narrow that 45 is the absolute maximum. Most cars do 30 to 40 mph. There's a speedometer on this bike, and I find myself doing 35 most of the time. At that speed you can see a lot.

There are quite a number of thatched-roofed houses yet, and very quaint they are, too. Also the many old homes stand out immediately because of the wall construction, using wood-end (or pegged) beams for structure, and a mixture of mud, straw, stones and sticks for the actual wall.

This beam work is very unsymmetrical and crooked, and rough-hewn. Otherwise, and in town, mostly brick is used, and the wide chimneys are often just a continuance of the wall at one or both ends the building, and sometimes at the sides.

The country through which I passed so far is just one hill after another with green fields, trees, (large, and mostly along the road) and many stone fences. There's a sort of a peaceful air here, and not very much noise. People don't seem to shout. Cars and motorcycles (and there's a lot of them, and bicycles, too) never blow their horns. And there's not so much visual noise, like billboards and signs, and so forth. So far, the impressions are favorable.

Monday, July 19, 1954

After a fine breakfast, I set out for the American Express office where everything was ready and waiting. Then I went the BSA factory. The accident had ripped out one of the bolts which was fastened to the back fender, and consequently the whole load was tending to fall backwards. I had improvised braces using the straps on the pack, but I was afraid to trust them. After visiting three or four cycle shops (BSA doesn't repair-- it only supplies new parts), I finally had some strong braces put on, and the whole shebang painted. After a little lunch, it was 2 p.m. again before I set off.

I passed through the Manchester area (coal and cotton) on my way to Wigan, and noticed many coal-fired power-plant stations. The big spool-like condensers for the water dominated the landscape. There is also a US Air Base near here, and although I didn't see any planes, I passed a couple monster trucks which were carrying wing sections.

There are no hostels in the Wigan area so I again stayed at a bed-and-breakfast. This evening after supper I decided to drive around town and give it a look-see. I ended up seeing Danny Kaye in *Knock on Wood* for nine shillings. Then I went out, it was dark, and I discovered—no lights! So I rode the few blocks back to the house without them.

Tuesday, July 20, 1954

I set out from the house to fix my lights and couldn't find a single place they could do it. Either the electrician wasn't there or they were too full up or something. In addition, it began to rain. I did indulge and bought a windscreen, because bucking the wind for such long periods was getting me down. So I set out in the pouring rain. Twenty miles further on, still raining,

I stopped at a small cycle shop and they fixed the trouble. The taillight wire had been shorted when the special heavy-duty carrier had been attached. The rear wheel had to be taken off, and in all it was quite a chore. But by this time the rain had ceased, and I had dry sailing all the way to Carlisle.

I passed through what they call the "Lakes District," and although the main road doesn't pass next to any lake, the scenery still is beautiful. The hills are endless in procession, and it's just like a patchwork quilt in different shades of green. The boundaries of each patch is a stone wall, and these walls (or fences) run all over the hills. There's not much crop-growing, but a lot of sheep and cattle. Then every so often there will be a small, dense, and very definite stand of trees on the top of a hill, like a giant crew-cut on the world's head. And those fences? It must have taken years and years to build them. There is only about three feet of sod, and the rest of the land is all rock, so you can see where they got the material. The stone houses are thatch-roofed, and the side roads are very, very narrow. In contrast to this peaceful ancient domestic scene, there are the occasional modern stone quarries, cement plants, and lime plants (I passed five of them).

I pulled into Carlisle about 7 p.m., and ate in a cafe. Then I set about looking for a hostel. I found one, and I managed to park the cycle elsewhere and walk in. Everything turned out fine and nobody the wiser. I hope I can get away okay in the morning. The warden said that there are about 30 hostlers here tonight. I bought a British patch, a Scottish patch and an international patch, so I'm all caught up on that score, except for Canada. The dorm sleeps eleven men, and were full up. I managed to do some washing and they have a nice drying room in which to leave them.

Monday, July 21, 1954

I got away from the hostel this morning and none of the wiser as to my mode of transportation. Good!

I went downtown to buy a sweater, and ended up buying a jacket. Waterproof, with a flannel lining and hood, zipper, and all for 27 & 6, or $3.85 (Army surplus)—not bad! I also got my shoe sewed up where I cut my foot at the time of the accident. The swelling is almost all gone now.

Then on to Edinburgh. I passed the Scottish border shortly and started climbing. Ah, it was beautiful. The hills are bare of trees, for the most part, and seemingly endless. The stone walls go running helter-skelter all over, uphill and down. The sheep keep the grass "mowed" on the hillsides. The stone fences make a checkerboard of the hills, and each field is a different color. I took a side road for a shortcut and found it was more aptly a cow path. But I really got away from the bustle of civilization that you find on the main highway. I didn't meet a single car or pass a single telephone pole. On the unfenced hillsides I noticed large splotches of brown intermixed with green. With the sun and shadows of the clouds playing hide-and-seek over those green and brown slopes, it was really pretty. At one point I came to the very top of a hill and I could see for miles around. The Firth of Forth was in the distance and I could see the smoke of Glasgow on the left and Edinburgh on the right.

I arrived at Bob's cousin's home just at teatime. Mrs. Bartholomew served tea, and then I set about to do some washing while waiting for Bob to get back. He had gone to Loch Lomond for the day. As he had a late start, he didn't get in until about 11 in the evening.

After supper, I went to the New Cavendish Hotel, where there was a class in Scottish country dancing. I tried out my foot and all seemed to work. I sat all I could and noticed that my foot ached like I had been walking all day on it, but otherwise it was okay. I "learned" five different dances, of which I imagine I can remember maybe two. I got the names of all of them. A very good evening, even if I did get slightly lost on the way back to Bartholomew's. Bob was in when I got there and of course we had to chew the fat until all hours.

Thursday, July 22, 1954

Bob showed me around Edinburgh today. We first visited the castle, and Bob took a snapshot of me on the castle wall, with a city in the background. Then the cannon was fired from the parapet at 1 p.m., and we were there for that daily tradition. We went to the chapel, which was dedicated to all the Scots who fell in World War I. They were all named, and a large wall space was given to each regiment, showing inscription, coats of arms, and so forth, and so forth—all very fancy. There was a museum of old British and Scottish weapons, dress and medals, and models of ships.

We went through Holyrood Palace and saw Queen Mary's private bedroom, the dining room of state, the ruined chapel, and so forth. Many pictures and relics.

Then we stopped for tea, and had it in a real English teahouse, complete with little sandwiches, cakes, scones, and so forth. Nice, but expensive.

We visited the museum. Bob had been there before, but wanted to continue where he had left off. It had the usual things, but in more detail and of more of them. The metallurgy and zoology departments received special notice, of course. We had just gotten to the physics section when the closing bell rang.

Then we went to a record shop and I bought all five of the direction booklets put out by the Scottish Country Dance Society, and one (I repeat, one) record. How I'll get it home is going to be a problem.

This evening we went again to the New Cavendish Ballroom where there was general Scottish country dancing in the main ballroom. Quite well attended, too. Then afterwards we met Tim Wright, the famous band leader of Scottish music, to whose records Bob and I have often danced. His band was there in person, as New Cavendish is his establishment.

During the evening, there was a tape recording made by two fellows who were putting together a program for the Armed Forces Overseas Network, and they interviewed us. So we're on the air. The trouble is, we don't know when.

We packed before we went to bed, planning to leave in the morning.

Friday, July 23, 1954

We rose early, but it was 11 a.m. before we got away from the house. The morning was gray and drizzly, and it looked as if we wouldn't be staying too dry. Before we left, we visited the Kilt Shop in Edinburgh, just for kicks. Well, as you might guess, both Bob and I are now fully-dressed Scots. We both bought an outfit. I'm now a Murray (I hope they don't mind), since that was the nicest tartan they had in my size and price range. A leather sporran, socks, flashes (garters) and the crest pin completed the outfit. I suppose that perhaps I should have gotten a pair of Scottish dancing slippers, but I wear regular shoes for other folk dances so I guess they'll do for the Scottish ones too. There's $28 down the hatch! Maybe. I'd better give up a camera to buy costumes and records instead? About noon we left Edinburgh in the pouring rain.

We intended to get to Fort William, but just outside of Lochearnhead I had a flat tire. In the rear wheel, too. And that, plus the slow going in the rain made us head for Crianlarich Hostel (near Tyndrum, north of Glasgow about forty miles). They were full up, and we pushed on through the rain to Dalmally, some twenty miles west. We got there just after 10 p.m., but they let us in, and we managed to dry out some and get some hot supper before turning in. By-the-by, Scottish hostels allow motorbikes and even cars, charging a penny for a bicycle, six pence for tandems and motorcycles, and a shilling for cars. Some hostels even have places for caravan (trailer) camping.

Saturday, July 24, 1954

We got underway by 10 a.m., and were the last ones to leave the hostel. But I couldn't find my pocket knife and pipe holster. Evidently someone swiped the knife, and perhaps the holster was swept up and went in with the discarded tire. Anyway I couldn't find them.

The sun shone briefly around 7 or 8, but it was well hidden and overcast by the time we left. We went up through Glen Orchy via a winding cow trail that was little more than a two-lane rut. We found out that life can be beautiful. Sun broke through fitfully, the mist hung on the hills like a shroud, and the stream we followed meandered its merry way over sheep and cow pastures with nary a car in sight. It was slow traveling, but pretty.

Then we headed up and up, and finally down the bleak wildness of Glen Coe. That is where the Campbells massacred the Macdonalds back in the days of the clan wars, and Bob wondered if he should tell anyone his name. "Maybe I'm not in safe territory." I could just see the Campbells swarming down the hills and rocky crags on both sides of the Glen, and feel the fear of the Macdonalds as they watched them come!

As we rounded a bend, there was a parking space by the side of the road, and an old Scot arrayed in a variety of tartans, with bagpipes and all. He had an upturned hat nearby, and would pose for a picture playing the pipes. Behind him was a very pretty waterfall, so we broke down and Bob snapped me alongside the old fellow.

We want across Loch Leven at Ballachulish via the ferry, and got to Fort William about 2. We were informed by a pamphlet that Bob had, that there would be Scottish games at Fort William today, but it turned out that was wrong. We were disappointed, but it was all for the best as we didn't have too much time to get anywhere near Skye.

We turned toward Skye at Invergarry, and followed a newly paved but very narrow and winding road into Loch Quiet. About supper time, we found ourselves on the shore of the loch at the Ratagan Hostel, in the pouring rain again. It is a building adjoining a small lumber mill and we were able to park our bikes under the shed.

Sunday, July 25, 1954

We ran into a most unusual situation today. I believe it will be the only time to bother us, though. In the western Highlands, they are very strict about their Sunday observance, which means that no business is carried on then. We had intended to cross to Skye today, but could only get to Glenelg, some nine miles down the road, seeing as no ferries were running. The road from Ratagan to Glenelg is the steepest part of our whole journey so far. We were in low gear most of the way. I snapped a pic at the top of the "pass" with the loch in the background.

The slopes of the hills around the loch are all heavily forested with evergreens, as part of the government's reforestation program. The sun was out, the loch was blue, and the hills very green. When we got to Glenelg, we unloaded our stuff at the hostel and went out to look at the Pictish houses nearby. We found two and both were marked and kept in repair by the Ministry of Works, but the disconcerting thing is about it was that at each one there was a large plaque saying that those who tampered with the buildings will be prosecuted, but not one word of how old the houses were, what the different parts were, what the habits of the people were, or what their former shape was like. I really don't understand it.

We met a hiker from the Glenelg hostel, and the three of us had lunch near one of the houses. Bob refused to drink the raw milk we got from a nearby farm. When we climbed to the top of the nearest hill to get a good look at the glen, we could plainly make out the rows of planted evergreens on the hillside, and the hills of Skye were blue across the firth.

We all three went back to the hostel, getting there just in time for supper. It seems that this is an old ferry house, the second house built on this site. Johnson and Boswell were guests in the house formerly here, and it left a very unfavorable impression with the locals.

It didn't rain much today at all, but the warden said there were five weeks of sunshine in May and early June.

Tuesday, July 26, 1954

We got up early today, and were ready and waiting for the ferry when it arrived at the hostel. The car ferry that used to run was discontinued last year, but there is a mail boat that comes around which carries hikers and cyclists across to Skye. It was a large inboard motor boat, but I'm glad that our bikes were light, because we had to lift them on by sheer muscle power.

And at the other side, the quay was a stone boat launch which sloped sharply into the water, covered thickly with wet moss, so it was a slippery struggle to get them on dry ground.

The road we took was the worst so far. No pavement at all, just gravel in a couple ruts leading inland from the ferry to the main road, a distance of some twelve miles or so. After we hit the main road, it began to rain, and continued for the rest of the day untill about five o'clock. We first came to Broadford and bought some petrol. Then on to Sligachan. Then it really started coming down! We got very wet as we battled our way through a heavy headwind, and we stopped at both Brachadale and Roskill to get out of the weather and rest awhile.

We bought some bread and cheese, intending to eat lunch at Dunvegan if we could find some shelter. But none afforded itself, so we stopped at a hotel at Dunvegan and had tea. It was high tea and cost is four shillings apiece which is a pretty fair price by British standards, but it was worth it to sit by a hot fire, drink hot tea and eat hot ham and eggs! We knew that we weren't the only ones there, of course, even though we didn't see anybody else (we had been ushered into a small sitting-room to be served our high tea), so we arose and went to the large lounge, where we met about a dozen other guests. We had a nice conversation with them, but when the rain let up after about a half hour, we excused ourselves and went on to Portree in a drizzle. By the time we got there it had stopped raining all together. At Portree we got some postcards, and saw a certain the Bill Andrews, who is a friend of Tim Wright, the Scottish music band leader and recording artist that we met in Edinburgh. We were hoping to be offered a free bed for the night, but no such luck. So we pushed onto Staffin where there were sixty-six other hostellers. We saw there the largest collection of motorbikes to date at a hostel; eight, including ours. We also met two of the hikers who had left Glenelg with us that morning.

Tuesday, July 27, 1954

Today we were to say goodbye to Skye, but changes had to be made in our plans again. Sporadic drizzles were coming down as we left the hostel, and we first stopped at Duntulm hotel, built near the ruins of Duntulm Castle, the ancient stronghold of the Macdonalds. We inquired at the hotel and the proprietress very kindly let us park our bikes, and also invited us into the sitting room to look at a book about Skye which had pictures and some history of Duntulm. We climbed up the hill to the ruins, and my imagination ran rampant. The Castle was built on the end of a high promontory, surrounded on three sides by the sea. It stood on the very edge of a high bluff, so that from the edge of the wall one looked straight into the water. The wind fairly howled around the place, and I can just visualize secret trysts, sinister conferences of war, and midnight raids. There were few walls left, the highest being at the corner of the old keep. One end wall of the chapel persevered, and a couple small cellar rooms. They were quite dark, and I imagined the chief of the Macdonalds torturing the McLeod plotter there. According to the book, they starved him, and satiated his hunger with salted meat with no water. He died, of course, in agonies. We went around the northern tip of the island and down to Uig, where we saw an old fire signal tower which was used both as the lighthouse and to send signals of approaching ships to places inland.

We went back over to Dunvegan because the castle is open to visitors on Thursdays, and went through it. It's the home of the chief of the McLeods but doesn't have much of its old glamour left. Although you notice the thickness of the walls, trophies, and so fourth, it still looks like a fairly recent building built to resemble a castle.

Then we pushed on toward Kyleakin and the ferry, but here fate stepped in to delay us some more. Between Bracadale and Drynoch I had another flat tire. This time we pulled out another nail, fixed the obvious hole, and put the wheel back on (the rear wheel again(!), but it seems I had other leaks, too, and the tire wouldn't hold air. So off it came once more, and I looked around until I found a ditch left by the cutting out of peat, and I used this natural water trough to find the leaks. I patched the thing in five different places before it was okay again. During this time the sun had come out, and Bob climbed to the top to get a picture. He saw a ways away, something that looked like a round building. As we were getting the bike back together, a shepherd came along the road with his two dogs and stopped to chat. He told us the round building was a "doune," used as a tower for some of the surrounding castles. We decided to investigate later. The shepherd told us all about the branding of the sheep (they use ear clips to distinguish the owners and colored paint to distinguish the counties).

Well it was pretty late, so we went back to the Gairloch hostel and there met five of the people who had been at Staffin the night before.

The sunset colored the nearby hills a rich orange, the sky was blue and not too cloudy, and it was a nice ending to such a trying day.

Wednesday, July 28, 1954

We had a good day today, for a change. Last night's beautiful sunset foretold it. We started early and took the ferry from Kyleakin to Kyle. We ate lunch on a high knoll overlooking the Strait of Kyle. We progressed as far as Invermoriston before halting for the night at the Altsaigh hostel. It was a beautiful place, situated right on Loch Ness. It was originally a road-house and cafe, and rather recently, too. The dining room was very large and had big windows on three sides, one of which overlooked the loch. The kitchen was big and had plenty of stove space. The dorms are many and quite adequate, each with a bathroom and washroom in the same building. There was a nice gravely beach, and I skipped some stones, trying to arouse the Loch Ness monster, but to no avail.

Thursday, July 29, 1954

We traveled along the edge of the loch northward, and passed through Inverness. While we were there, we indulged in a haircut which both of us needed badly. We looked around some and then pushed on to Elgin, where Bob's relatives, the Griersons, lived. He had made arrangements for us to stay overnight there. Mr. Grierson is a judge, and they are quite well off. We met Mr. and Mrs. Grierson and their two daughters, Susan and Nikki, and Mrs. Grierson's mother.

Friday, July 30, 1954

We didn't get started too early, as usual, so only got to Corgarff. We left Elgin around 9 a.m. and took a walk to the nearby ruined Cathedral before we quit the city. It was a beautiful place, and well-preserved by the city. The grounds were filled with gravestones of both recent and ancient vintage. The former inside was also filled with graves. The building itself dated from 1400. Do you remember the New England Contra Dance called "Monymusk"? Well, we went to the town of Monymusk to see one of the girls that Bob met on the boat on the way over. She was going there to learn Highland dancing. She wasn't there, but the people she was to stay with welcomed us, and wouldn't let us go until we had tea with them. The husband was a logger in the reforested pine woods that cover the slopes nearby and was also an a-one piper. It was then late, so after a very pleasant visit, we went on, through the small village of Lumsden, (Remember Roy Lumsden from high school, Jane?) and we started looking for the Corgarff hostel. We finally found it, and boy, was it in an out-of-the-way place! We started down a country lane from the main road, and I thought that was the hostel. But no, we had to go on for another half mile through a sometimes trackless, sometimes miry, sometimes wood-flanked sheep pasture, through two more gates, ford a couple streams (small ones), and finally arrived at a small redone shepherds cottage. The warden was a fella who was doing a thesis for an advanced degree in ancient history and who wardened in the summer to get the privacy he wanted. (hostels, you remember, close during the day.) There were six hostellers at Corgarff, all men, and one, an associate of the warden's, had a small portable radio so we lived in style. Our motorbikes, by the way, were just the ticket for getting into this place; they pulled us through everything and we didn't even get wet feet.

Saturday, July 31, 1954

From our trackless abode at Corgarff, we pushed on to Dundee. We had directions from the warden as to the best place for seeing Balmoral Castle, so we took this side road and went up a hill, and through a break in the trees got a wonderful view, although rather a distant one, and not a good one for Bob's camera.

We then went to Braemar, and took a side road over to the "Linn O' Dee," where the Dee river is forced into a three-foot-wide channel. The river itself was only as big as Gill Creek and not as deep, so I really didn't think it was such a wonderful thing, although it was a strange rock formation. Just before Bob snapped a picture of me straddling the stream, he saw a fish leap up the falls behind me. Too bad he didn't catch him in the snapshot.

Then we turned south and went through Glen Clunie up a stretch of very steep winding road called "The Devil's Elbow." The height of the pass is 2199 feet, the highest road in the English isles. We noticed a line of tank barriers, concrete, extending across the pass, leftovers from WWII invasion preparations. On the barriers the Scottish Nationalists had written, "Elbow the devils out! Home rule now!" From what I hear, their voices are pretty ineffective.

We arrived in Dundee in the rain and a day late. We thought we could get to Dundee yesterday, but a late start from Elgin and a long tea at Monymusk delayed us. George McMillan welcomed us at the door, and introduced us to John Taylor, from Aberdeen, who was also there visiting for the weekend. Mr. and Mrs. McMillan were away for the weekend, so there was room in the small apartment for us. Jean came home from the store and we all had a high tea. Then we all cleaned up and went to a dance hall. George had a date with his girlfriend, and the rest of us tagged along.

A word here on the etiquette differences. There were plenty of stags, both male and female, and a lone person is not considered a "tramp." The place was well-lighted and spacious, and quite crowded. Coats were checked (required) for seven cents (two pence). There was none of this "sardine" dancing and slow cheek-to-cheek stuff. Everyone kept moving around the room counter-clockwise, and if you didn't move you got trampled. There was a was definite program of dances, announced over the loudspeaker, and some were ladies' choices. There was one old-time medley, in which the "Gay Gordons" (a Scottish country dance) was included, but that was the limit of the "folk dancing" for this evening.

Sunday, August 1, 1954

Well, we had originally planned to be in London by this date, but we somehow lost four days in Scotland and found them irretrievable. We got up late, and George whipped up some dance tunes on the fiddle, accompanied by two harmonicas when he played in the right key. We left around noon, sternly refusing the proffered invitation to dinner. We would never get to Edinburgh if we had accepted. We took a turn up the firth to see the ancient earth-dwellings, and were completely buffaloed again when we ran into those placards saying not to disturb anything, but giving no hint as to who or what had lived there, or when.

We went through Perth, then crossed the Firth of Forth at Queensferry in the very shadow of the Forth Bridge. It is a spectacular structure of tubular steel entirely, and barely supports its own weight, in comparison to which the weight of a train passing over is negligible. They don't make a roadway across it because it wouldn't stand the weight of the road bed.

We got to the Bartholomew's in time for supper, and this time met John and Robert, two of the sons. The two Bobs stood John and I at a game of English croquet "they pronounce it "cro-kee" here), and were thwarted in their attempt to best us.

Monday, August 2, 1954

This morning we left as early as possible for Darlington, first stopping at the music shop so Bob could get copies of the directions for some Scottish country dances. On our way down, the weather was pretty good and we didn't hit too much rain. We stopped off on the way to see Hadrian's Wall and an accompanying Roman fort. We were expecting something like the Great Wall of China, but found a wall which is only as high and twice as wide as the stone fences which divided the landscape. In addition to this disappointment, we got lost trying to find the place and lost a couple of hours. We arrived in Darlington about 9 in the evening and dear Ada and Harry Hayman were still waiting supper for us. Well, it seems that they were expecting the Redmonds at anytime but they hadn't arrived yet, fortunately. We slept the sleep of the weary.

We did get the one shock, though, when we tore the paper from the toilet roll. Whoever heard of music boxes in the bathrooms? English toilet paper was the worst I've seen. It's glazed on one side, like a slick magazine, and like sandpaper on the other. The "water closet," a separate little room with only a toilet, is common in English homes. At Hayman's, two choices were given the user: English paper on the left, and American paper, in a decorated wooden holder, on the right. This is a no-brainer. But when the roll revolves as you tear some off, you are actualy winding up a music box, and as you wipe, you are serenaded. In my case, I heard gales of laughter coming from the kitchen directly below. They knew just what I was doing!

Tuesday, August 3, 1954

We decided to stay at home today. Ada would have loved to have shown us all around, but the Redmonds were coming and she'd have her hands full then. Besides, we both had a stack of correspondence a mile high to answer. I got straight with the insurance company and I guess there will be no claim, so that's finished. I filled out the application for a new bike "licence" (British spelling), and sent a whole batch of postcards. Then I wrote a long letter to Liz and did some work on this diary.

In the afternoon, Ada got a message that the Redmonds were arriving at 8 p.m. so we couldn't dodge them. It was a beautiful sunny day all day and I sat out in the yard to do my writing. Ada's twice-a-week help came in, and did all of mine and Bob's washing, and it was only with the greatest difficulty I kept her from ironing all my underwear and overalls. She and

Ada got a big kick out of this, and Harry a bigger one when he got home.

So the Redmonds were here for supper and Bob and I didn't dress up. After they went upstairs, I talked Ada into winding up the bathroom music box and removing the second (British) roll of paper. But then we four got to playing a couple of Ada's records "The Lass With The Delicate Air," of course, and had a gab fest. (Harry is the funniest thing on two feet!) We made so much noise we didn't hear the music box. Oh well, they still must have been startled.

Wednesday, August 4, 1954

We left this morning early, but not early enough to escape being recorded for posterity on John Redmond's movie film.

We hustled on down to Nottingham, stopping at York and going through the cathedral. It's a beautiful place. There are extensive repairs going on, as is usual for these old churches. About half of the stained-glass windows are still replaced with clear glass after being dismantled during the war. We went on a guided tour of the place with a "verger" (church caretaker) who was really interested in his work. We found out that York was the fourth church to be built on this site. The first was of Roman architecture, of which the base of a pillar was left, the next two were Norman, of which the crypt is the remains, being incorporated into the present building. We also climbed the tower, but nothing afforded a good camera shot. And this kills me! One of the best places in England to see, and after spending two hours in the place, we didn't get a picture and didn't get a postcard! So we have nothing to show for our pains!

We got to Nottingham by 6 p.m., and found that Mr. and Mrs. Colquhoun were in Bournemouth for their holidays. At Nottingham was Eileen Colquehoun, wife of Joseph, and Betty, Margaret's sister. Betty's son and husband were also there. Eileen wasn't feeling too well (she's four months pregnant), so Betty and son Ian stayed overnight. We had a good talk about taxes and the "never-never" (installment buying).

Thursday, August 5, 1954

We left early after taking pictures. A fine breakfast got us started, and four-year-old Ian, who had been quite unsociable earlier, got a little more friendly. It really was a shame to have missed the Colquehouns, but that's life.

We made plans to go through Cambridge on our way to London, but this plan also went astray, due to an incident at Stanford. Bob was ahead of me leading into the town, and I was aghast, upon rounding a bend, to see him sprawled on the side of the road, his machine damaged and a car set at an angle across the road. I quickly stopped, and Bob was by this time standing. Then he sat on the ground, and I and the driver of a nearby lorry and Mr. Davis, the fellow who was responsible for the accident, inspected him for damages. His shoe was torn, and he was a little bruised and shaken up, but otherwise all right. It seems this X-ray man from the hospital was turning around, and instead of picking out a suitable driveway or side street, he chose to turn into this drive which had the gates closed, and back out onto the main road. Well, if he had looked, he would have seen Bob coming. Also, if he had chosen a deeper driveway (and there was one, right across the street), he could have left room for Bob to pass. What's more, it's illegal to back out on to the main road!

Well, he went into the office of a laundry company nearby and called the police and an ambulance. When they came, the policemen took down the details and Bob was carted off to the hospital. I hung around while the policeman was getting a signed statement from the car driver and then I drove Bob's machine to the garage. (My cycle was driven to the garage by the passenger of another motorcycle which had stopped—a friend of the policeman, I think.) Then I went to the hospital to get Bob. They put three band-aids on him and told him he was okay. So I showed him how to get to the police station, and went back to the garage. They had straightened somewhat his leg shield, but told us the front fork was bent. We called the BSA works in Birmingham, and they assured us that there were places in London which had complete parts for his machine. Well the windscreen plastic was broken and the bike steered crookedly, but it was rideable, so we went on to London.

We got there by 7 p.m., but it took us two hours to get through the city to where we wanted to go. Peter Bartholomew, another son of the Bartholomews of Edinburgh, and Lynn Sandeman, whose father is a partner of the Sandeman Brewing Company (you have seen their ads in Time magazine, no doubt), share a comfortable apartment in West Norwood, between Croydon and Wimbledon, London. They pay a guinea (one pound plus one shilling) a week apiece for two bedrooms, living room, kitchen and bath. Not bad. We had supper from a can and hit the sack. It's the first time so far I've used my sleeping bag. One sleeping bag was furnished by Peter; Bob used it and slept on the couch. I slept on a camp bed.

Friday, August 6, 1954

Well, London certainly is a town to get lost in. It wouldn't be so bad if I they had any system to anything, but as it is, it's hopeless. Not only do the streets go every which way, without rhyme or reason, but if you do by some miracle hit upon a straight stretch, the name is changed every other block. Then there's a multitude of one-way streets, which further louse you up. But trust ol' Budrow with his handy little road map (plus two atlas road guides of London)—we never got lost once!

We shopped all over for parts for Bob's bike, but with no success.

Saturday, August 7, 1954

We shopped some more this morning, and visited Bob's insurance company. No luck at all on either score. Bob's insurance company is interested only if they are sued for damages, and as the car wasn't damaged and Bob doesn't have comprehensive insurance, they won't do a thing for us. Sweet!!

All the shops were closed this afternoon so we went down to Whitehall and through the houses of Parliament. Boy, it's beautiful, with statuary, paintings, wood carvings, gold, and so forth, and so forth, all over the place. It must cost a mint to keep up. I've some postcards which I'll send home. The one thing that really struck me was that there was no statue of Disraeli among the scores I saw. I was told there was one in the park opposite, but we didn't find it. We had a guided tour through the Houses and were led by a very enthusiastic fellow who held up the crook of his umbrella so we could see where he was going.

After leaving there, we went across the street to Westminster Abbey, and were sorry we hadn't come first thing in the morning. The place was mobbed, and with all those chairs blocking the floor, you just couldn't move at all. We saw the Coronation Stone and several of the more important graves. Like all the other churches, Westminster is falling apart. They've raised about a million pounds to save the place, but that's still too small a figure. The Great Hall in the Houses of Parliament was suffering from an infestation of termites, and Westminster's roof will have to be entirely replaced because of the same thing.

Tonight we went to the Cecil Sharp House, the home of the English Folk Song and Dance Society. It is a beautiful new structure, with the name of the society lettered on a concrete frieze across the top. On the inside it's very modern with a good-sized dance floor, good acoustics, and all the conveniences to go with it. There's a large refreshment hall and good-sized locker rooms with showers. They did all English country and American square dances, and I got some good ideas. We met a fellow from the SIFD (Society for International Folk Dancing), and got the right address for their session, which is held tomorrow night. Guess where we're going to go?

Sunday, August 8, 1954

Today we got up and went to church at the neighborhood parish church, a Romanesque-style place which is very pretty, but had lousy acoustics. One of the things that impressed me was the fact that there was a small congregation but a large choir, and an all-male choir, at that. Another thing that impressed me was that they read off the "banns," which is simply a public announcement that two people are engaged. This isn't so bad, but all the girls are referred to as "spinsters."

Then we got on the train and went to town to have dinner with Bob's cousins, the McKays. Mrs. McKay put on a really good feed, and we had a good talk afterwards. Mr. McKay is a doctor, and took care of Bob's finger, bruised in the accident, which had a bit of a blood clot under the nail.

Then we headed for Sloane Square and the Society for International Folk Dancing's Sunday session. We did a lot of dances we knew and a lot we didn't know, all to the tune of an accordion (no records to speak of). Then we heard of a Folk Ballet coming to the Sadler's Wells Theatre, and were also invited to dance on the grass in Hyde Park next Wednesday. An interesting day!

Monday, August 9, 1954

We had another day of fruitless searching in the motorcycle shops. Well, not quite fruitless—we found a set of front forks for the bike, but no petrol tanks. Everywhere we go they say that repairs would take about a week. Much too long! So we figured out a scheme: we'll get the forks and put them on the bike, then we'll order petrol tanks and have Bob's cousin pick them up and ship them to Rotterdam, where Bob can get them before he sails for home. We'll see how this works.

As we came home from the center of town, we noticed a darkening cloud approaching, but hoped to get home before the storm broke. About one block farther on, the cloud burst and it came down in rivers. It was like someone was pouring water on you from a pail. We got drenched, and took cover on the front porch of an apartment house. There we found a bobby (policeman), who said that at the beginning of the storm it was coming down so hard that he couldn't see the face of the clock across the street. It let up as suddenly as it started, and we got dried out later in front of the gas fire. No dancing tonight; we actually got some letters written.

Tuesday, August 10, 1954

Today I bought a few things to keep me dry. I bought a real motorcycle raincoat (long, with straps to hold the tails to my legs) from Len, who shares the apartment, and some bicycle oilskin leggings. I also invested in a crash helmet. About Bob's cycle—the usual "no luck" story. He bought another sleeping bag to replace the one he lost, and I bought some baggage insurance. I also bought a switch with a battery case and batteries for a brake light.

Tonight was the best night we've had anywhere, as far as I'm concerned. We went to the Sadler's Wells Theater and saw "Les Ballets et Choeurs Basques Etorki," (Basque folk music) and was it swell! (See the enclosed program.) I just can't describe the costumes, as they were too beautiful and too varied. Nor can I describe the music very well. The "Txistu" (you pronounce it—I can't) sounds like a recorder. It is played with the left hand, the little finger across it holds it against the mouth, and there are three holes top, and one on the bottom for the thumb. The fellow who played it was excellent and although one would think that he could only get five tones from it, he ran all over the scale even played two-note chords. The girls all wore braids (only one girl's braids were her own). Underlined on the title page of the program are the names of those whose autographs appear inside. Sorkunde Laya and Nekane Lasarte are the two girls who sang the duet, and Maritxu Zubiaurre played a part in "Andoniñe." The two ballets used ballet to carry the story along but the folk dances were integrated cleverly. A lot of the background music was supplied by the cast singing a capella off or on stage. The only other bit of explanation is that what they call "voices" in the chorus section means "parts." It was a beautiful show and I only wish you could have seen it. They didn't have any pictures, unfortunately.

Wednesday, August 11, 1954

Another fruitless day of searching for a petrol tank.

Tonight we danced on the grass in Hyde Park with the SIFD group. We had a good time, although the ground was a little bumpy. We were invited to go with them for coffee afterwards but we couldn't find the cafe. Oh, well . . .

Thursday, August 12, 1954

We went to the motorcycle shop today and put on the new forks, but lo and behold, the new forks were out of line, too! So we deduced that it wasn't the forks, but the frame. So we put the old forks back on, packed up, and got all set to leave for Birmingham in the morning.

Friday, August 13, 1954

We got to Birmingham about 2 p.m., and they told us it would take a week to get the frame straightened, so we left the bike there and took off for Stratford-upon-Avon. Bob hitched and I rode the bike. Before I left, I bought a pillion seat and footrests. I got to Stratford around 7, and looked for the youth hostel. I made the mistake of asking for the hostel right in front of the place, and the warden saw me and wouldn't let me in. So I headed back to the Memorial Theatre because I knew I would find Bob at the festival. You see, we got there just in time for the last performance of the English Folk Song and Dance Society's annual Stratford-Upon-Avon Festival, where there is Morris, sword, and English country dance exhibitions, and plenty of opportunities for the onlookers to participate. It's held in the front of the Memorial Theater. Bob came and we both had a wonderful time. After the show we went inside to the conference hall in the theatre building and danced some more. We met Kenneth Clark, regional (Birmingham) secretary of the society (this is a job?) and had a terrific time. We also met a family from Philadelphia who had come over expressly for the Stratford Festival. We made arrangements to go the following night to the Stratford branch's annual After-the-Festival square dance. And then I worried about a place to sleep. I finally ended up rigging a tent out of the tarpaulins we had and sleeping out in the city's caravan and camping park. It was bumpy, but at least it didn't rain.

Saturday, August 14, 1954

I left the bike at the campground, packed up and went to the hostel to see if I could get in. Without my raincoat, leggings and helmet, I looked different enough to get away with it. I saw Bob and helped him pack, and so forth. They told us both that we would have to come back at 5 and take our chances, that no reservations were accepted over the phone or early in the morning. So I went to town to see about seats for a matinee. The play didn't let out until 5:30, so it was either the play or the hostel. We chose the play, and spent the rest of the morning looking for a cheap bed and breakfast. We went to the Catholic hostel, but they were full up. Then we looked in at the old church where Shakespeare was buried. We stopped at a garden to talk to the gardener who took care of all the gardens belonging to the Shakespeare Trust. He gave us each a small marigold to wear in our caps and told us to go to the British consulate. We went there and got a list of all the rooming houses in town. We finally got a place at eight shillings, and headed back for the theater.

We got there just in time for the performance and saw a very well-acted Troilus and Cressida. During intermission we met some children from Germant, Germany, and the girls of the group were all wearing very pretty embroidered skirts and vests, a sort of costume, all alike. Afterwards we went backstage to see this actor that Bob had met the last time he was in Stratford. We had a good chat and he invited us to tea the next day. But as we were planning to leave early Sunday for Dorset, we couldn't accept.

We headed back to the hostel, had some supper, picked up our packs went to the bed-and-breakfast. A wash, and off to the dance. We saw some girl hostellers from the US, about 10 of them, and they just got back from Norway. They were at the dance but left early. It's not like a real square dance, they said. The dance was mostly English country dancing, with about three squares. Bob and I met the caller, and saw lots of folks who were at the festival the night before.

Sunday, August 15, 1954

We left today for Jan Macdonald's in Dorset. Bob set out hitchhiking about noon, and I, having to fetch the cycle and whatnot, set out about 1:30. It was an uneventful trip; everything went smoothly and only a couple rain showers were encountered. As I progressed toward Dorset, the land got more and more hilly. By the time the coast was reached, low gear had been used quite often. I made inquiries at Bridgeport and had no trouble at all finding Jan's house. Neither Jan nor I thought Bob would make it that night, but about fifteen minutes after I pulled in, Bob came up the walk. It seems he had very good luck, and one ride took him all the way from Cheltenham to Blandford. It was a young couple on a holiday and they invited us to stay with them when we got back to Birmingham.

Jan's cottage is over three hundred years old, and of the primitive mud and wattle construction. When she was fixing the place up, her carpenter pulled an oak beam about two feet long right out of the wall! They used anything and everything, back in those days. We got ourselves set, and settled down for the night. Bob had the second bedroom upstairs, and I enrolled my sleeping bags on the couch in her study

Monday, August 16, 1954

Last night we had tentatively mapped out a route for ourselves, but we found it was too long for one day's looking. We made ourselves a lunch, and set out for Askerswell, near which was Egerton Hill, on which there was a prehistoric fortification. (Don't bother looking for any of these places on the map; we had to use a half-inch-to-the-mile survey map to find them.) We went up to the hill, and saw a Chevy station wagon sitting there. The driver turned out to be the French ambassador to Lebanon, on leave of absence from his job. His family, and some friends of his children had come up for a picnic lunch. We walked all over the hill, and saw the place where the old dwellings were supposed to have been. The folks there were all very nice, offered us tea and all, and we spent much more time there than we had planned.

Then we pushed on over the fields to the little town of Sydling St. Nicholas, where nine tenths of the buildings are thatched-roofed. Then on through Maiden Newton to Cerne Abbas. There we saw the ruins of the old abbey (dating from Tudor times), and ate our lunch by the "wishing" well. The gardner's little boy took us around, and told us all about the place—and a very good guide he made, too! (He was only about nine years old.) Then his father came along and filled in on the finer points. The only parts of the abbey still intact, more or less, were the main gate, part of the wall, a small garden gateway, the graveyard and the wishing well.

We headed back, and stopped for a few minutes to see the Cerne Abbas Giant, one of the most famous monuments in England. It is the figure of a naked man carved in the hillside so the underlying chalk shows through. He is brandishing a very wicked-looking club. His genitals show as a huge penis, because it is a phallic symbol, and has to do with fertillity rites. There are also many horses carved in the hillsides in like manner.

Then we came back to Jan's via the old Roman road, which has been resurfaced since it was first made, but otherwise unimproved. A fine supper greeted us, and after dinner we made plans for the next day.

We had a very fine day today. It was sunny and bright, and didn't rain once. The best day, in fact, soince we left Darlington.

Tuesday, August 17, 1954

Today we went sightseeing in the rain, something to which we are pretty used to now. We continued where we left off yesterday, completing yesterday's schedule. We first visited the museum in Dorchester. In Dorset and surrounding countryside lived many people in prehistoric days and the museum had cases and cases of relics that have been dug up. There were displays of the evolvement of the metal spearhead, stone axes, methods of chipping flint, and so forth, and so forth. There were photographs and charts of excavations, showing the different civilization layers. The most interesting, biggest and most excavated spot was Maiden Castle, just outside Dorchester. It had been a fortress and dwelling place for three thousand years, and they trace the civilizations back to the Stone Age. There was a very complete write-up on it, showing excavations and all, and we both read the complete story.

It's really too bad that the Ministry of Works doesn't have enough money to go around. The very extensive excavations at Maiden Castle all had to be filled in because they couldn't afford to keep guards and repair workers on the job. The whole place is a cow pasture now, and just a few service markers remain to show where some of the buildings and roadway sites were.

Imagine a large oval piece of ground about a half-mile long about a thousand feet wide surrounded by two or three deep trenches with steep sloping sides. All this done with hand tools in prehistoric times. Some leader must have had some great dream to fulfill, and a great hold over his subjects, to have such a fortification completed. I said that Bob and I were disappointed in the size of the Roman wall; well, this is immense and done long before the Romans set foot in the country. Each trench was it least 30 ft deep! We were at the museum all morning and then went to the park to eat lunch (we found some densely-leaved trees to shelter us), then went back to the museum after lunch, and stayed a couple more hours.

Then we went next door to see Saint Peter's Church, and to the edge of the town to see Saint George's Church. The latter was the older, and over the doorway was a tympanum, or bias-relief carved stone block, of Saint George Castle, depicting St. George helping to defend two Crusaders from the Saracens.

Then we went out to Maiden Castle, and we sure were glad we had the cycle. The road for the last half-hour was a sea of mud, but we plowed right through without a hitch. We walked all over the place, saw the cemented remains of the foundations of the Roman Temple that was the latest structure built there. We saw the drawings of the distinctive traverse mound and long burial mound; the sunken pits, one round and one square, which mark the sites of the two prehistoric dwelling places, and noted the depth and width of the protective trenches. We also noticed the complicated turns through these trenches one had to go to get to the living site proper.

It was raining all the time and a strong wind was blowing. I was glad I had this motorcycle rain coat and oilskin leggings. We went back to Jan's to eat a good hot meal and talk.

Jan had done considerable relief and social work of one sort or another, and spent quite a few years in Palestine. From all her talk, the main thing that I could get was that she thinks the formation of Israel was a big mistake, and frowned upon the grouping of the Jews in any form. She would like to see them more well dispersed so they wouldn't "grab up" all the jobs on stores, TV, radio, stage, movies, entertainment and politics. Because Jews always look out for fellow Jews, she says she doesn't want them to be able to that. It seems to me that the root of all trouble, according to her, is the Jewish religion. And yet she told us many times not to misunderstand her, that she was "pro-Jew, but anti-Zionist." It sounds a little mixed up to me!

We looked at an article that she wrote for a magazine, in which she describes the Palestinian costumes, and saw the original pictures of them. Jen seemed to be a well-thought woman who realized the value of seeing both sides of the question. She certainly has made up her mind about the Jews though, and is convinced that there is more prejudice against them in the States that anywhere in Europe.

Wednesday, August 18, 1954

We left Jan's today and went back to Birmingham to see about the bike. Bob hitched, and got a ride to the Bristol Street YMCA hostel tonight. I didn't. I went to Abbotsbury and visited the famous Swannery. It was marvelous. The flowers in the gardens are beautiful, and several magnificent fuchsia bushes, ten feet or more tall, were covered with blossoms. There are hundreds of white swans there, and I walked right through them. They come to this place because of a certain weed that grows in this particular inlet, where the water is half salt and half fresh. Then I went to the Dorchester Museum to get a postcard of Maiden Castle.

Finally I set out. It didn't rain too much today. Darkness found me approaching Gloucester (I went by way of Bristol), and I had to go to the Cheltenham YMCA nine miles away for a room. The "Y" was actually a makeshift dormitory, shared with two others, and I just got in by the skin of my teeth.

Thursday, August 19, 1954

I went into Birmingham and straight to the BSA Works, and made arrangements to get the 600-mile service check, which is now three times overdue. Then I went to the YMCA to look for Bob. He wasn't there. They had charged him nine shillings for a bed and breakfast, and he was rather disgruntled at that, so he left. Well, I knew he had a friend in Dudley, just outside of town, so I figured he might have gone there. Sure enough, he arrived at the Dudley address a few minutes after I did. He met this fellow at Llangollen, but the man wasn't home now. He was on the second week of his holiday and wouldn't be back until Sunday, but his father came up while we were talking and told us to come back Sunday. So we called up the bed and breakfast place where I stayed before then went there. We went to a local movie, hoping to see the fall of rock at Niagara Falls (on the opening newsreel),* but no such luck.

Friday, August 20, 1954

I spent all day writing, catching up on letters and this diary. Bob spent all day in town buying some leggings and seeing about the bike. We planned to go to a square dance at Muntz Park, put on by the Birmingham branch of the English Folk Song and Dance Society, but it was utterly rained out. So we both sat home, wrote, and watched TV for a while before turning in.

---

* On July 24, 1954, a huge section of Prospect Point observation area at the brink of the American Falls collapsed, sending an estimated 185,000 tons of rock thundering into the Niagara River Gorge. Engineers determined that more rock had to be blasted from Prospect Point to make the famous point safe for tourists and workers alike. On August 12, 1,800 tons were blasted away, but it only removed two-thirds of what was needed. On August 16th 1954, a dynamite charge at Prospect Point sent 900 tons of loose rock to the base of the Niagara Gorge, ending a chapter in Niagara history. Since then there hasn't been another rockfall at Prospect Point.

Saturday, August 21, 1954

This morning I continued with my writing. Then in the afternoon we called Cadbury's to see if we could go through the chocolate works. We made an appointment for Wednesday morning. Then Bob and I went to town to shop and sort of look around. Besides, I froze yesterday in that fire-less house. I wore two jackets all morning, and my hands were icy. We saw crowds of shoppers around the second-hand open-air shops in the Bull Ring. We looked up the hill and all we could see were people. There wasn't an open patch of pavement anywhere. Then we went out to Birmingham University, but it was closed Saturday afternoons. Tonight Bob went to a dance and didn't have a very good time. He had to pay four shillings admittance, too. I stayed at home, wrote and watched TV. I'm very glad, after hearing Bob's report, that I didn't go.

Sunday, August 22, 1954

Bob, that ambitious character, got up in time to go to church. I didn't. I had a good bath and was all cleaned up to go to Dudley when he got back. We thought that since it was only two of them rattling around by themselves in that house, that they might invite us to stay for a few days (aren't we mercenary, though?). So we packed our stuff. Then Bob came home and said that we were invited to dinner by the folks he met at church.

So off we went to the home of Mr. and Mrs. Hill and daughter Kathy. It was a very nice warm home, and a very good dinner. They showed us all around their "allotment" (public ground divided up for gardens) and all around the community. Then a few turns of the wind-up gramophone, playing really ancient dance records, and it was time for tea. Kathy showed us her medals she had won for ballroom dancing, and I said that if it didn't rain, and if we were still here, we might make arrangements to take her to the square dance next Friday. She has never done any, and I know she would enjoy it. We left, finally (I thought we wore our welcome a little thin), and went home to the rooming house. More letters, TV, and bed.

Monday, August 23, 1954

We packed up, left our stuff in the hall, and went to town. First we went to BSA and left my bike there for the check-up. Then we went to American Express and picked up a letter from the insurance company and the invitation from Cadbury. The estimate for Bob's bike had been received by the insurance company, forwarded to the Birmingham office, and an inspector arranged for. Good! We went to the insurance man and got everything straight.

Then we stopped at a news theater and saw them blasting away Prospect Point. Back again to the BSA Works, and we were taken on a tour through the factory. We saw everything, from the making of chains to the complete assembly and shipping. When they test-run their engines, they use regular stove gas, not gasoline, and no carburetor. All the frames are hand-welded and all the painted parts hand-dipped. We had a large tea with hungry company (three motorcycle-mad US mechanics from Burtonwood air base) and then went back to our bed-and-breakfast.

We packed up our stuff and went out to Aston, to the home of the people who gave Bob his long lift on the way to Dorset. Well, it turned out that the fellow, Alan, shouldn't have asked us to stay with him at all. There wasn't enough room. He and his wife lived with his parents over his mother's grocery shop. His folks had a sitting room on the ground floor and a bedroom on the first floor. The young couple had a sitting room on the first floor and a bedroom on the second. And they shared the ground floor kitchen which was also the lavatory. That was all the room there was. Alan hadn't told his parents that we were staying overnight, and left to work the night shift. His wife ended up sleeping on the couch, and us in the second-floor bed. Not the best for the wife.

Tuesday, August 24, 1954

We did just about absolutely nothing today.

Tonight, Alan's wife slept in her bed, and Bob and I slept on the floor of the upstairs sitting room, using foam rubber cushions and the couch cushions. Not bad, and much better for the wife.

Wednesday, August 25, 1954

This morning we hustled ourselves out to Cadbury's in Bournville. We had a guide all to ourselves (each party had it's own guide), and we saw all the operations, from the roasting of the cacao beans to the making of the chocolate; from the mixing of the flour to the finished chocolate-covered biscuits; from the making of the cans and pasting of the labels to the boxes of cocoa waiting to be shipped. We watched the chocolate being wrapped by a machine doing over a hundred pieces per minute. We saw liquid chocolate exuded into molds and then passed through a cooling room on a conveyor belt, being shaken all the while to get rid of the air bubbles. One of the most satisfying things—I found out how they got the chocolate all around the centers, They pass over a screen-like conveyor which oozes chocolate from below while pouring it on from above. Only one thing still puzzles me -- how do they get the chocolate around a liquid center? We also saw the biscuits and wafers being baked, sandwiched and cut to size. They work day and night from Monday morning to Saturday morning and constantly produce the stuff. Many packaging machines get fouled up if the next piece of candy isn't there to be wrapped, so they always work at full speed.

They took us on a motor coach tour of Bournville and showed us all the low-cost houses that Cadbury's has built. There was nothing there when Cadbury's started and they built the town. The government is separate from that of Birmingham. The folks who founded the company were Quakers and their heirs are also.

We noticed an ad for an Old Tyme dance tonight, so we decided to come back after supper. When we got back to Aston, Alan's father was arguing with his son for asking us to stay there in such crowded conditions, so we left and went to the YMCA. We got to share a room with two others at a cheaper price than Bob was charged before.

Then off to the Old Tyme dance at Cadbury's. We had a good time but found an awful dearth of young women. They do what they call Modern Sequence in the Old Tyme style. We didn't like it too much. We also did some we thought we knew, but they did them different here. Someone has been balling everything up, I guess. Before we left we each bought a ticket to another Old Tyme dance Saturday at Cadbury's.

Then went to BSA and got my bike back. A lot more GO, now!

Thursday, August 26, 1954

We spent most of today writing letters. In the afternoon we called the insurance company and then went down there. We were very surprised and pleased when the fellow offered to make a cash settlement on the spot. So we did. Then we rushed to BSA to tell them to get it done as soon as possible. They told us five days, which, including Saturday and Sunday, makes a week. We got back to the "Y" and called Mrs. Colquehoun at Nottingham and she was very surprised to hear me on the phone. She invited us down, so we decided to go there Saturday. That meant, of course that the Old Tyme dance is off, so we went back to where we bought the tickets and got a re-fund. We had a nice talk with them and I got directions for the Moonlight Saunter dance. Then we stopped off at a movie and saw a comedy.

Friday, August 27, 1954

We again spent the morning writing letters. Then this afternoon we went through the Dunlop Tire factory here. We saw the complete show, from the mixing of the raw rubber to the finished product. Tonight we went to Muntz Park to the square dance, and although a little rain did fall it wasn't enough to stop the dancing. So we had a full evening of dancing and did some of the more complicated squares.

Saturday, August 28, 1954

Today we packed up and set off for the Colquehoun's and it was a nice day for the second day in a row! Now there's a real record! I got to Nottingham about 1 p.m. Isabel met me at the door. Both Mr. and Mrs. Colquehoun were out, but Pop came in while I was unloading the bike. Bob came in a few moments later. Mrs. Colquehoun was late so we sat down to lunch without her. She walked in just as we were finishing. Both Mr. and Mrs. Colquehoun are looking fine. Mrs. Colquehoun tells me she's better now than she's been in a long time. Isabel looks like Margaret; she tells us she's determined to be an old maid—that her work is more important. I don't believe her.

Bob and I went to an Old Tyme dance at the fire hall. Again, most of the dances were Modern Sequence ones, and we didn't know them. We talked to the emcee afterwards and it seems he's just in the game for the money. It's a rather narrow-minded attitude if you ask me. There were, however a number of younger girls present so we had a better time.

Then—wouldn't you know it?—we got back to the bike only to find a flat tire! One of the patches had worked loose. We went to the police garage nearby and fixed the thing in comfort, but it was an hour's job.

Dear Mom:

Well, we're in Nottngham now, and expect to pick up the bike Thurs-day, then on to France. Whew! Do you really think we'll make it? I think I better invest in a new inner tube; this one has six patches in it now. We're going to a lace factory tomorrow, so I'll go to bed.

Love, Ted

Sunday, August 29, 1954

This morning we woke up just as the folks were going to church, so we missed our chance. We continued writing letters in the morning and again in the afternoon, when the rest were taking naps. This evening Isabel took Bob and I to the Methodist Mission service held at Albert Hall (owned by the Methodists), which is the concert hall of Nottingham.* The place wasn't packed as usual because the regular Minister wasn't there, but it was fairly nice, with a large choir, a good organ, and five hymns during the service (I never found one I knew).

Monday, August 30, 1954

Today we visited Castle Rock. In the center of town there is a huge sandstone rock protruding from the ground, and years ago there was a castle on top of it. The rock itself is honeycombed with tunnels and passages. Ye Olde Trip To Jerusalem Inn, which claims to be the oldest pub in England, is built right into the rock and many of the "rooms" are carved out of it. There is a very terrific museum where the castle used to be, with many relics from prehistoric times, including two wooden canoes carved from trunks dredged from the river Trent and two stone cels (axe heads) from Brentford. We went through the tunnels on a short guided tour and got sand in our hair along a formation. In the basement of the museum was a very good display of lace and lace-making machines.

Tonight Mrs. Colquehoun took us all to the movies. *Halt! Who Goes There?* is a satire on the Grenadier Guards, and very funny.

Tuesday, August 31, 1954

This morning we went through the Boots Chemical Company's plant. Boots is a large chain drugstore outfit, like Rexall. We saw them making

---

* Albert Hall in Nottingham (not to be confused with Albert Hall in London) continued to function as a Methodist mission until 1984. Nottingham City Council purchased the Albert Hall in 1987 and a major refurbishment was set to task in order to link the venue with the adjacent Nottingham Playhouse for use as a multipurpose centre. The work was completed in 1988 and Her Royal Highness the Princess of Wales unveiled a plaque on 23rd February 1989 to commemorate the refurbishment. The Nottingham Playhouse managed the Albert Hall until July 1990 when the Nottingham City Council leased the building to the Albert Hall Nottingham Ltd for use as a Commercial Conference and Entertainment Venue.

pills, capsules, talcum, bath salts, and so forth. No prescription drugs are made in their Beeston plant (where we were), but they do make them. We saw their packing and shipping department (quite big and mechanized), research labs, controls, and special prescriptions department.

Tonight we went to the best Old Tyme dance yet. It was at the Victoria Ballroom, quite the best dance place in the city. There was a good crowd and quite a number of younger girls. I really had a good time; so did Bob. They did a standardized version of the Florentine Waltz and I got the directions. They did something called "The Marine Four Step" to (get this!) "The Happy Wanderer" music.

We got home with no flat tires!

Wednesday, September 1, 1954

Today I finished my writing. My diary and letters are completely up to date let's hope they don't get behind like that again. Bob is still a month behind.

Today we thought we were going to a lace factory, but actually went to a lace finishing place connected with a manufacturing company. We saw them carding lace (winding it up on bolts or on cards) and saw how they made the lace so that it could be divided into narrow strips for veils, edgings, and so forth. We visited the room where they're embroidering bridal veils. This was by hand, with a special attachment to the regular sewing machine. The head lady took a couple pieces of veiling and embroidered "Bob" on one piece of veiling and "Liz" on the other. (Bob just wasn't quite quick enough on the draw).

The we went to the council house, home of the Lord Mayor, but found we had to have an appointment to see the place. Both Bob and I bought three-shilling books on Old Tyme dancing and we came home.

It was one of the hottest days of the "summer" today, bright and sunshiny all day long. It was wonderful. Do you suppose we'll get some summer after all this?

Thursday, September 2, 1954

This morning we left at 7 a.m. for Birmingham in one of the trucks of Mr. Colquehoun's company. We loaded my bike and all took off. Bob's bike was supposed to be finished today, thank heavens! Well this Bob is a lucky fellow! On his way to Nottingham he was picked up by a family from Birmingham and they invited us both to dinner today.

We arrived at the BSA works at 9 and we're told the bike wasn't ready yet, so we left the packs and went to look around at the University. We stepped into the buildings for a while and a student who was there showed us some of the latest gadgets they had in the Metallurgy and Chemistry departments, Then out to the Pynes, the folks who invited us, and found no one home. Just as we were turning from the door, the next door neighbor came out and said, "Oh, you're looking for the Pynes, aren't you? Well there's no one home, but Mrs. Pyne told me to let you in and for you to make yourselves at home and have some tea." We were overwhelmed!

Along about 4:30 we went back to BSA and had to wait until 6 p.m. to get the bike. After figuring expenses, and so forth, we guess we came out about even as far as the insurance settlement was concerned. So we finally got the bike and headed back to the Pynes, where we found supper and bed waiting for us. Mr. Pyne was a mechanic so we took advantage of the equipment he had and tightened chains, and so forth, before going to bed.

Friday, September 3, 1954

Mr. Pyne said goodbye last night, as he got up early this morning to go to work. Mrs. Pyne also works, and she breezed in and woke us up on her way out. So we got ourselves some breakfast and left for London. Bob's bike felt queer to him -- he had to get used to riding an unbent machine. Peter Bartholomew wasn't home when we arrived but the landlord let us in. We picked up our stuff, and I rescued my shoes from the repairman, and we headed out to the McKay's.

Saturday, September 4, 1954

Today we got all our business taken care of. It took us quite some time to get all the papers together. We inquired about getting comprehensive insurance but found it would be twice as expensive as the third party, fire, and theft that we already have.

We took Liz (that's Elizabeth McKay) to the Cecil Sharp House of the English Folk Song and Dance Society for the weekly dance. She picked up the English and American dances quite easily and had a good time.

Bob and I went shopping and picked up some pins, I bought some postcards showing the dancing at Stratford, and I replenished my supply of bells on the zipper pulls on my jacket with some genuine Morris bells.*

---

* "Morris bells" are tiny bells traditionally worn when doing Morris dancing.

Sunday, September 5, 1954

We got up early and saw the changing of the Horse Guards at White-hall. It was quite a show, with all that shiny armor and spotless white trousers.

Then we went to St. Paul's for church. I couldn't follow the order of worship at all, but the sermon was pretty good.

After dinner at the McKays, we went to the Tower of London to see where Anne Boleyn "walks the bloody Tower with 'er 'ead tucked under-neath 'er arm." It was quite the place, but we stayed so long in the White Tower looking at the old torture devices that we didn't get to see the Crown Jewels before they closed shop. I was surprised to find the Tower was really a well-fortified castle with many towers inside. But the towers inside were just names given to the many buildings that were built there, one smack-dab up against the other. The chapel was interesting; there were all the graves of those who had been executed in the courtyard just outside. In the White Tower we saw one of the old chopping blocks and its accompanying (shudder!) axe.

Tonight we again took Liz dancing, this time to the Society For Inter-national Folk Dancing group. We again met all the kids we had seen before and had a good time. Liz said she enjoyed this more than the Cecil Sharp dance, so we were happy. She often didn't know what she was doing but she did it well and she had fun doing it.

Monday, September 6, 1954

We got off to an early start and went to Dover today. The bikes worked fine and the weather was pretty good too. We pulled the wool over the eyes of the warden by driving at night and parking our bikes, then walking into the hostel. Yes, the things we do so illegally!

Tuesday, September 7, 1954

Today dawned bright and beautiful, nicely enough. I went to the American Express office to pick up my papers and there they told us we had to be to the boat in ten minutes. I had my suitcase to pick up and Bob had a sleeping bag waiting for him at customs, so we missed the boat to Calais. Luckily there was boat to Bologna at 2 p.m., so we decided to take that one. We had some time on our hands, so we hightailed it to a music shop and bought a couple records and a couple copies of sheet music, all of "The Happy Wanderer." Now I can learn the Deutsch words.

The White Cliffs of Dover are really white and with the afternoon sun they were quite pretty as we sailed from the harbor. Bob went around snapping pictures like mad. And behold, he found that there was a hot water and a shower on board so of course he had to take a shower before landing, seeing as he was paying so much for the crossing.Remember I told you about the English toilet paper, which was glazed on one side and like sandpaper on the other? Well, we found that there was soft American-style toilet paper on board, so we became thieves, and stole as much of it as we could find!

We got our passports stamped on board ship, and when we docked they just filled out a carnet* and waved us on. So we got our first glimpse of France in the sun, which is nice. If the weather holds to what has been predicted for us by others (i.e., what it has been all along), it will probably rain all the time we're in Paris.

We went to a youth hostel in Frévent, it being the closest, around 6 p.m. Our limited French being understood, we found the place easily. They all told us that the French hostels were dirty and if this one was any indication, they're right. It wasn't too dirty, but quite a bit dirtier than the English or Scottish hostels.

"Squat john" is the name I'll give to the toilets we were forced to use while in France. They are made of porcelain, about three feet square, set into the floor, with two raised areas where you are supposed to rest your feet. There is a porcelain flange around the perimeter, from which water flows to wash the excrement down the hole in the center. A pull chain is attached to a tank on the wall. Toilet paper is also on the wall to the rear. Don't lose your balance!

I met a couple English fellows driving by motorcycle. They said their seats are becoming too hard, so they were traveling by train after Paris. The chickens! We had heard of straw ticks and pillows, and I'll say that they are okay, but rather bumpy. But it'll be better here than in Dover—the gulls won't be screaming outside the windows at 5 in the morning!

Wednesday, September 8, 1954

We got off fairly early this morning, although still the last to go. This place was dirtier than I thought. When we swept, the dust rolled in clouds. I hope it's better in Paris.

---

* A carnet is a customs permit allowing a motor vehicle to be taken across an international border for a limited period.

We bought our first gasoline on the continent. It's more expensive than England.

We arrived in Paris and went first to see if Claude Michele's parents were home. But it turned out they were in Britain, as you warned us, so we had something to eat and went to call on the fellow Bob had met at Llangollen. We found his place rather easily, but he lives on the sixth floor (seventh, in our vernacular), and we were actually winded when we got up there. He must have a big appetite when he gets home at night. He welcomed us and invited us to stay for supper. We accepted, of course. We had a good time, and they invited us again for a time when they would be prepared for us. They were all there: Marcel, his wife, his mother, and his daughter.

Then as it was getting late, they showed us the way to the hostel at Port de la Chapelle. We got there, and found the place booked solid. So what to do? They fixed us up, though. They called Malakoff, a small municipality just over the city line and that hostel said they had plenty of room. So we took off. Well, according to the tourist maps we had, the streets had names, but it turned out they really had entirely different names. With the help of a fellow on a motorbike who led us, we finally got there. It was the field house of the town stadium, and was run by Les Amis de la Nature, a sort of socialist youth hostel organization. Our American Youth Hostel cards were good here, though, and the price the same as the others, so we stayed. We slept in rows of 20 or 30 on army cots on the floor of the gymnasium, with wooden partitions separating the sections. They had only cold water for washing, but you can come in any hour of the night as long as no one complained of being disturbed. This suited us fine.

Thursday, September 9, 1954

Today we inspected our surroundings. I actually figured out how to find this hostel on the map, after renaming half the Malakoff streets. Then we set out to go to Notre Dame, but decided to buy gas first. Bob was completely empty, and I was on the last bit, but was all right for me. I went first, and purchased a full tank with money borrowed from Bob. Bob went second and asked for only one liter because he was now short of funds. The proprietress gave him five liters. He had a big argument and a gendarme came over and we had a jolly time. So we wheeled the bikes into the garage and walked around for a while waiting for the bank to open, It did, in a few minutes, and we paid the lady, but she was still mad at us, so she wouldn't let us have any air for the tires. The next time we'll watch more closely.

Notre Dame is unique in that it is built on an island, so it doesn't have too many buildings near it to obstruct the view. We went inside and took pictures of the windows. They certainly are beautiful! All the best ones have been replaced since the war. Then we went up the tower, our student cards getting us in for half price. Boy, you get quite a view from up there! And more pictures—we took some of ourselves posing next to some gargoyles (Look, Ma—no horns! Look, Ma, no wings!), and went to look at the bells; five were missing; melted up or bombed out, I guess.

Then we went for a walk along the Seine, and saw the sidewalk libraries and art galleries (anyone for a nude?). Bob's camera, I'm finding out, has too narrow an angle. He has to get a mile away from anything to get it all in. This is all right with Notre Dame; it's not near another large building. Butt what about other places? I think our Kodak Bantam is better, even if it does get only eight pictures to the roll.

This evening we spent four hundred francs apiece and went to the Casino de Paris. It is not a gambling casino as we think of it, but a theater with a regular show. Well, you see, we were told it was practically the same as the famous Folies-Bergere, only not likely to be so crowded. So we found standing room, and moved into empty seats after intermission. All I'll say about the show is that anything you've heard about these Paris shows is probably not too exaggerated. There was lots of nudity, yes, but not too much lewdness, and plenty of burlesque humor.

Friday, September 10, 1954

Today we did a lot of concentrated sight-seeing. First, we went to Les Invalides. It's a magnificent structure from the outside and even more magnificent from the inside. The windows are all transparent but tinted blue and it gives a sort of eerie light to the place. We looked over the rail to see Napoleon's tomb and trailed a guide around as he told of each of the little side rooms. The only two windows that weren't blue were those on either side of a big high altar standing on the far side of the crypt. These were yellow and another eerie light was the result. The building is a mass of polished marble and pillars, very pretty but it had a cold feeling. It was good to get out into the sunlight again.

Then we went up the Eiffel Tower. Cheapskates that we were, we walked up to the second landing. We had to take the elevator up to the top, there weren't any stairs. Really, the filigree and lace work that resulted from the building of this thing is lovely. Bob and I were noticing on the way up the stairs that there were big steel plates every so often which held together a number of angle irons and each had a shaped hole cut in the center, and each of these holes fit into a large design that ran from the top of the tower to the bottom. Some planning! The view from the top is undoubtedly the best one in Paris. You can see absolutely everything, but everything! I mailed a couple postcards from the top of the tower (no one can say that I'm not the typical tourist), then we left, several photographs later, and went to the Arc de Triomphe.

It was there that we learned that everything they say about Paris traffic is true. We parked the bikes on one of the streets leading to the Arc and walked across the traffic circle to the monument. The cars were coming every which way, and pretty fast, too. We had to judge on which side the car was going to pass, then jump the other way. Yes, we learned how to drive in Paris. You always try to make the other fellow think that he has to stop because you're not going to. "He who hesitates is lost" is the byword here; you have to be a good fake-out artist. A recent regulation for Paris trafic is to not blow your horn because of the complaints of too much noise. (If you remember, Gershwin had car horns written into his *An American in Paris* opus.) We found out later that there are underground tunnels to get to the Arc. The price to the top of the Arc was high, and they were closed, anyhow, so we didn't go up, but we looked at the massive sculpture work, saw the tomb of France's unknown soldier and several other graves, and took some pictures.

Then we went to the home of the Rouffianges, where we were Wednesday night, to find out when they wanted us to come for dinner. This was a big mistake. We should have phoned. Driving takes such a long time. We were told 8 p.m., but by the time we drove all the way across town and changed our clothes and took the subway back, it was 9. On the way across town we ran into a rainstorm (really, a cloudburst, and every bit as bad as the one we hit in London), then my machine wouldn't go and I had to change the spark plug. Well the folks were just finishing eating when we arrived. I guess they had just about given us up as lost, but they had kept our plates warm, and a very good meal ensued. Then Bob and Monsieur Rouffiange talked, while I and his daughter Lucille got together over some phonograph records she had, of a negro quartet singing Negro Spirituals. Later on we went up to Montmartre, Marcel and Lucille showing us the "painters paradise." We went inside one of the wine gardens just to see what it was like. The place had vines on trellises, forming a roof over the entire garden. Outside on the square it was an outdoor cafe, and two or three men were singing and playing guitars. The city looks beautiful from there, the best lookout being from the observation point in front of the onion-shaped towers of L'eglise de Sacre Coeur. After that terrible cloudburst, it was a beautiful night.

Saturday, September 11, 1954

Today I made a most disheartening discovery—I lost my little brown book that contained all my European addresses. It also contained directions to a few dances and notes on the places we've been. So the first thing we did was go to the Eiffel Tower where we last remembered having it and ask if it had been turned in. No soap. We figured if it wasn't there we wouldn't find it, so it looks like I'll have to rely on the addresses that Bob copied. RATS!

Then we went to the Place de la Concorde and walked up the Tuileries Garden to the Louvre. It was raining slightly, but we could still appreciate the beauty of the gardens. We walked for about an hour through the galleries of the Louvre, enjoying it very much. To be brutally frank, I mostly enjoyed it because it was dry inside and raining hammer handles and pitchforks outside. But I did get a thrill seeing the Mona Lisa. Such a famous painting, and to think I was actually within touching distance of it! I sort of had to pinch myself.

When we got outside it was positively pouring. We turned up our collars and pulled down our hats and set off our splashy way down the Tuilleries Garden to our cycles. By the time we reached the Place de la Concorde it had let up some, so we headed for the American Express office to pick up our mail and leave forwarding addresses.

After that Bob wandered off in search of a post office and I wandered off in search of a soap case (my old one finally gave up the ghost and broke on me). I went down one of the side streets and found a store which stocked them. I also found something else. It so happened that I stumbled onto one of the streets where prostitutes were pling their trade, and as I walked down the street, the girls walking there would smile and say, "'Allo?" "Oui, Monsieur?" and so forth. Well, I didn't stop. But when Bob came back, I took him back and walked the street again. We got quite a kick out of it.

Sunday, September 12, 1954

Today we left Paris. We first went to Versailles Palace to see that famous place. The building was a massive thing but I thought it not particularly pretty from the outside. We showed that we were students and got in for free, and then we saw the real beauty of the place. The guide said all his spiel in French, so we couldn't catch much—just a date or name here or there, but the rooms were beautiful, if unlivable. We walked around the gardens and noticed all the colored lights in the pools and fountains. It's too bad we couldn't stay until nightfall when the fountains begin playing.

Then we headed east, in the general direction of Reims. But that's east of Paris and we were on the west side, so we had to go across the city. Then, of course, I had another flat tire! I always seem to get them just when it's important not to get them. We stopped and I put in that new inner tube—enough of that old one! And it rained quite heavily while we were doing it, just to add to the fun. But that wasn't all. My clutch, all of a sudden, decided to go out of adjustment. So I had to fix that. Since I had no idea how it worked it took a little time. In fact, it was dark before we finished, and we were just on the fringe of Paris. So we holed up for the night at the hostel at Neuilly-Plaisance, just a little ways away. A rather nice-looking place, even if it was rather muddy from the rain, and Bob (the lucky guy!), found an innerspring mattress on one of the bunks.

Monday, September 13, 1954

Today we went to Reims. The journey itself was uneventful. But when we got to the cathedral I was more than pleased. It was simplest and most beautiful church I've seen yet on this trip. The only statue in the place was one of Jeanne d'Arc, in bronze, and the Stations of the Cross were just simple brass crosses, about 10 inches high, with the numbers on them. I tried to take some pictures of the stained-glass windows, but I have my doubts as to how they'll turn out. But even if the pics are lousy, I'll remember their beauty.

The hostel was easy to find and quite an elaborate place. It was a made-over wealthy home with a winding staircase, a glass-roofed porch, and more. We met a couple of real interesting fellows from Deutschland, up near Köln (Cologne). One played the guitar quite well and sang too; out came the harmonicas and the record of "The Happy Wanderer" and we had a real good session.

Tuesday, September 14, 1954

Today journeyed on toward Metz. The two Germans we met last night were also heading there by "auto-stop" (hitch-hiking). They left before we did and we met them on the road about a half hour after we started. When we got to Metz we had a devil of a time trying to find the hostel. Oh, how I wish they had street signs on the corners like in the good ol' US! When we finally found it, there were our two German friends. We had heard there was only one sleeping room at Metz; that the women and men sleep in the same quarters. But as there were no females there, the story remains unproven.

Wednesday, September 15, 1954

When we awoke this morning, we found that the other half of the long barracks in which we stayed was occupied by an all-negro athletic team. They were up bright and early, dressed all in blue and yellow sweat suits, batting and kicking soccer balls all around the place. Now we know why the windows were boarded up on one side of the building: to avoid breakage.

We passed right through Sarrland today. Just like the Sudatenland, Kashmir, and the Polish Corridor, the Saar Protectorate* is a "displaced country." Everyone speaks German, but they use French francs. What a mix-up! We got all our money changed to deutschemarks and noticed that the Bundesreich (German government) has put some really good metal into their coins, not like those aluminum things in France.

We stayed the night at Kaiserslautern, just over the border in Germany at the end of the Autobahn, a rather recent building that was built just for a youth hostel. Nice! And it only cost $0.12 (US) to stay. Wow!

Thursday, September 16, 1954

We went via Autobahn from Kaiserslautern to the small village of Kirchheim an der Eck just off the Autobahn, where a cousin of Bob's girl-friend's father lives, one Fritz Hammel. He owns a wine factory and drives a Mercedes-Benz, so he's pretty well off. He had pressing business just as we arrived, so he referred us to his cousin, Frau Wintner, in another village not far away. He phoned ahead and she was waiting for us when we arrived. Well, it was a good chance for me to use my German, as she couldn't speak a word

---

* France partitioned Saarland at the end of WWII. The French returned it to Germany in 1957. Today it is a federal state of Germany.

of any other language. However, with the aid of my small lexicon, we got on admirably. She showed us around the farm, and it was a typical one—a large courtyard surrounded on four sides by buildings all joined together wherein the animals and people live and the the produce is stored. The animals are kept inside the pens the year 'round (except for the chickens) because there isn't enough land to use any for pasture. The farmhouse was very nice, newly painted. We had a really first-class feed for lunch,and talked and talked. Later on in the evening, Fritz took us all out to dinner. We went to a restaurant at Bad Dürkheim, where there was an agricultural show going on. We had a good look at all the Massey-Harris and McCormick-Deering stuff.

It was very interesting to talk with Frau Wintner—the first American soldiers that came to her village were all Negroes. The people there had never seen them before, and they were scared stiff.

Friday, September 17, 1954

Today we took our leave of the Wintners', and headed for Karlsruhe. On the way, we stopped at Heidelberg to look around. We first went to the American Express and did a bit of business, then wended our way up to the Königstuhl, lookout out at the top of the hill overlooking the city. It was somewhat hazy; we couldn't make out too much, but Mannheim was quite clear and we could trace some of the Rhine.

Then we went half way down the Berg and visited the castle. We were very pleased; it was the most "castle-ly" castle we had seen yet. There was a really deep and wide moat, drawbridges, bastions, ramparts and all the things you usually thought of with a castle. It was terrific! We even found a set of spiral steps that led into the ground, and followed them to the end, where a doorway to a passage was filled with dirt and stones.

But the trouble was, we spent too much time at the castle and were late in getting to Zerr's. We looked in at the famous Zum Roten Ochsen (Red Ox Inn) and saw its hundreds of deer horns steins, clocks and names-all-over-the-walls (ceilings, too). It seems to be quite the thing to do to, to carve or write your name, university, fraternity or date somewhere. Even those in chalk aren't washed off.

When we got to the Zerr's, we were utterly crushed to find that Helga, Herbert's sister, was not at home, but was out folk dancing! She came home just a little while later, so it would have been no use for us to go so late. Rats! There won't be another dance for two weeks!

Herbert immediately got on the phone with his friend Jurgend, and made plans for us to tour the Schwarzwald (Black Forest) tomorrow and Sunday, Mama Zerr and I took to each other immediately; she's so nice! So we ended up with Bob sleeping on the couch and I in Herbert's bed. Herb slept on the floor on a mattress. Actually, I should have been on the floor, but the Zerrs were as stubborn as my mother in making me take the bed and giving Herb the mattress. Can one fight it?

Saturday, September 18, 1954

We set off on the Autobahn about noon, Jurgend with me and Herbert with Bob, on our way to the Schwarzwalt. For the first part of the afternoon it didn't rain, and a couple of times we even saw the sun. But in the evening we ran into a lot of rainy fog. We passed a sign that said, "Blick an der Rhine" ("Glimpse of the Rhine River"), and when we looked, there was nothing but white. It was most discouraging. We stayed the night at a Naturfreunde ("Friends of Nature") house in Knebis. It was a bit more expensive than the Jugenherberge,but newer and more comfortable. I hadn't worn my Army jacket, and consequently was pretty well wet through. A good hot meal soon got me to feeling better. Oh, but that bed felt good!

Sunday, September 19, 1954

Today, unlike yesterday, was wonderful. We awoke to a leaden sky, but by the time the breakfast was over, the sun was alone in a startlingly blue sky. It was so warm that I rode along without my raincoat., letting my jacket dry out. The Schwarzwalt is like the Adirondacks, only more so. And the houses, naturally aren't the same. A typical Schwarzwalt house is built in three stories up against the side of a hill. The "driveway" comes down the hill and enters the top story via a bridge. This is the floor of the barn. The family lives on the second floor and the animals are kept on the first floor. This is a holdover from the days when snow shoveling wasn't so easy or neighbors so close, and everything had to be under one roof when the house was snowbound for months each winter. We saw many such houses as we drove.

There's a certain kind of evergreen that's a lot darker than the other species. This one predominates here, and the hills really are almost black. You know, when Miss Miller, our German teacher in high school, told us all the woods in Germany were clean and free of undergrowth, we all pooh-poohed her, but she's right, even if she did give us a stupid reason for them being that way. To look beneath the trees, you'd think you were in someone's living room.

Our route was from Pforzheim through the back roads to Sand and Knebis yesterday, and through Freudenstadt to Freiburg today. Oh, it was beautiful! Bob got a picture incorporating a waterfall and a few houses in a picture-book setting. Seeing as it was Sunday, you saw a number of women in costume (Bob got a picture of one) one and a lot of nice dirndls, too (girls inside them, of course). At Freiburg we went up to the tower of the church. It's unique in having a hollow spire of filigree-worked stone. Quite unusual. I don't see how they ever got it together. The church was lucky—bombs completely devastated a large section of buildings next to it, but left the church itself unharmed. Of course, the usual renovating and repair work is going on.

From Freiburg we went on to Breisach where there is a famous carved wooden altar in the church. In the fading light we saw it. It, too, is unique in that the center portion shows Mary between God and Christ, and higher up. The story that goes with this altar is that a poor artist was in love with the mayor's daughter, and the mayor said that it was as impossible for his daughter to marry the artist as it was for the artist to build an altar that was higher than the church. Thereupon the artist proceeded to make the altar, bending it over at the top to fit into the church. ". . . and they lived happily ever after."

We stopped at Herbert's uncle's house just in time for supper (what makes you say that we planned it that way?) and had some good hot soup. They were quite disappointed when Bob and I didn't like their home-made apple wine. I tasted it and I said to Herbert, "It tastes like vinegar." Well, the guy sitting next to me had been a prisoner of war in United States and understood my English, and he announced to everybody there that I said the wine tasted like vinegar and they all laughed and I was a little bit chagrined.

Then back to Karlsruhe, at night, on the main road and the ever-present rain. I thought perhaps we had ducked the jinx for one day, but you see I was wrong.

Monday, September 20, to Thursday, September 23, 1954

These were catch-up days. We looked after the bikes, saw some of Karlsruhe, and made some interesting purchases. I bought a chromatic harmonica, key of G (I had to order it and have Herb send it on to me in Graz), and it only cost me about $3.50 US. A ridiculous price, isn't it? But Bob bought even more. The first: a button accordion. The second: a paddlewheel arrangement of six tremolo harmonicas in six different keys: A, B, C, D, F, and G. He'll really start them talking when he shows that around!

I think I got to know Herb a bit, although seven days is not too much (not all day every day, either). He's like Mom in some ways, interested in the same things. He said that he didn't date my sister Jane more at College of Wooster, because he didn't want to get too familiar with someone with whom he could too easily fall in love. Now that's a nice compliment, because he is such a terrific guy.

Karlsruhe September 23rd 1954

Dear Mom:

Well, you see we did finally get to Karlsruhe and see Herbert. we went with him and a friend for two days in the black forest, and spent some nice here days here in Karlsruhe checking the bikes, seeing the sights and talking with the family. Mama Zerr is so nice, and she and I get along quite nicely on my German (with the help of a small pocket dictionary occasionally). The daughter, Helga, is a folk dancer; we've exchanged notes with her. Papa is a toolmaker, and we only see him in the evenings. I've talked a lot with Herb, and I can surely see why you see so much in him.

We are going to Graz, through Konstanz and Lichtenstein and Innsbruck. We will spend one night in Switzerland. We should be in Graz by the first of October.

Love, Ted

Friday, September 24, 1954

Well, the rain is ever with us! Will we never get good weather? I shoulda brung my water-wings!

We got up early (this is a minor miracle) and packed, but a week of unpacking caught up with us and we didn't get off until 3 in the afternoon. That's not very good. In addition to that, my bike didn't seem to have any power, and they going was slow. We went to Baden-Baden and took a quick look-see around that famous resort town. It sure was loaded with dough! Nothing but expensive hotels and shops as far as I could see. Then we headed for the Schwarzwalt and Schramberg. But the night came and we only got as far as Sand. We stopped there at the Naturfreunde house. It was a nice place, about a mile deep in the woods off the main drag. Hot tea again! I think I'm living on it this summer.

Saturday, September 25, 1954

We passed by the same road this morning as we did on the 18th and the same fog was still there so we couldn't see the scenery. Rats! We got to Schramberg about 3 p.m., and Edmund Moser wasn't there (he was my roommate last summer at Syracuse). He was on vacation in France and wouldn't be home for a week. But his sister was there and she insisted that we stay the night. I didn't see where we were going to sleep, but she insisted they had room. Her little brother came home from school and immediately set out on his bicycle to tell his parents who was here. Evidently, Ed had spoken of me, for I was well-known to them. In the evening after supper we all had a real good folk sing (Ed's sister plays the guitar quite well). Of course the Mosers were all questions and we were all answers. My Deutsch got another good workout.

Sunday, September 26, 1954

Today we bid our farewells to the Mosers and set out for Zurich. They wouldn't let us go until we had dinner with them, so who were we to object? My machine wasn't running right, so just this side of Switzerland I stopped to fix it. My points needed adjusting and it made all the difference in the world.

Switzerland is much more expensive, even though the exchange between deutschmarks and Swiss francs is one-to-one. We bought a couple of cloth badges on the German side of the boarder that cost sixty-five pfennig apiece, and saw the same thing in Schaffhausen for two Francs. We stopped in Schaffhausen to see the Rhine Falls, then on to Zurich. It got dark and started to rain after a while. We arrived around 7:30 p.m. and found, on a large city map at a gas station, just where the hostel was. Then we went to a couple of the addresses that Bob had but they didn't pan out. So we went to the hostel. We didn't stay in the hostel proper, but in an addition located in the rear of a very modern grade school. But I didn't think the bedroom set-up was that good, even if it was so modern.

Monday, September 27, 1954

Today we went around some of Zurich. We got up rather late, and the first thing we did was to go to the national office of the Schweitzer Jugendherberge (Youth Hostel) to see if they had any badges or pins. We ended up buying song books. Then on to Dreilinden Restaurant, where we were taken to lunch by Bob's friend. This fellow, Ed Berkmeyer, was a basso in one of the choruses at Llangollen. The lunch was superb, veal and chicken with rice, served on a little two-burner candle-warmer. It must have cost him twenty-five francs at least.

We spent a lot of time in the afternoon at the BSA dealer, puttering. In the evening at the hostel we talked with a Canadian from Toronto, and with the many, many Australians who were there. There were six Aussies traveling in an Austin van. And two girls and a fellow, who, along with a guy from South Africa, were going overland from London to Adelaide, via Greece, Turkey, Arabia and India on a Vincent Motorcycle. I'm glad I'm not doing that!

Tuesday, September 28, 1954

Today we were almost the last to leave; we first watched the Aussies go off. The six in the van looked awfully crowded—three in the front seat in three in the back, with the rear doors open. They had a piece of leather strap across to keep them from falling out. They said it wasn't so bad if it didn't rain, what with sitting on blankets, sleeping bags, etc. Then the three going overland! They were traveling by motorcycle and sidecar. The sidecar was a specially-built one, with lots of nooks and crannies where they could stow their stuff. They had practically a whole new motor along with them and all the other spare parts they might need. What they're really using up are spokes. They had so much power in this Vincent motorcycle (more than 1000 cc's) and so much weight, that the rear hub would turn and leave the wheel behind and broken spokes were the result. They didn't have to worry about tires; they had new tires waiting for them in Athens, Tehran and Calcutta, from the Avon Tyre Company. They also had two rifles and a pistol with them!

We had a good ride to Buchs. It was just 60 miles, and we didn't hit any rain until we got there. We even hit some sun on the way. As we came through this one valley, the sun broke through, and we got some pictures of a picture-book scene just like in the travel photos of the mountains. There's a lot of activity there with the military—we passed a lot of soldiers on the road.

At Buchs the hostel is a couple of outbuildings associated with a non-alcoholic restaurant and hotel. We there met four Canadian girls, hitch-hiking, and five Australians (who else?), girls who were traveling in a Jeep with a fellow from New Zealand. These Australians—the continent is crowded with them! We also met two Australian girls whom we had met previously—in Scotland!

Wednesday, September 29, 1954

It was still raining when we left—will we never get good weather? We went over to Liechtenstein, just to say we've been there and to get some stamps, and then out the other side to Feldkirch, the Arlberg Pass and Austria. Well, I should have shipped my suitcase on to Innsbruck. If I go this way again, I'll not forget. You see, my little machine, with it's heavy load, just wouldn't putt up the steep hills of this pass, so I had to run the thing at idling speed in low gear while I trotted beside it. That was exhausting! I had to stop and rest every so often. I thought I was in shape, but at 10,000 feet it was puff, puff all the way! Anyhow, I wasn't cold going up the pass. We ran through our first snow of the season at the top. The Aussie girls in the Jeep came this way. I'll bet they got a thrill—some of them had never seen snow before.

We rode into Innsbruck (raining still) as it was getting dark and found the hostel without too much trouble. And what a hostel! It is in the basement of a school and has hot water, large washrooms and showers! Terrific! We met all of our Australian friends from the night before, also an interesting American character. He was a "ski bum," who was an instructor at Sun Valley (after many years of ski-bumming there). He wanted to go to Innsbruck University on the GI Bill and ski, but Innsbruck wouldn't take him (no BA or BS degree, same as with me) So he was just on his way to the US Consulate in München to throw himself on the mercy of the people there, trying to get a passage home. He had a $40 pair of ski boots with him—he's going to try and be a personal agent of the maker in the States.

Thursday, September 30, 1954

We awoke to a wonderful sight. As I said, the hostel is in the basement of this building, so the windows are at the top of the wall. On our way from the sleeping room to the washroom, when we looked out the window we were looking up, and saw the sky behind a beautiful sunny mountain with snow at the top. So we knew what we were going to do, and after breakfast, we did it! We took the cable car up the Hafelekar mountain. It was wonderful, swinging a couple hundred feet above the trees. There was about three inches of snow at the top. Bob got some pictures, but sadly, the camera went kerflooey and started tearing the film. So he went into a dark closet that we found, and took the film out. He didn't waste too much; it was at the end of the roll. But I hope it didn't tear the film beyond redemption—it had all the pictures of Karlsruhe, Schramberg, Switzerland and Innsbruck on it, so we had to complete our day with no camera. We spent a lot of time on top of the mountain, and it was pretty late when we got down. So we decided to stay in Innsbruck until tomorrow. We were late for our showers last night, and there was no more hot water. But tonight—Ah-h-h-h-h!

Friday, October 1, 1954

We sent a second postcard to Graz, saying we would be another week in getting there, and set out for München (Munich) and the Oktoberfest (beer festival), in the hopes that we would see some folk dancing. We went via Mittenwald with a 20-degree grade uphill. I had to walk up again! We got to München just as the hostel was closing (how do we take so long?) A new hostel, but no hot water.

Saturday, October 2, 1954

Today Bob and I went to see what we could dig up at the Oktoberfest. Actually, it's a big beer party. There is a big amusement park, with more rides and shows and other money-costing devices than the Canadian National Exhibition, and every other tent is a beer hall set up by one of the many brewing companies, and serving all sorts of food. Bob and I stuck our noses in a number of them, but no folk dancing.

We went on a couple of the rides. The "Rotor" is a big steel drum that revolves in a vertical position. People line the walls, and when the drum is going so fast that the centrifugal force holds them against the wall, the floor drops slowly for about 10 ft leaving them stuck on the wall like so many flies. It's really fun to watch, as the drum slows down, and the people start to slide down the wall, leaving, in some instances, their clothes behind.

The "Teufelsrad" ("Devil Wheel") was another ride. It is a polished convex circular disc in the center of a large padded ring. People would get on, and as the disc rotates, the centrifugal force would make them slide off. They would call for all boys or all girls, or perhaps a couple of fellas with boxing gloves, for example. The last ones left on would get pummeled with a large pillow on the end of a rope, swung back and forth.

These two rides can be ridden as often as you want for one entrance fee, and each has a large viewing gallery, so they were the most popular rides, being chock-full of people even in the slack period in the afternoon. It only goes to prove that the most popular rides are the ones that rely on the people themselves to provide the fun for the others.

I also liked to watch the swings. They are a regular swing, but are connected to a fulcrum about fifteen feet off the ground by rigid metal bars, so that when you pump them high enough, they go a full 360 degrees around. Natrually, the riders are upside down at the apex of the swing, and the girls are in danger of showing their underwear, but that didn't stop them from volunteering to ride.

But the best thing about the whole fest are the little portable organs all over the place. There was one by every merry-go-round, ride and food stand, all going full blast. They all had drums, cymbals and bells, with little figurines that moved, and lights that flashed on and off in rhythm to the music. They're all run by a series of cards with holes in them that ran through the machine. The actual power usually came from an electric motor which ran the mechanism and pumped air. They were wonderful. We saw one really old-fashioned merry-go-round with scenes from Wagner operas painted all over it. We looked for and saw many costumes—I think Bob got some pictures of them.

We were told to go to the "Platzl" restaurant, to see schuhplattlering.* So we went, but were told we had to have a ticket for admission, and they were all sold out. But they did let us stand long enough to see one dance. Then the people sitting near us talked to a waitress, and a couple chairs were produced from somewhere, so we stayed for the rest of the show. The yodeling was very good, although pretty high for my taste.

Back to the hostel just at closing time—we had a pretty good day!

Sunday, October 3, 1954

We left pretty early for Salzburg, but stopped by the home of Bob's friend Dr. Hoffa, to leave the map Bob had borrowed. The Hoffas wouldn't let us go until we had lunch with them. It was about 3 in the afternoon

---

*Literally, "shoe-slapping"—a folk dance popular in Bavaria and Tyrol, where the men slap their shoes at certain points in the dance.

by the time we got started, and we didn't get to Salzburg until after dark. I called Kurt Bacher's parents from the gas station outside town, and they said to come on down, because they had plenty of room for us.

Herr Hoffman is a very busy man, with all his teaching, and speaks English very well. His daughter, Monica, helped quite a bit to maintain our impression that most of these young girls are pretty, and she, too, spoke English well. They put us up on a couple of couches in a spare room. (Actually, they have only five small rooms in the apartment, but increase it to seven by the use of curtains).

Monday, October 4, 1954

The rain came down in bucketfuls today. Monica stayed home from school (I don't know why—she didn't appear to be sick), and so told us of all the places we should see in Salzburg. We went first to the Mirabelle Schloss to see the famous stairs there. The Schloss was built by a Catholic arch-bishop for his mistress and eight illegitimate children. It's a big place—now full of offices. Then on to the American Express and the old part of the city. We went to see the old graveyard at St. Peter's, with all the wrought-iron crosses. It's really fabulous—very well kept up, and still in use. We saw the inside of St Peter's, the Franziskaner Kirche, and the Dom. They're all baroque churches. At 6 p.m. we went to see the Glockenspiel. It's quite old, about four hundred years or so, and it's very unique—it's a huge music box sort of an arrangement with a big steel wheel about four feet in diameter having a lot of little pegs on it. The pegs flip levers as they come around and the levers in turn pull other levers, wood slats and chains which finally make little hammers hit the bells. There's a great deal that can get out of adjustment, so consequently not all the bells chime at exactly the right time. But it still is terrific. The man let me wind thing up afterward, too.

Tuesday, October 5, 1954

Today was a little better—at least it didn't rain any. We spent all morning walking around the castle, Hohensalzburg Fortress. It's just like Heidelberg, a real storybook castle. It stands like a king on the top of the Festungsberg. There are a lot of narrow doorways and crooked stairways, many passages and very thick walls. First we walked around the outside and the courtyard, then we paid our fifty groschen (only about two cents) and took the guided tour. It was one of the nicest we've had here on the continent. The guide spoke very slowly and distinctly and I could translate most of the spiel to Bob. We saw the dungeons, torture chambers and towers. We walked the beat of the guard, and had a look at the automatic organ that plays every day at 6 p.m., just after the Glockenspiel.

Then we spent all afternoon decarbonizing the cycle engines. We had gone well over 5,000 miles and weren't developing maximum power at all (our two-stroke engines deposit carbon inside the engine). After that we had supper and we packed up and went to the youth hostel. Frau Kauffman had developed some sort of sickness while on vacation in Kärnten, and had to stay in the hospital there. A friend was going to stay to help out at the Kauffman's, and there wasn't enough room for her and us, too, so we left.

Wednesday, October 6, 1954

Last night we met an Australian fellow who is traveling the same way we are, by BSA Bantam motorcycle. He stayed in Salzburg today because of the rain, but we, hardy souls that we are, went on to Linz.

When we got there we went to the police and they, with their information on everybody, told us where Frau Zeller lived. But she wasn't home and neither was her son. They had left just yesterday for a little trip.

The jugendhergerge here was very new. In fact, it was not yet completed. The sleeping rooms were small and Bob and I had one all to ourselves. Boy, it was nice to get in out of the rain.

Thursday, October 7, 1954

We went on to Wien (Vienna), and it didn't rain much until we were just about there. We passed the border of the Russian Zone and saw a few of our first U.S.S.R. soldiers just a few miles this side of the line. I skidded on the slippery brick of the road (that's one thing that's so terrible about Europe: they will use paving stones and brick for roads, and it's extremely slippery stuff when wet), so I fell and broke my mirror. That was the only damage, but it's rough riding when you don't know what's coming behind you.

We went to Walter Michalitsch's fraternity house (Remember him? He was with Jens Tschebull and Erika Oberlander, who saw me in Syracuse. He stayed at the Macdonalds), but no one was there. So off we went to the police again. We found out where he lived in short order. His girlfriend was there visiting him and and volunteered a camp bed for one of us to sleep on. She went with me on the cycle to fetch it. Bob slept on the cot and I on the couch. It was all very comfortable.

Friday, October 8, 1954

Today we got underway early and made a little tour of the city before Walt had his first class at the University. We passed by Saint Stephen's Cathedral and Karlskirche, the Houses of Parliament, the City Hall, the Winter Palace, the Opera, the Art Museum and, of course, the University. Walt still had a few minutes before his class, so he showed us around the University. It's all in one building, but it's an enormous one, with many courtyards and corridors.

We signed in at the American Consulate, then set off with our newly acquired map of the city to the Opera ticket office. There we bought a couple tickets for that evenings performance of Die Walküre.

Then we visited St. Stephen's Cathedral, a fine example of Gothic. It has a terrific tile roof with a gorgeous design in all different colors—red, yellow, black and white. The old crest of the Austro-Hungarian Empire is there—the double-headed eagle with a crown overhead, and appropriately enough, St. Stephen's cross.

We passed by the Opera—they don't have the performances there yet, because they're still repairing the bomb damage. As we watched, they were at it, full steam ahead! Walt says that it will be finished by the end of next summer. From the front you can see a little bit of the ceiling of the second-story balcony. There's paintings all over and a lot of little golden curlicues. Looks pretty.

Karlskirche is a fine example of Baroque architecture. While we were there the choir was rehearsing with a small but complete orchestra. Pretty fine! We also stopped for a minute in the chapel, which used to be with the old original University building, and the organ was playing. So we had two free concerts.

As we passed by one of the squares in the city, we noticed that there were a lot of bells on stands sitting around, and a lot of people. It was just noon and they all began to ring. There are about five bells in each set, and when one set stopped ringing, the next began. We were deafened for about fifteen minutes while all this went on. We learned that this was because of the meeting of the "Kongress von Katholische Kirchmusik" ("Congress of Catholic Church Music"), and that all the churches would be having especially terrific music at mass Sunday. So I guess we'll go to a Catholic church Sunday; we've just hit it lucky.

Then we took a drive to the north side of the city to Kahlenberg, where the view is especially fine. There was a lot of haze but the sun was shining, for today has been swell all along. Will it last?

We high-tailed it back to Walt's because the opera started at 6 p.m. No one was home, so we couldn't change our clothes. We decided to go as we were. It wasn't very becoming, but it could have been a lot worse. We grabbed a bite at a cafe and caught the subway, which never gets very far below the surface here. Then we found out we are on the wrong line! We got to where we were going, but it took longer.

So we didn't catch the first scene entirely. The program explained the story but it was slow translating. Then after the first act, we started talking to a university student who had been to the US, and he told us the synopsis. The music was very good. I found that the cartoons we always see of operas with Wagnerian characters aren't so far wrong, after all. During intermission we saw at least a half-dozen people eating sandwiches in their seats. I presume they brought them with them. The place was sold out, as far as I could see—even the standing room was limited.

Saturday, October 9, 1954

Another good day today. We went to see the summer residence of the emperor with one of Walt's fraternity brothers. Schönbrunn Palace lived up to its name and was very pretty. While we were walking through with the guided tour, we saw where they were making a movie inside: *The Eternal Waltz*, with period costumes, and all. They have some beautiful Baroque architecture to use as a background. I think the place is more beautiful inside than Versailles. Several rooms were entirely filled with porcelain collections, inlaid wood walls and so forth, with a Chinese room, a Japanese room, etc. We spend some time inside, and went to the old carriage house to see the wagon collection. They had everything there from sedan chairs to chaises, hearses to hacks, sleighs, harnesses, children's goat-carts, and so forth. The guide knew about every one; each belonged to some famous person.

Then we rushed back to the city. We were late. We met Walter at the fraternity house and proceeded to take the windscreens, Great Britain plates, and auto club insignia off of the cycles and to leave our helmets behind, for we were going to Walt's home in the Russian Zone beyond Wien!

From this side of the Donau (Danube River) to the village, we didn't do any talking and didn't stop once. We saw quite a few Russian soldiers and hoped that they didn't see us.

Walt's father is a farmer and his land is very fertile, being an old river bed. Perhaps that's not the whole story because they impressed us as being rather well off, for Austrians. A new house, all paid for, a new tractor, new stoves in the kitchen and hot running water. We had a belated lunch there and looked around at the rest of the farm. One huge building houses the entire farm. Bob took a picture of the cowshed with it's window boxes. We stopped for a minute on the way back to look in at the local church, where Walt was raising money for new chandeliers, then back to Wien without stopping or talking. Walt said we were the first Americans to visit his town in sixteen years.

This evening we went to the Sophiensaal, a ballroom where the people from Sudetenland were having a yearly celebration. The were many costumes, but very little folk dancing. Only a couple of very simple things, repeated often during the evening, and lots of Viennese waltzes and polkas. We paid ten shillings for admission, and it really wasn't worth it. We danced a bit with the girls there (there were plenty!) and went home about 11. The shindig went on until 5 in the morning, the posters said, but we didn't stick around to find out, because to Wallt's house from the Sophiensaal is a long walk. We missed the last direct trolley, but with a little running, we managed to catch the one that came somewhere near the house.

Sunday, October 10, 1954

There is one church in town where the music is always exceptionally beautiful, and it is so popular they charge admission, with tickets and everything. We tried to go there, but the streetcar was so slow we couldn't get inside the door by the time we arrived. So we walked around and got some pictures of wrought-iron work, and then Walt took us down some narrow alleys to show us some out-of-the-way statuary. Afterwards, Walt took us to dinner.

After dinner, he left for his home. We said goodbye, for we might not see him tomorrow morning if he comes late, which might happen. Then we went back to the room, picked up the map, and went to Belvedere Palace, the former home of the nobility. The place was closed by the time we got there, so we just got a look around the grounds. We went to The Winter Palace, where Bob snatched a picture of a Russian soldier. It was almost dark by this time so he went back to Walt's room.

Monday, October 11, 1954

Walt arrived this morning before we left, so we had a chance to say goodbye all over again. Walt's money-raising campaign was a success, and he also said that the whole village was talking about the two Americans that had been there.

Then we went to American Express (where we met a couple of Australian girls—hitchhiking, of course), and to the BSA dealer. We thought we should get some new gaskets for the cylinders, since we had just decarbonized them and it's always better to put on new gaskets every time the cylinder head is taken off. But we spent a lot of time looking for the shop and then they didn't have any. He did fix Bob's front brake, though, and didn't charge anything. Then we tanked up and took off.

Night fell as we started climbing the Semmering Pass, and we had to finish our journey in the dark. We pulled into Wartburg, a very small town in the Murztal before you get to Bruck, at the home of the parents of one of Bob's friends from Carnegie. The father was the president of a small sheet metal factory, and pretty well-to-do by Austrian standards. They had a Volkswagen and a Vespa Scooter, a big house and plenty of hot water, also a deep freeze. The wife was Yugoslavian, and could really spread the board! She said, "Would you like a little meat?," and gave us four big hunks of beef steak in rich gravy. This, on top of what we thought was the whole meal, but that was only the "vorspeise" (appitizer).

She said she wasn't feeling so good, so the doctor came and brought his wife, and the four of them sat and talked and drank wine until all hours. Bob and I were conversing with the daughter and playing Yugoslav records, then we went to bed. It was quite late, but we were the first to retire.

Wien, October 11, 1954

Dear folks:

Well, I'm slowly getting caught up. We leave for Graz tomorrow. I don't think we'll get there all in one day, because there's a friend of Bob's we want to visit on the way.

Jane, give me some advice. We've heard here in Austria that the Italians will steal you blind, and we're worried about the safety of our packs on the cycles when we leave them to go sight-seeing in Italy. We asked some Austrian girls just last night, and they said that if we lock the cycles we would still have them when we got back, but no more duffel.

Perhaps we should leave the bikes in Austria and hitch-hike down and back, but the more we think about it, the less appealing it seems to be. Can you give us a clue, Jane?

I'll hit the hay now. I'm putting a variety of stamps on here in case you know someone who would like to have them.

Love, Ted

Tuesday, October 12, 1954

They woke us late this morning. Bob was in seventh heaven because he had hot water to shave with! Breakfast took us by surprise—there was a terrifically big "vorspeise," which we just took for the main course, and then the wife brought in a huge dish half full of omelette with pieces of ham all through. And she made us eat every bite, too. It was an effort to get it all down, and it lasted us straight through until supper, and then some. We had fine weather and got some pictures, and went on to Graz. Yes, we finally got there!

Putz answered the door. Tante (Aunt) Nora and Onkel (Uncle) Alex Rollett were upstairs and so glad to see us! We put the bikes inside the front door, and brought the luggage upstairs. They said we could use the girls' room on the third floor, but of course we didn't, but slept on a couple couches in the living room. Gerda and Dorli came home together about 6 p.m., and we all had a grand reunion. We talked our heads off until bedtime. Onkel is sick, and has been home from work for three weeks. Tante must go to the hospital as soon as we leave, too.

Wednesday, October 13, 1954

We made plans to go up on the Schlossberg this morning, then stop by Gerda's drug store, and then buy some tickets for the opera (Don Giovanni), but Burli showed up (he's not living at home because his school marks are down, and two kids in the house are too much for Tante), and we didn't get away very soon. Tante telephoned and found out there was folk dancing, so we decided to go to the dance instead. Then we walked home with Gerda. It was another beautiful day. This makes the sixth!

The colors on the Schlossberg were lovely and bright. We made a little experiment: The red ivy on the cream-colored walls of the schloss (castle) looked beautiful against the bright blue of the sky. Bob doesn't believe his light-meter and range-finder are accurate, so we took two shots of this scene, one with me in it and one with Bob in it. Bob guessed the distance and "interpreted" the meter reading, and I used the rangefinder and set the stops exactly as the meter indicated. If I'm right, Bob's will be under-exposed. If he's right, mine will be overexposed.

Gerda took us to the little palace nearby, where the Alpenverein (Alpine Club) has the folk dancing every week. We joined in with a will. We didn't know any of what they did but most of the dances were quite simple and we could follow okay. They asked us to show them an American folk dance, but there aren' t any that take only men, so we taught them the Zaplet Kolo (a Croatian line dance) instead. Afterwards, the accordion player wrote down the melody. He played it over a couple of times and had it pretty good. I'd love to stay here for a while and dance with them—I want to learn all those ländlers they do, and I could teach them a lot, too. They had dances where the boys yodeled and sang and did a simple schuhplattler. It was really good.

When we got home we found a couple slices of apple pie waiting for us, and the girls were still up. They invited us to eat the pie in their room, so we went up and talked a bit before retiring.

Thursday, October14, 1954

We spent the entire day with Tante Nora. We took the trolley out to the edge of town, then rode the brand-new Sessil-lift up to the Fursten-stand. We just sat and talked and enjoyed the sun (another good day!). The haze was pretty bad and made taking pictures difficult but we enjoyed the sun and the view. Tante bought us lunch (we weren't quick enough on the draw to grab the check), but we paid for the trolley and the lift. It was getting on toward sunset when we got back, but Bob dashed off to get some pictures of the Schlossberg.

Then Burli dropped in again on his way from school to the place where he lives. We got a picture of him and me. We weren't in the backyard a minute before he started to roughhouse. I'd like to spend a couple of days with the boys alone—we'd have a small war going on all the time.

We went over to the Stellers for coffee and sandwiches and talk. My, what a handsome family! Ingrid, Klaus, Uti, Karin, Frau and Herr Profes-sor—they were all there. We had a look at Klaus's model cars—he sells them for 20 shillings apiece. We had a good talk—Frau Steller says that Mother must learn her German well because Frau Steller is going to start learning English, and when Mom and Dad come to Graz, they can all speak together.

Friday, October 15, 1954

Today Gerda got the whole day off by taking half-days for the next two weeks. Then she remembered that the Sunday between these two weeks is her day to maintain the emergency services. So the poor girl works every day for 13 days solid. Too bad.

She went with us as we bought the town out, and it's a good thing she did, for we would never have gotten everything done by ourselves.

Bob bought a silk handkerchief for a cravat, with a silver slide, a Steirischer jacket, three pairs of lederhosen (small and large for himself, and a pair for his friend Fred), a knife, a pair of suspenders for Karl Heilborn and about three pairs for himself. I bought seven "dirndltucher" (scarves)—one for my cravat, one for Liz, and five to sell to the girls at Syracuse—a beautiful knife with a staghorn handle, a pair of long lederhosen, a pair of gray and green steirsocken (socks), and a red, white, and blue "lumber jacket" like Dad's. We came home loaded. I don't know where we're going to put all the stuff.

We met Dorli for lunch, and afterwards the girls took us to one of the nice cafes in town to have some "espresso" with them. It is very strong coffee, like drinking a bitter soup. Bob and I couldn't stomach it, but the girls thought it was the very best.

We put on all our new stuff tonight, and Tante, not to be outdone, also wore her dirndl. Ingrid Steller came over, and we all had some tea and cookies and talked. Ingrid is a cute one—I got her attention once by saying, "Hey, you!," and now she says a it to me all the time.

Graz, October 15, 1954

Dear Folks:

Here's a short note just to let you know of our plans and activities, and to show you that we did finally make it to Graz. We left Wien Monday late, and stayed overnight with a friend of Bob's in a small town in the Murztal. Then Tuesday we came on to Graz. Putz answered the door and was just beaming. Then Tante Nora and Uncle were waiting at the top of the stairs. I tell you, it was just like landing at Darlington. I really felt like I had arrived!

We had afternoon coffee with them and then brought up our stuff, talked and got settled. Then Gerda and Dorli came home, and loud were the greetings! Bob and I slept on two extra cots in the living room and were very comfortable.

Then Wednesday Bob and I got up late, and then Burli dropped in for an hour or so. We saw his stamp collection and got a picture before he had to go.

Then Bob and I went up to the Schlossberg and Uhrturm (clock tower) and got some wonderful pictures. We met Gerda at the drugstore where she works and came home. We went folk dancing with the Alpenverein that night and taught them a Kolo. Thursday we went up to the Furstenstand (at the top of the new chairlift) with Tante Nora and took life easy, eating and talking.

That night we went with the girls to Steller's for coffee and sandwiches, What a beautiful family! Like the Olsons, as fair as the Olsons are dark. We saw a few of Klause's model cars and met the youngsters, too. We had a really good evening.

All day today we spent money, and bought the town out. Well, we got a lederhosen and dirndltuchers and all, and knives and a pipe and a good sweater jacket, and so forth. Gerda and Dorli were with us and we had a very good day.

And now this evening Bob and I are wearing our new clothes. Tante Nora put on her dirndl to get in the swing of things; Ingrid came over, and we're sitting here talking and drinking homemade soda. It's been a very good time. I hope I'll return. Here's a few words from the others.

Love, Ted

Dear Mrs. Budrow:

I will write to Jane next week if I are in the hospital. Now I will only say to you that I am very happy that Ted is finally here and we do understand us very happy. I am very sorry that I have to go tomorrow (Saturday) in the hospital and cannot keep Ted his friend in our home longer.

Best greetings to you all with much love.

Nora Rollett

Saturday, October 16, 1954

Tante's doctor called today and said she must go to the hospital this afternoon. It was hard saying goodbye to Tante. I'll surely have to come back. So Bob and I packed up and left, and went over to the Hascheks.

Eve and her mother had just come back from their annual business trip by auto to Switzerland and France. Eve had a cold, and doesn't look too good. (Gerda says she looks "used"). We got a picture, then Eve went to bed with her sniffles. Bob and I took a ride out to Rosenheim and back. Then we delighted in a hot bath and went to bed. Well, Bob did—I stayed up until 4 a.m., writing a long letter to Liz.

Sunday, October 17, 1954

We were supposed to meet the Rolletts at 9 a.m. to go to church with Gerda and Ingrid, but Frau Haschek said that she couldn't keep us another night and we had to pack up this morning. We got everything together and left it in the hall. Then we were late for church. There was now no use in going, because the worship part would be over, and the place will be jammed anyway—there was a pretty good guest preacher, been holding seminars all week. So we had a good little walk around and arrived at the end of the service. It's another good day today, as well as yesterday. We got a picture of all of us (we got someone to take it for us). We transferred all our stuff to the Steller's and had lunch there. Then we all (Dorli, Ingrid,Gerda, Bob and I) went to Dr. Rosanelli's for a little talk and folk sing. We took the harmonicas along and did a couple exhibition folk dances for them. The doc's quite a joker and teaser. A lot of the stuff I didn't understand, but the girls translated. Poor Bob! He nearly had a fit when the doctor exclaimed over his six-barreled mouth organ and immediately started to play it. (Of course, Bob couldn't play it now—it had to be washed with alcohol first!) I explained to the others what was wrong, and they all thought it was quite funny. Then the doc had to try mine, too. (My new one. It is a honey! It just came yesterday.) We got out the song books and sang a bit, ate a bit, talked a bit, drank a bit. Doc couldn't understand why I didn't like wine. He gave me, out of a clear blue sky, a book about Steiermark (the state Graz is in). I don't know if I can read it, but I'll try. It's a great big book—going to be hard to pack. We went to the Steller's for for supper and bed.

Monday, October 18, 1954

We got off just about noon today, after a wonderful lunch prepared by Frau Steller. Burli dropped by on his way to school, and we got pictures of all the Stellers who weren't at church Sunday. Gerda and Dorli came over just before we left, and Onkel Alex, too. Oh yeah, it's so hard to say goodbye to these these people.

It was good weather today and we traveled right along. Our first stop was the hospital in Voitsberg, where we visited Ruth Steller. She sure is yellow, all right. It is the first case of jaundice I've seen. Three or four weeks more, the doctors say. I hope her job in the States can wait that long.

We visited the Naturfreunde office in Graz before we left, and they said there was a house in Sankt Andrä. But when we got there we couldn't find it. Even the police had never heard of it. But we got a room in a fairly nice gasthaus (inn) with a ridiculously low price of seven shillings each. No hot water, but they did have feather beds.

Tuesday, October 19, 1954

Dear Folks:

Yes, we did finally make it to Graz! And I don't know how we did it, but we haven't had a single cloudy day since we arrived at Wien! Today is the 12th day in a row of bright, sunny weather. Jane, did you get out into the hills here at autumn? Today we drove from Sankt Andrä (just above Klagenfurt) and the scenes that spread before us were just breathtaking, even more than the Schwarzwald. The colors really stand out when they are scattered among the dark green of the nadelbaum (conifers).

Bob and I went folk dancing at the Alpenverein (taught them a Kolo), spent one whole day with Tante Nora (went up on the brand new chairlifts to the Furtenstand), went to church with Gerda and Ingrid, stayed one night with the Hascheks (Eve is sick, doesn't look good, but knows all about Bert), stayed one night with the Stellers (what a beautiful family!), talked and sang with Dr. Rosanelli one afternoon, and got pictures of everyone. We also saw Ruth Steller at the hospital. She's getting well; she just needs time (three or four weeks yet).

So now we go to Venice and Milan, but no further south.

Love, Ted

Wednesday, October 20, 1954

We started from the Villach hostel about 10. Just outside the city, we stopped and chatted with two hitchhiking Australian girls for a minute or two before they got a ride. We saw the loveliest colors today, but the air wasn't clear and it was too cloudy to take any pictures (we took one, anyway!). To pass between really jagged mountains, the lower slopes covered with lovely colored trees mixed with the evergreens—terrific! We went through Tarvisio and Udine, and ended up at Vittorio Veneto, straight north from Treviso and Venezia (Venice). All the land from Udine on is as flat as a billiard table, with lots of poplars predominating. We had to do a bit of night riding, and found that the roads are extremely well marked with white posts (plus reflectors) all along the sides. We found the hostel after quite a bit of asking, and it turned out to be a hotel with some rooms turned over to be a hostel. The warden was a real crazy-type woman. All the time we were eating she kept ranting about how much better Italian food was than any other, and she kept wanting us to put all of our eating stuff that we weren't using in a different place than where we wanted, then she started playing the radio so loud you couldn't hear, and after that she started the same procedure on records. All the music was modern jive stuff and we were getting deafened, so we went to our room to write. Then her son came to tell us not to go into the courtyard at night because of two police dogs patrolling there. He wasn't kidding, either. He brought them up to the door and let them have a good sniff when he turned them loose. They have been setting up a terrific noise so far, and I wonder if we'll get any sleep tonight. It's a queer feeling, sort of like being a prisoner. We were charged 230 lire apiece, too (37 and a half cents), which is the most expensive of all the countries that we've been in.

Thursday, October 21, 1954

When we awoke this morning, the dogs, which had barked themselves hoarse all night long, were chained and the warden (bless her little pointed head!) had gone to Venezia on the bus. We ate in our room and cooked tea on Bob's pocket stove. They charged me fifty lire last night for the hot water to make tea—using my own tea leaves!

We were on our way about 10 a.m. and made our way towards Venezia, via Treviso and Mestre. We had a good journey, no rain, although the sky was overcast all day. Just a little ways from the hostel I discovered that the outside sheath of my speedometer cable had broken, just as the indicator reached six thousand miles. I patched it with rubber bands and electrician's tape and it went the rest of the day okay.

To get to Venezia, we crossed a long causeway built out from the land, about nine miles of it. We got to the city just after the noon hour closing had begun, so we parked in front of the AAA office and went searching for someone who spoke English. I found a newspaper vendor who spoke German, and he gave me the address of a student-home. I thought that he said it was a "kloster" (monastery), but evidently he was telling me that it wasn't a monastery, for who should show up but our ill-fated friend, the warden of Vittorio Veneto hostel! She gave me the name and address, and told us where to park the bikes there.

It's costing us one hundred lire per day to park and 255 lire per night at the student-home, which isn't bad, considering that we were offered several rooms by various people for about five hundred lire per person per night. Still, it's more than any hostel or Naturfreunde house we've been in yet.

We walked to the ferry station instead of riding a boat, and were glad we did. It saved a few lire and we got a good worm's eye view of some of the city. It started to rain this evening (our first in thirteen days!), and the bricks were quite slippery. Then we met some students who were going to the Casa San Giorgio, where we are booked, and they led us right to the dock. We found the place just crawling with Australians and Englishmen, and one Canadian. But the girls we saw at Villach yesterday aren't here—I wonder if they made it.

We went out to buy bread, milk and tomatoes this evening, and had a good little walk around. I wouldn't say the town was dirty—it's just filthy, is all.

Friday, October 22, 1954

Today we reverted to type, and were the last ones out of the hostel. The first thing we did was to head for St. Mark's Square. We took our own sweet time and nosed in a lot of the back alleys along the way. ("Nosed" is really the word to use—often it was better to go in holding one's nose!) Bob swiped the tax stamps off of a number of posters along the way, as souvenirs, and we had a jolly time. When we got to the square we had a terrific time feeding the birds. I went and bought some bread, but the stuff they really go for is dried corn sold by the vendors. A couple of handfuls of that stuff brings them in flying. Bob got some pictures of me and the birds, one of them on my head for a while. Inside Saint Mark's we tagged along, as a guy told a busload of English all about the place. It's entirely mosaic on the inside, a great deal simpler and more majestic than the churches we've been in so far. The main altar is supposed to be solid gold and silver, and they say Saint Mark himself is inside. Hm-m-m-m? A lot of the building dates from the ninth century, the oldest we've seen except for Dorset. We continued with this bus group to visit the glass exhibition. There were just wonderful things there; it's a good thing I didn't have enough money to buy anything. We spent about an hour just looking. When we got back to Saint Mark's Square a vendor tried to sell us some jewelry. It was a scream! He kept saying, "I give you present—two dollars the whole lot," and kept adding to the pile. Well, we finally convinced him we didn't want any at all.

We went up the bell tower to get some pictures, and then went through the Doge's Palace. There was quite a collection of arms there, old swords, helmets, armor and so forth. We went through the dungeons, too, which are below sea level when there is a really high tide. Then up to the Rialto Bridge, via all the smelly, little side streets. Then we just wandered for about an hour, picking up a little fruit here and there, some bread, cheese, and so forth, eating as we went and just taking in everything. We finally went back to the hostel about 7:30 p.m.

My impression of Venice so far is that it's an interesting city but very dirty and smelly. Sanitation must be a real problem here. And, by the way, it was a pretty good day, weather-wise. No rain, and even some sun at times. Tomorrow we'll take a gondola ride and hustle out of town. Bob has a only about a week and a half left before he has to report to the Army.

Saturday, October 23, 1954

It was pea soup with fog this morning, but lifted by the time we got away from the hostel. We said "so long" to all we saw there (the Aussie touring by BSA 125 whom we met in Salzberg, the three US boys and one Canadian, and the rest of the Australians) and shoved off in a gondola to cross to the main island. Then we took the water bus all the way down the Grand Canal to the place where the bikes were parked. We passed a lot of these "barber poles" and fancy houses, but it still didn't look as nice as the travel poster pictures. Venice is different and interesting, but I was glad to leave. At the place we parked the bikes we got rooked out of a hundred lire apiece because the sign said "100 lira" and meant "from 12 midnight through 12 noon," not "per night," so for two nights we had to pay 300 lira apiece instead of 200. I guess you have to watch these Italians—they'll play you for a sucker every time.

We had an uneventful trip to Riva del Garda on the north end of Lake Garda, with the exception of going over a small pass. It was hazy and cloudy all the way to the top and we were wishing it was sunny so that we could capture some of the lovely colors on film. Then just at the top we broke through the cloud bank and got some pictures. But the sun shortly went behind the hills, and we finished our trip in the dark. As we rolled into Riva we came upon a curve, banked like a bobsled run. It would be safe to do 40 mph around that hairpin, since you could travel on the wall! The hostel was brand-new and, of course, we met a couple Australian girls hitchhiking. We had a good time eating and talking along with an Austrian fellow. We five pooled all our food, and had quite a variety menu.

Sunday, October 24, 1954

This morning dawned bright and dry (how do we do it?), and although there was a lot of haze, we had a beautiful ride down the western side of Lake Garda towards Brescia. The road ducked in and out of tunnels along the water's edge. It was clear and looked awfully cold. We got a bit of sun the last part of the day as we came into Milan.

Then the fun started! First the rain, then getting directions in a foreign language through a town as big as Paris. I don't know how we did it, but we finally got to the cathedral. Then, as we were looking for the hostel, we picked up a self-appointed guide who climbed aboard my cycle (he sat on the petrol tank) and led us on a wild-goose chase all around the town. I felt very unsafe, as Milan has very large paving stones, and with the rain it was like driving on ice.

We finally found the place, and it wasn't open yet, so we talked with the Austrian, Belgian, and South African who were standing there. We gave our guide fifty lire. He hung around, expecting more, I suppose. But we were firm (Hurrah for us!). Then the place opened and we booked in. The warden wanted an extra twenty-five lire for cooking that Bob wasn't planning on doing, and we finally got that back. And we weren't allowed to take our packs into the sleeping room.

Having been warned that a parked motorcycle on the street is like an invitation to steal in Italy, we parked our bikes inside the walled hostel and walked to do our sight-seeing. We went to the cathedral, which in the rain is still pretty, but the day was dark and we could see nothing much. The ceiling, with with its filigree work, is the nicest part.

Then we went out looking for bread and didn't find any. We got some roasted chestnuts and drank a half liter of milk each, but still no bread. We ate a slice of pizza from a vendor, but "It sure ain't like good 'ol American pizza!" I led the way, and seemed (to Bob) to wander as the fancy took me. The the poor boy—up until we were within a block of the hostel, he was confident that we were going in the wrong direction. Oh, well, we have our fun! We met one of the American boys who was at Venice and gave the poor, broke soul some of our spaghetti. We also met a girl from New Jersey who was puffing on a pipe!

Tuesday, October 26, 1954

Today Bob and I parted company, he to go to Interlaken and then to his ship and home, and I to go to Salzburg to look for a job. The weather was absolutely gorgeous!!! I went over the San Bernardino Pass, and I tell you, it took my breath away! The sky was blue, the snow was white, the trees were a riot of color, backed up with the dark green of the pines! It just goes to show you what God can do. Lovely! It was cold, too, although I rode entirely in the sun. The road was all dirt (I'm lucky it was dry), and it went up to 6,778 feet, the highest I've ever been. (Or were we were higher when we were on horseback in the Tetons in 1946?) I first stopped at the hostel but it was full of soldiers, so I'm writing this from a very dirty place in Bonaduz. I don't think the hostel inspectors would keep the place open if they knew about it. Of course, it isn't as bad as Frévent, France. I'm the only one here, too, so I'm really getting ahead with my writing.

Wednesday, October 27, 1954

Well, back to normal—it rained all day today. I left that foul-smelling place of last night without even stopping to eat. I arrived at Buchs and got to the hostel around 10 a.m. There I ordered a couple pots of tea and had breakfast. Then on through Liechtenstein to Feldkirch. I went I to the bahnhof (railway station) and shipped my suitcase to Innsbruck, remembering my previous experience of pushing the bike up the Arlberg Pass. I met a couple of American soldiers there who were rather optimistic about my getting a job. Then on through the fog and rain over the pass, and I didn't have to push! Well, well, goody for me!

But by the time I got to Landeck, I was frozen to the core, so I stopped at the hostel there instead of going fifty miles more to Innsbruck. The hostel is small and cozy at Landeck, and there were two people already there, a boy and a girl. The girl I had met four days ago, at Venezia. The boy was a

Swede. We had some really interesting talks, but the height of comedy was when the girl tried some of my nice soft American toilet paper and came back wreathed in smiles. She was Hungarian, and had been living in Australia for the last six years, and had never used such soft stuff before. So I gave her a wad, enough to last her until she reaches Canada, I hope. She's going to Canada to try and find work long enough to come back next summer and finish touring the continent. I gave her our address; perhaps she'll stop by.

Thursday, October 28, 1954

The Hungarian girl used my down-filled sleeping bag last night because she said she was cold even under seven blankets. This morning she reported that she was very comfortable inside all that down. The Swede, Bent, departed first, heading for Innsbruck, then I and the girl about the same time. It was pretty good weather—no rain—when I set off about 10. I passed Bent, the Swede, on the way. I picked up my suitcase at the Innsbruk train station and headed for the hostel to snatch a hot shower before continuing. There I met a South African lady whom I had met before in Milano.

About 2 in the afternoon I finally got under way, but decided to run a few errands before continuing. I bought an Österreichische Jugendherberge (Austrian Youth Hostel) handbook, and got some information from the Naturfreunde office. Then I bought a pocket stove and cook kit, seeing as how Bob was no longer with me. By this time it was dark, so I went back to the hostel.

There I met Bent again, and I also ran into a girl, Jane Johnston, who lives near us on the River Road, Youngstown! She was hitchhiking with a Canadian friend. Later on in the evening, the girls and I and a boy from Colorado (he had met these two girls before in Copenhagen) got into a quite hilarious discussion about continental toilets and toilet paper. Ye gods! That's a conversation? I also found out where the foam rubber mattresses were kept, which fact I didn't know the last time I was here, so I slept in comfort.

Friday, October 29, 1954

Today dawned bright and clear. I almost yielded to temptation to go up the cable lift on the south side of the valley, but I resisted and pushed on. The ride was quite beautiful, and around 3 in the afternoon I found myself just outside Berchtesgaden, so I decided to go in and have a look. No wonder Hitler liked the place; it was very pretty. I went up to the pile of rubble where Adolf's house used to stand; he had a good view. Then on to Salzburg, where I met a couple of American kids who are art students, and actually thought Montmartre was not conducive to painting! Back to normal—it started raining in the evening.

Saturday, October 30, 1954

I went to the civilian employment office, but it wasn't really open until Monday morning. So I have two days in which to see the rest of Salzburg. I parked the cycle and went by foot through the old part of the town, just wandering and looking. I broke down and brought a record of zither-playing and one of a schuhplattler. Later on when I got back to the hostel, I collected the two American artists, and we went to a gasthaus I had come across in my wandering, where they had yodeling and schuhplattling in the evening. They brought their sketchbooks, and we had a good time drinking apfelsaft (apple juice) and watching. We told the leader of the group (there were four: an accordionist, a guitar player, a singer and a girl yodeller) that we had to leave by 9:30, and he very nicely had the tables pushed back and did a shuhplattler for us. I hope I meet up with these kids again—they said they'd make a sketch of me in my Austrian costume.

Sunday, October 31, 1954

I hoped to see some of the Kauffmanns at church this morning, but they weren't there, so I called them on the phone. Monica answered. Her mother is better since I was last here, and Herr Kaufman was rushing around, leaving in a few minutes to go to Karnten to see her. So I went back to church and sat through the English Army service. It wasn't very well attended. The German service, on the other hand, was very crowded, with people standing all around. I was listening hard, and understood some of the sermon. "Zuruck zu Luther" ("Back to Luther") was the topic (it was Reformation Sunday), and the minister kept talking about what went on at Evanston, IL at the World Council of Churches convention.

After church I wandered around the newer parts of the city looking for places that might be open where I could buy some bread, but no bread could I find. So I finally ended up eating the cheapest thing on the menu at a second-rate restaurant.

Back at the hostel, the director of the Jugendherbergsverband (Youth Hostel Association) for Salzburg was talking to the warden and told of a folk dance this evening. So off I went with the two art students to "Alkoholfrei Volkshaus," where we found a bunch of younger kids, 13 to 18 years old, doing a lot of the same dances that I did at the Alpenverein in Graz. We had a good time; we all got into the act. At Graz, all of the girls could waltz, but not so here. But we enjoyed ourselves, and later on at the hostel we sat with two more US girls and I showed them all my loot. They oohed and ahhed over my scarves, and so forth, and a German fellow played his harmonica (very good!) for us.

Monday, November 1, 1954

My trip is exactly four months old today. It hardly seems so long. I went to the employment office, and was told there wasn't a thing. Then to the special services office where they hire all the entertainment, thinking they might use a folk dancer or a square dance caller, but no, they didn't want any. They gave me the phone numbers of the two local service clubs. I called them and they were interested, but they only wanted me once a week, and at less than $5.00 a throw. I wouldn't mind working for less if it was more often, but $5.00 a week, even in cheap Austria, is not enough to save any money with. So I guess it's on to München (Munich) tomorrow.

Dear Folks:

Well the prospects for a job didn't pan out. However, all the Germans here say it's much better in München, Heidelberg and Köln. If I get a job in München, I'll try to audit some courses. If not, well, I'll keep trying until I buy my ship ticket.

Love to you all, Ted

Tuesday, November 2, 1954

It was a good weather today, and I made good time on the Autobahn between Salzburg and München. I arrived at Ed Mosers room about 3, but he wasn't home. So I left and went out to Doctor Hoffa's where Bob and I were before. They all greeted me with open arms and bid me come in for tea. Their married daughter, Trudy, was there with her two children—Annette (two years old) and Kristoff (8 months). They were lovely kids—I had a good time playing with them. We talked and talked; and I told him of all our adventures since we saw them last. Then it was supper time and they made me bring up my stuff and stay the night. It wasn't too elegant—mattress on the floor—but it was very nice.

Wednesday, November 3, 1954

After a huge breakfast (hot toast!) I went to Ed's and found his note that he was in a travel bureau just down the street a ways. I found him— he and a friend were visiting another friend who works there. We went to lunch at a nearby restaurant, then I left them to go to McGraw Kaserne, the Army HQ. They had nothing to offer, but the lady there gave me some good tips and some leads in Heidelberg and Nuremberg. She said that on my application my summer jobs wouldn't mean a thing. But my recreational work should be all included in bold type because they needed recreational leaders. She thought that my talents could be used in Nuremberg for sure, and a strong possibility in Heidelberg. Well, let's hope.

I went back to Ed's and we talked and talked and talked and ate supper. Then Carl, another American friend, showed up, along with Oskar, the boy who was with Ed on his trip to France and who worked at the tourist bureau. Joachim, another friend, also came, and plans were made to go with Carl and his friend Polly to the Hofbrauhaus, one of the local brand beer halls. So off we went, five of us in Carl's very small English car. We all had a good time talking and watching Polly and Carl eat. Then off to a new bar for some after-dinner liqueur (I with my usual apfelsaft), and then home about 12. Ed and I stayed up until about 2, talking and looking at pictures. He has some good pics of Advani, the Indian student at Syracuse, and me, and he's going to send me some prints. (But whether he really will or not is something else again, if I know Ed.) He had some extras of some of the Outing Clubbers, which he gave me, then I sacked out on his fold-down couch. Pretty nice, and a good day!

Thursday, November 4, 1954

I packed up and left today. I had some business to attend to, and a breakfast date at the Hoffa's, so I got up and out pretty early. After another gigantic breakfast Annette and I invented a new game, which consisted of my letting her fall on the bed, so she bounced. It delighted Kristoff too— he was laughing at us. Then I said goodbye; it was getting late and I had promised to meet Ed at the University at noon. So I did, and he showed me all around the place. Joachim, who knew somebody who might know of a job for me, didn't show up, so I said goodbye to Ed and went to Joachim's house. He wasn't home, so I gave that up as a bad job and went on to do my other business at American Express and the Naturfreunde office, where

I got a map showing all their houses. Then the motorcycle started acting up. I couldn't make the engine go fast. It was something wrong with the adjustment of the points (I think I need new ones), and I had to go to a garage to have them set. By that time it was pretty late so I changed my plans to go to Ulm, and headed for Augsburg instead. By the time I got to the Autobahn it was dark, clear and cold, and I nearly froze for those 30 miles. I was the only one in the hostel at Augsburg, and I got some letters off to Liz and Graz.

Friday, November 5, 1954

Today was bright and clear, and I decided to stay over here a day to rest, write letters and give my letter to the Zerrs a chance to get there before I arrive. I finished a long, seven-page letter to Liz, and then went to town. At the post office they told me that airmail envelopes weren't good for letters going by normal mail. How stupid! And I had to walk all over creation to find them! I bought a tea cozy for a present for the Zerrs, some bread, cheese and wurst, and stuck them all in the string bag. That thing sure holds a lot! As I passed by a music shop I saw an ad for a Bach concert this evening, so I bought a ticket. I had a hard time talking the warden into letting me come in a little bit late, but I finally succeeded. I'm the only one here again, anyway, so it shouldn't make much difference. The concert was terrific, even if I did miss the last piece, a triple concerto for two flutes and violin. A fourteen-piece orchestra (six violins, two viola's, two cellos, one horn, and a harpsichord) and two soloists (one flute and one violin) made just about the loveliest music this side of heaven (my apologies to Guy Lombardo). The first piece was a flute concerto, the next two were violin concertos. I could have stayed all night. It was three marks well spent!

Saturday, November 6, 1954

I got up and out this morning, and rolled out on to the Autobahn at exactly 11 a.m. Three-and-a-half hours later I had covered 140 miles and was tanking up at the first gas station in Karlsruhe. Wow! That's averaging 40 miles per hour—probably the best I'll ever do! I didn't stop the entire way, and was running full throttle all the way. I noticed that there was frost on the grass this morning, and the trees are beginning to look naked—winter's coming! The Zerrs left a note saying they'd be home at 6, so I went to the American Express office. Closed! Then to the Army office to see if there was a civilian employment office here. No! Then to the music store where I bought my other harmonica, to buy a bass harmonica (ever since I played that one in München, when Bob and I met this Swiss fellow at the hostel who could play so well, I've been meaning to get one). Then I went to see Herb's friend Jurgend. He was home, and we had a bit of a talk before his parents arrived. A bit of tea and bread with them and it was time to go to the Zerr's. Then the cycle wouldn't go again, and we had to fuss with it a long time. The Zerrs were glad to see me, and not too surprised because Bob was here just last Sunday. We talked and talked. Bob hadn't told them much of our adventures. I showed them all my "loot" and they were properly impressed. Now I've had a hot bath and cleaned my shoes and sit in the kitchen, where the delightful aroma of apfel kuchen fills the air. Ahh-h-h-h!

Dear Dad:

Gee, Hallowe'en came and went, and I forgot your birthday! Well, please forgive me—here's belated greetings!

Sunday, November 7, 1954

I went to church this morning with Mama and Helga It was a good service. The church building is very new (five years), and modern. It is entirely brick and wood and very simple. No stained glass or any place for it, and a very simple platform, There's a balcony, but altogether the church can only hold about 300. They have a new organ, only one week old. When they get it paid for, the next item is a belfry and bell. Then they'll be complete. The trouble is, they are already overcrowded; the place was filled this morning. (But not so jammed as at Salzburg—nobody was standing.) The preacher was very good—he didn't read a word of the sermon. He talked about independence—that we must all account for ourselves when the Judgment comes (Romans 14: 7-10). In the afternoon, Papa and I walked around the city and visited the city gardens, including a zoo and botanical gardens. The park is built around a small hill—man-made to to cover a water storage tank—atop of which is a small ruin of a fort (also recent vintage), and the "ruins" overlook a couple of pretty man-made lakes (actually ponds), but it's still very nice, even when you know all this. This evening Helga went to a school dance (stag, like all the others). Mama and Papa say that she's very independent. She doesn't like the boys to take her out—she just likes to dance with them when she gets there. Tomorrow—Heidelberg!

Monday, November 8, 1954

I left early this morning for Heidelberg, where there are no jobs available. The sky was overcast all day, but no rain. I spent a long time pleasantly in the waiting room of the civilian personnel recruitment office, reading Time, Newsweek and The Saturday Evening Post. I read about the big flood out there in Texas—you really get separated from the news on a tour like this.

Tomorrow I'll go to Neuhofen, where Anni Fittler lives. That's the German girl I met in New York City at the YMCA folk dancing group. I mean to be back in Karlsruhe Thursday or Friday to go folk dancing with Helga.

I wonder what I've run into in this youth hostel. There's a whole group of young girls, about 30 of them, here. They all ate together and sang a thanks before and after the meal (I guess they're "Evangelish"), and sang some later on, too, with a guitar playing. Very pretty. I wonder if it's a chorus. From the shrieks of laughter I hear coming from the next room, I guess they're having a good time.

Tuesday, November 9, 1954

I met the most interesting character last night of the whole trip so far. He was in the same sleeping room as I. He wore a low-cut double-breasted vest of gray corduroy, and a pair of trousers of the same material which were very tight to just below the knees, where they flared sharply outward in an exaggerated bell bottom. He wore a long gold bangle-type earring in one ear (pierced) and a very broad-brimmed fedora hat. He carried a very twisted and knobby walking stick, and his small pack was all done up in bandanna. He was a journeyman, traveling for three years and working at his trades (carpenter and mason) as he went. All his tools were in his small pack, all of them dismantled , and they had to be reassembled to use them. His dress was required from from his guild. It's the only remaining guild in Europe, for carpenters, masons and cabinetmakers.

This morning, as I was packing up the cycle, a girl came up and said she was an American. It turned out that she was one of the Cornell folk dancers, class of '51, and we had a lot of friends in common.

I went to Neuhofen. When Anni came home, it was a big surprise because the letter I sent only arrived today, after she had gone to work. I mentioned in my diary in June that I met Anni in New York City at the YMCA folk dance, and that at the time she was very unhappy and homesick. I urged her to visit us at Niagara Falls if nothing else (she had never seen any of the US besides New York City and a bit of Long Island), but she was so homesick that she never went, but grabbed the first ship for home as soon as she earned enough money.

She lives in a very small house here, with her mother, brother, sister, brother-in-law and a baby nephew and baby niece. The place is in a bit of a constant uproar, with the kids and all, but it's real homey.

Wednesday, November 10, 1954

I got up around 9 and put the pillion seat on the cycle. It was about 11:30 by the time I got ready to go. I went to Mannheim, to where Anni works, and went out with her to lunch. In the afternoon I did a little business, one part of which was getting the cycle fixed. It was just a minor adjustment—the thing was running badly because the points were pitted. So I had them cleaned. It sure feels nice to be running high, wide, and handsome again! I picked up Anni at work and brought her home. In the evening I showed everyone all the stuff I bought, and Anni and I did a little folk dancing for them. Then she mended a couple holes in my pants while we sat and talked. The weather was good today, but you can just feel the cold more and more. Mannheim and Ludwigshafen are just big cities, that's all. But I think I shall never get used to seeing street cars coming toward me on the wrong side of the street.

Thursday, November 11, 1954

Tomorrow night is the folk dancing in Karlsruhe and Anni wants to go, too. So I went to Karlsruhe this morning to see about where the place was, if it was exclusive, when it started, and so forth. Helga was home and told me all I wanted to know. She also had some good news, that there were three letters waiting for me. Mama Zerr had them at the house where she was working so I went and got them. One from Mom, one from Jane, and a card from Mary Lou Cramer. I'll have to write Mary Lou and tell her I may not get to see her. Five bucks in Mom's letter was good. All Jane's advice about Italy, and we're through there already. I read the card which Mom enclosed from the Kindlers, and after lunch (and a nice talk with Mama Zerr) I went to their place in Heidelberg. But they had gone off for the day and were not yet back, so I left a note saying I'd visit Saturday, and came on back to Neuhofen.

Dear Folks:

I'll go to Nuremberg Monday (arriving Tuesday or Wednesday) to see what the Special Services branch of the Army has to offer. I'll also have a look-see at the teaching situation, although I think it is nil. If nothing breaks, I'll go on up the Rhine River to visit Herbert at Bonn and on to Köln and Koblenz to see if the steel mills have anything. If nothing there, I'll call for enough dough for my ticket home and see you all for Christmas or soon after.

Love, Ted

Friday, November 12, 1954

I went up to Mannheim about 4 to pick up Anni and we froze (it was cold!) down the Autobahn to Karlsruhe to go to the folk dance at the jugendherberge. It's a new hostel in Karlsruhe—really something, modern and with all the facilities.

The folk dance was held in the common room—not too big a place for the amount of people who were there. I got in seven good dances with Helga Zerr and Anni, since most of the dances were repeated often, and everybody changed partners two or three times. We were all well mixed. They did some pretty complicated dances and I got the names of some of them. One accordion for the music, as usual.

Saturday, November 13 1954

Anni poked her head in the room and woke me up at 5:15 a.m., and we got ready to go. I took her to catch her train, and went back for breakfast. I headed out towards Heidelberg on the Autobahn and had some of the same ol' trouble with the cycle. A passing motorcyclist took a look at it and discovered that the axle that my contact breaker was pivoting on was moving slightly, throwing the whole thing out of whack. Well, I tied it up with a bit of wire and it was better. I went to the Kindler's at Heidelberg and talked a bit with Frau Kindler. Dr. Kindler wasn't home—he was away this afternoon on some sort of business. I promised Frau Kindler (she insists that call her "Tante Fritzi") that I would stay with them when I came back from Nuremberg (this over a cup of coffee and a piece of apple strudel at a nearby cafe). Then I purchased some steel wire and made a more durable makeshift repair on the bike and headed for Neuhofen. Anni's friends Inga, Ludwig and Dieter came tonight, and we all went to a special dance at the local ballroom, where the highlight of the evening was the election of the carnival queen for the coming year. To hear the music, you think it would be a folk dance, but no one did any. It was just like at the Sophiensaal in Wein—all waltzes and polkas. We piled in bed (I don't know where Anni put them all!) about 2 a.m.

Sunday, November 14, 1954

After a long sleep (a couple of the kids were eating lunch in their PJ's), we joined Annie's cousin Lisl and her fiancé Emil for a long afternoon walk. I took along the harmonica and we had a good time as we walked. We all went to Lisl's house for coffee and cake and Dieter played Lisl's guitar while we sang, and I did a couple folk dances with Anni and Lisl. Then Anni and I went to Mannheim on the bus to hear a Bach concert. They had it in a church (Konkordiankirche), and nobody clapped at all. I wasn't too happy with the whole thing—I liked the concert in Augsburg better. Perhaps it was the acoustics where we were sitting or the fact that the group playing was very small, but it didn't sound quite harmonious to me. The church has a very new and modern interior, after being destroyed by bombs. It is quite simple, with Romanesque arches and no stained glass. A huge polished wooden cross (without Christ on it) dominates the front. A little bit of marble and hard wooden benches complete the scene. The concert let out early so we took the streetcar to the end of the line and walked the remaining three miles to Neuhofen. The people here all walk on the right hand side of the road, not facing the traffic. I felt awfully unsafe, but "when in Rome do as the Romans do." Anni sounded quite bitter. She said that the Americans weren't liked over here because they weren't friendly and civil enough but were too "fresh," with a sort of superior air. Well I suppose she's right. I've met a lot of those people myself.

Monday, November 15, 1954

I got up early, said my goodbyes to Anni and her family, and when I started out the sun was shining, but it started to rain before I got to Speyer. I got some money changed from the $5 from Mom, and while I was getting gasoline it snowed a bit. It's getting late in the season, so I'd better hurry. I thought I was going on, but I was so cold I decided to stay in the jugendherberge here. It's only four years old and very nice inside. They said there were 80 people here yesterday, but I'm all alone tonight.

November 15th 1954

Dear Folks:

To Nuremberg, then back to Heidelberg to really visit with the Kindlers. Then Bonn, Köln and Koblenz. I get more pessimistic about a job every day.–

Ted

Tuesday, November 16, 1954

I left the Speyer hostel and went to Schwäbisch Hall today. It was quite cold—I counted the miles all the way. At Schwäbisch Hall I had a hard time locating the hostel because I was given directions to the warden's house instead, and there was no sign on the door. The hostel is a tower built on one of the old city gates. It was marvelous! The hostel was redone after the First World War, and a master iron worker fashioned all the door locks and wrought iron railings. The wrought iron locks were big, with little people or animals for on the face plates and in designs on the hinges. The keyholes for on the dorm rooms were cute, showing little boys peeking in on the girl's room, and little girls peeking in on the boy's room. There's a couple common rooms done in real folksy style—real nice. I, being the only one here, was invited to the living quarters of the warden to eat my supper where it was warm. There are three children—very nice. The father has talent in his finger-tips—he makes wonderful pen-and-ink landscapes. He has a hobby of keep-ing a sort of monthly or yearly diary with drawings instead of photos. They have some big pictures on the walls—really lovely! Trees are his specialty. He did a small memory sketch of the hostel here and gave it to me as a souvenir.

Wednesday, November 17, 1954

Everything went wrong today! Well, not everything—I was pretty well straightened out by bed time. But I didn't get far—only 20 miles from Schwäbisch Hall to Crailsheim. I had been noticing a decided lack of power all yesterday afternoon, but today it really hit. I couldn't go up even the tiniest hill, not even in low! I fiddled and fiddled with the points, thinking this was the trouble, but to no avail. Then someone on the main street in Crailsheim said that the muffler was clogged. I didn't see why it should be, but anything was worth a try, so off it came and I tried driving without it. Power! I had it!

So it had to be cleaned, but it was 5 p.m. and time to head for the nearest hostel. The warden there struck another cheerful note—he himself owned two motorcycles. His profession was repairing motorcycles, he said, and in the morning he would take a look at mine. The youth hostel here consists of two rooms in the school; the whole thing is modern and built since the war. I scouted around and got a fire going in the stove and really got warm.

In the morning, I took my bike to the warden's shop, and proceeded to pull the inside baffles out of the muffler. What a mess—all crudded up with a gooey, greasy deposit! I washed it all off with gasoline and reassembled it on the motorcycle. The warden said that as long as it was here in his shop, we might as well do another head-cleaning. So we did, but as we removed the head, the gasket broke. I was at a loss when this happened—where to get a head gasket for an English bike in Germany? No problem! The German DKW 125cc is the mirror image of the BSA 125cc, and he stocked DKW parts, so all we had to do was use a DKW gasket upside down, and it fit perfectly! So now I had plenty of power—just like new.

Dear Folks:

I send this from Heidelberg, where I'm having a good time with Tante Fritzi and Onkel Werner Kindler.

Ted

Thursday, November 18, 1954

The herbergsvater (hostel warden) at Crailsheim really did me up proud this morning. He set the points and adjusted the spark plug gap, and told me what had been wrong. My spark plug gap was too big so the spark wasn't hot enough. Thus too much unburned carbon was deposited in the muffler. Well, it's really working well now. I awoke to a pitiful sight—there were a couple centimeters of wet snow on the ground. But the warden assured me that the streets were free of snow, so I set out. I didn't go very fast, because the first ten miles or so there was a lot of slush on the road and gravel, and where the roads were bare, they were wet.

But in spite of all this, I arrived at Nuremberg at noon. The hostel was closed until 2:30, so I had a look around, bought some souvenirs (three decals, a patch and a pin), and ate. The youth hostel here is really terrific—built three years ago right up next to the old city wall and incorporating one of the old towers. On the first floor is a "jugend gestaltet"—a big eating hall and ping pong tables. On the second and third floors was a "boy's home," sort of a place like the Rolletts put Burli in. The fourth and fifth floors are occupied by a "festhalle"—a small auditorium with a balcony. The 6th and 7th floors are the jugendherberge, and the tower is a girls' home. The whole thing (with the exception of the tower, which is real stone) is made from molded cement blocks, quite large, which look like stone, with wrought iron, wood lamp fixtures, large wooden beams, staircases, walls, and furniture. Really terrific!

I ate a hot meal in the spiesesalle (dining room) for a very low price. The place was overflowing with school kids who were eating their lunches. Really, "the joint was jumpin'!" In the evening when I ate, there were also a lot of them. I went and checked in at the hostel, then went out to the Special Services office in the Palace of Justice. You know, by this time I ought to be immune to people saying "no," but I'm not. I felt pretty low when I was told that to teach crafts I'd have to have a BA in fine arts, a BA in physical Education to teach sports or recreation, and BA in theater to work with any entertainment groups. They gave me the address of the professional entertainment branch in Wiesbaden, but I'm afraid that I'm not professional enough for all that. The more people I talk to, the more I'm told that it's hard to find a civilian job in Germany. So perhaps I'll be going home soon, after all. Darn!

After supper I put my new decals on the windscreen. This makes six of them, now. I noticed that there was something going on in the festhalle, and asked the ticket-taker what it was.

"A Musicabend (concert). You're from the hostel? Go on in."

So I heard the concert for free—a Handel violin sonata and a modern piece by a former Nuremberger. Naturally, the Handel was good. The modern piece was something different—it had a narration going along with it which told the story. So it was much more enjoyable than just the music alone. The artists were Nuremberger students and did very well, especially the narrator, who really acted it out with his voice.

Friday, November 19, 1954

This morning I met an American, an older man, a photographer who also had stayed in the youth hosteL. He was quite interesting—he travels, takes colored movies, and then lectures in the US. (This is a living?) He was very interested in folk dancing as a movie subject—he said he might just drop around sometime at Syracuse. He's trying to sell a travel movie (and lecture) to some of the American schools over here, and almost hired me to be a salesman for him. But of course that wouldn't work because I had no idea what I was selling. Then I scooted my cold way back to Schwäbisch Hall. I stopped in Crailsheim to eat lunch and buy a pin and it got to Schwäbisch Hall around 3 or 4 p.m. Before I went to the hostel, I bought some plastic and made alterations to my machine. I tacked on some additional plastic to the windscreen so I'd have more places for decals and I put some extensions on the top of the leg shields so the wind wouldn't hit me in the stomach so much. Then on to the youth hostel. The children were glad to see me. This evening we all sat in the combination living room/dining room and I and the little girl got together on some songs, she on recorder and I on harmonica. I was going to write in this diary, but somehow it just didn't get touched.

Saturday, November 20, 1954

I walked around the city a bit, after a late arising, to look for some souvenirs. I ended up with only a pin. Souvenirs are hard to come by this time of the year. Besides, I won't buy any except city coat-of-arms, and if they are patches, the design must be woven in, not printed. Then I bought a large pair of warm and waterproof mittens to wear over my gloves. I finally got under way about 12:30. Two hours later I pulled into Heidelberg, after a not-so-cold and rather sunny trip. The plastic extensions on the leg shields really paid off, and so did the mittens. I bought a pin of Heidelberg's crest, then called on the Kindlers. They were both here, and insisted that I bring all my stuff up—they had a room all waiting. I cleaned up a bit, then had tea with them and Doctor Krahl, an assistant, his wife and a visiting doctor, a former assistant in Berlin. Tante Fritzi (she insists I call her that, so I guess I shall) and I took a little walk and bought some things. I washed, shaved (there's hot running water in the room—wow!) and changed clothes, but it turned out that Onkel Wiener ate alone (he's very busy) and Tante Fritzi doesn't eat much (watches her figure), so I had a bit of cold supper and talk with Tante. This room in the hospital—boy, it sure is luxury! A radiator that is really hot, hot running water and a good mirror, and a corner room with two sets of windows, a couch, an easy chair, a table, a clothes press—wonderful! I washed out socks and underwear—they were dry (on the radiator) before I went to bed. The bed—that's something else—is soft, and a big, thick feather-bed really keeps me warm! Mmm-m-m!

Sunday, November 21, 1954

I got up real late (9:30) this morning. Tante and Onkel came at 10:30, and we went for a drive. I saw their house that's being prepared for them, then waited in the car (a new Opel, a GM car, the biggest made here in Germany) while they went to pay a few professional calls. Then lunch (roast chicken—Mmm-m-m! The best I've had in a long time!). Tante and Onkel are busy again this afternoon so I'm finishing up this diary, putting the new Heilbrom decal on the bike, washing out a few things, and improving my harmonica playing. These cold days Tante Fritzi has loaned me a fur-lined overcoat that she thinks came in one of the packages from Mom. It's big and heavy and really warm! When Onkel and Tante came back, she talked to me while Onkel performed an operation. She told me all about her refugee work in Berlin and told many interesting stories about it. She's really a wonderful person—a Quaker, too.

Monday, November 22, 1954

I decided that I better see about shipping accommodations if I wanted to catch a ship which would get me home before Christmas (the possibility of work getting dimmer and dimmer). So I visited American Express and got the latest schedule. I also tried to book on the Holland-America line for December 7th or 9th. As of 6 p.m., when the office closed, the Holland-America office had not called back to say what was open, so I'll have to go back tomorrow. I rode about a bit in this fur coat that Aunt Fritzi gave me to wear—M-m-m-m-m, warm! I didn't do much—bought some soap and writing papers. I had a little leather band put on my knife sheath to hold it on. I spent a lot of time in the American Express office, waiting for that phone call which never came. Aunt Fritzi came down to talk this evening and I showed her all my stuff. She keeps bringing me food—she thinks I'm not getting enough to eat. Actually, I'm eating much better than I have for a week or so. They moved me today into another room because they had someone else coming into the room I was in. The only thing this place lacks is a lavatory, otherwise it's just as luxurious as the other. I had a talk with one of the nurses this evening—they have the same setup for becoming a nurse as they do an England. It isn't really because they feel that so much practical work is better then studying first and practicing afterwards, but because it's so much cheaper when you work as you study. Most of them here don't have so much money.

Dear Folks:

I'm going to stick this in the mail right away to let you know the latest. I have a berth on the *New Amsterdam* for December 7th , and will arrive in New York City on the 15th. Don't come to meet me unless you really feel like it. I want to stop in Syracuse for a day or so on my way home. They had a spot open on the ship, but said I could not cancel later than the 25th, by which time I can't possibly explore all the possibilities of jobs. So I sent Dad a cable today at his office. I sure hope he gets just the right amount sent off, as I'm not there to receive it. It goes directly to the American Express company. So "I'll Be Home for Christmas"! See you all there!

P.S.: Urgent News will get to me, if you send "Care of Amexco, Rotterdam, at 120 Meet," or "Amexco, New York City (65 Broadway)."

Tuesday, November 23, 1954

I went to the American Express office this morning and found that I could get a berth on the *New Amsterdam* leaving Rotterdam on December 7th so I took it, paying a little down to hold the reservation, and wiring home for the rest to be sent to American Express in Heidelberg. Then back to the hospital where, after a good lunch, I said goodbye to the Kindlers. They're wonderful people and she's awfully devoted to her husband, He, in turn, is awfully devoted to his work. Aunt Fritzi says that we must compile a list of places to go in the US which are not too expensive. She's toying with the idea of coming to the States in a year so. I sure hope she does!

I posted a letter to Koblenz, Bonn and Köln, and lit out for Neuhofen, where I had left my pocket knife. On the way, I noticed that my rear tire was soft but paid no attention to it after it was blown up again. I checked it once, and it seemed to be okay, so I let it go. I stopped at Speyer to see the "Dom" there. The grave of one of the Kaisers is there, otherwise it didn't have much charm. The whole style is Romanesque, which is different than anything I've seen before. They were redoing some of the inside—the place left me with a big, cold feeling. There didn't seem to be much life in the place.

I pushed on towards Neuhofen, and on the way, it happened! A flat tire! Rear, of course! So I pulled off the road, unloaded the whole shebang, laid the bike on its side and proceeded to take the whole wheel off to fix the thing. Two little boys were very helpful—one watched the bike while the other took me to his home so we could spot the leak via water bath. I pulled out a 3-inch nail and found four holes. It was necessary to cut a small patch from one of the big ones, and as I didn't have my pocket knife, I had to use the Austrian knife. Well, sad—I didn't see it again. One of those little boys must have taken it, or it was picked up by a man who came along and helped. Darn! It cost about $2, which isn't much for such a good knife. But even if I get the money back (insurance) and have the Rolletts send me another, I'm sure it won't be as nice. And it kills me, too. Just yesterday in Heidelberg I had a little strap put on that would hold the sheath on the blade, and now it's gone! I looked everywhere and went back and questioned one of the little boys. No go.

So I picked up my pocket knife in Neuhofen and went on to Karlsruhe. The flat tire was one delay, and a big detour was another, so I didn't get to Karlsruhe until about 10. Luckily the Zerrs were still up. I ate, said good-bye to Herr Zerr (he leaves for work very early in the morning) and hit the hay after telling of my further adventures.

Wednesday, November 24, 1954

I didn't bother to unpack anything, not even my toothbrush, so I was up and away with Mama Zerr early in the morning, at 8. I said goodbye and went to American Express. There was a letter from London and a letter from home that came to the Zerrs yesterday but they sent them on to American Express before I arrived. I was too early at the office—they hadn't arrived yet. But I didn't want to wait for them, because I had to be in Mannheim in time for lunch with Anni Fittler. There was, however, a letter from Liz and one from Emma Spade. Emma invited me to Cosenza for Christmas. Gee, I sure would like to take her up on it. But now of course, I can't. Well, that's life.

I got to Mannheim in plenty of time, so I sat down and wrote to Emma while I waited for Anni. She's a nice girl—she keeps saying maybe she'll come again to the States. She certainly ought to—she got such a sorry version of the States before. After lunch, I finished my letter to Liz and set out for Frankfurt.

On the way, I stopped at Lörrach, a little town just off the Autobahn just above Mannheim, for a look at the oldest complete German church. Built by the Benedictine monks as a monastery in 774, it now is still there, with the original paintings on the walls—1180 years old! Pretty good, eh? But the place was closed, and I could only look at the outside. What's more, I couldn't find a postcard in the town, so I came away with only a memory. It was very nice though, what I saw of it. There was a sort of checkerboard pattern in the walls because they were built with red and gray stone placed alternately. The Arches were Romanesque and the two towers were, I guess, Norman.

Then I took the Autobahn to Frankfurt. That warden at Crailsheim certainly must know his his stuff—the machine is running like a clock. I stopped at a gas station on the outskirts of town and they were very helpful in finding out where the Hoffmans were. We asked the telephone operator for the Methodist church and there someone told us that Dr. Hoffman is now in Karlsruhe. So he was just around the corner and I didn't know it. For future references the address is:

Dr. Gustav Hoffman, Auerstrasse 20a, Karlsruhe-Durlach, Germany

I'll write him a letter and offer my apologies.

I got directions to the hostel, which turned out to be a brand-new and very modern building. These Germans certainly do things up proud! If they would only allow motoring between hostels in the States, I think the movement would catch on more.

Then the second blow of the day! I found out that I had left my hostel pass in Schwäbisch Hall! Well, they let me stay here, and I don't suppose I'll need it again until after Köln, so I'll write the Schwäbisch Hall warden to send it there.

I met an interesting fellow here, a Canadian from Kitchener, Ontario. The really funny thing was that he had met Bob McDonald in the Rotterdam hostel! Wow! It really is a small world.

Thursday, November 25, 1954 — Frankfurt

Dear Folks:

I'll send this on to keep you posted. I hope that letter of yours didn't contain anything too important, because I won't get it now until Rotterdam. The Rotterdam address is again:

c/o Amexco, 120 Meent, Rotterdam

Also I'll stop in at the American Express Office, 65 Broadway, NYC immediately after leaving the ship, and I'll stay overnight at the Sloane

House (YMCA). You'll see the address on my first letters home (diary) that I wrote From New York (I think it's there). The Kindlers and the Zerrs send their greetings. Remind me to send everyone here Christmas cards when I get home.

Love, Ted

Thursday, November 25, 1954

Well I didn't awake to a very appetizing kind of day. It was sort of cold, muggy, foggy, rainy—the kind of day that a good book, good friends and a warm fire are nice for. But I went to Koblenz from Frankfurt—90 miles—on a motorcycle!

I had a little talk with a fellow who was visiting the hostel "parents." He had been a prisoner of war in the States and England and had there changed his mind about a lot of things. He said the Germans take their politics too seriously and showed me in the newspaper where some speaker for the Adenauer Party was beaten up last night at a rally. This POW was working in an office in the US during the election campaign of Dewey versus Roosevelt, and said that he couldn't understand how or why the men in the office could smoke and joke while they were listening to the speeches on the radio. He also got a year of schooling in London University, later, at the expense of the English government. I asked him if the whole program was good (the way the POWs were treated in the US in England) and he said "very good." Of course, he said, there were a lot of men who kept saying that it was all propaganda, that it wasn't really this way, and that they would never become democratic. But he thinks that most of them did see the light. He said that he himself has learned not to get so hotheaded and wrought up about things—to stand off and view them from a little distance and to cast his vote quietly, and he hopes that the others here will someday do the same.

I talked with Gisela Kefer about this later on tonight and she said that it's because over here the religious life and political life of a person are so closely interwoven—that political issues become personal and moral issues. She thinks it's good that way. I don't.

I left Frankfurt (after making sure that I got a letter off to the hostel parents in Schwäbisch Hall to send my AYH pass on to Köln), about 11 a.m., and most of the way to Koblenz was a nightmare! It's the most tiring bit of road that I've traveled so far, in all my 7,500 miles of this trip. Why? Well, practically all of the pavement is made from black stone bricks, old and shiny with use. When the road is dry they're just "all right," and when the weather is the least bit wet they are TERRIBLE! (they are never really good). Gray or red or yellow stone bricks aren't so slippery—but these? It's just like ice! I didn't go more than 20 mph on any of them, and I could feel the back wheels sliding around underneath me all the time.

When Bob came this way, I hope he had better weather. He probably had a better time of it anyway—his load wasn't so heavy, and he had a much lower center of gravity than my top-heavy load. I finally got to where I used the bicycle path on the edge of the road where I could. It had a macadam surface most of the time, and I could go faster there, on mud, even, than on those d____ bricks! But I did make it to Koblenz, finally, without any mishaps.

I had a look at a few of the castles, but just from a distance . I couldn't see much, anyway. because of the fog and mist. I also noticed some of the shipping on the Rhine. They often use a very large tugboat to pull two, three and sometimes four barges. Going against the river current, of course, the barges are really boats without engines, not square like those in the Erie Canal. Two interesting things I noticed: One—these large tugs all had side paddle wheels, just like the old Mississippi steamers, and if they used a screw too, it wasn't obvious. Two—the barges are all towed by extremely long towropes—twenty to thirty yards long. Why? An interesting question. I just got another one of my few real thrills of this trip as I looked at the terraced and grapevine-covered hillsides along the river. Because here, too, was something you always see in the travel posters and which, to us in the US seems so remote—more of a fairy tale than reality. But there it was, and I was right there with it! I got to Koblenz around 6, and Gisela was home. We had a good talk. Her mother came in around 8—she had just spent a long and, I imagine, happy afternoon with the mother of her oldest son's fiancée. After she went to bed, Giesela and I kept on talking—about politics, philosophy, and so forth until it was pretty late.

Friday, November 26, 1954

The two sons of the family are both away from home—one at school, the other at work, so there is one room vacant and plenty of room for me. I slept in until about 10, then awoke to find a fairly nice day. I lounged around—Gisela prepared for tomorrow's classes—until after lunch. Then Gisela went to her seminar. Frau Kefer went to visit with a girlfriend in the hospital and I went out on the cycle to look around. I headed back up the Rhine a ways to get a better view of some of the castles I missed yesterday. The afternoon sun lit them up beautifully. Then I went back to Koblenz, crossed the bridge and went in the same direction up the other side of the river to look at a couple of them more closely.

Then the bike wouldn't go. I knew exactly what the trouble was—my makeshift wire had broken. I shortly repaired it and got going again, but the sun was already beginning to sink. I took the winding road up to the first castle and found no one there and the place locked up tight as a drum. I walked around the outside a little then left. It was a very small place—not very impressive. But the front part of it was a terraced outdoor restaurant. Probably very nice in the summer, with its excellent view of the Rhine. Then I went out to the Marksburg Castle, a few kilometers away. It is unique in that it has a double tower that's very prominent—a small, round tower rising out of a large, square one. I started looking around and came upon some workmen just leaving, so I walked out on the rampart they were repairing and around to the other side of this quite "castelly" castle, and the groundskeeper or someone closed the gate behind me and locked it! Fine! How was I going to get out? Well, I jumped over the wall and beat my way through the brush to the road. It was built on a very steep hill—I can see where it was quite a stronghold.

Saturday, November 27, 1954

I slept late again this morning—ain't luxury grand?—and the day was also nice again. Gisela came home from her teaching, and after lunch we went for a walk around the town. We went under the newly built (since the war) bridge across the Rhine and walked on the old horse path past the city castle and old city wall. We contemplated taking a short trip on the river, but decided against it. It would take too much time. We had a good view all the time of the fortress built in the 1700s, on the other side of the river. We visited the oldest church, parts of which date back to the ninth century. Romanesque, with modern stained-glass windows—I didn't like them. Then we walked down to the famous Deutsches Eck and climbed the monument. A nice view. Gisela says that the river always overflows its banks a little each spring, and on the depth-recording station there were some marks indicating where the water level was in previous years. They had quite a flood, I guess, in 1764. Then we went through the town and saw quite a few bombed ruins. It was pretty bad here in Koblenz, but the slum area got it the worst, which gives the city a good excuse for cleaning them up now. There are a few of the really old buildings still standing, where you could you see the outward-leaning walls and narrow streets. We had coffee at a cafe and talked for quite a while before going home. We found Frau Kefer resting in bed when we got there—she has a weak heart. Gisela and I ate our supper by candlelight—the power went off for an hour or so. We talked, and I showed her all my souvenirs. Ho-Hum! Bedtime!

Dear Folks:

Please find out what Bob paid for his bike on the boat and cable that amount to American Express Rotterdam. I don't know if I have enough to cover the cost, and the money was only my fare. I'll be in Rotterdam December 5th or 6th. Gee, now that I'm thinking about going home I'm all excited and anxious. I suppose Bob got home all right, and had a wonderful time at the Kolo Fest in New York City. Did he ride his bike home or ship it and take the bus? I imagine it'll be too cold for me to ride.

See you all,

Ted

Sunday, November 28, 1954

I arose late, and, after a good dinner said my farewells and headed for Bonn. I got there around 5 but Herb didn't answer his bell. I waited until 6:30, and he still didn't show up, so I went to the jugendherberge. They said they were only open in summer, but there was another just five kilometers away. So I went there. But, of course, I didn't have my hostel pass. It's awaiting me at Bickenbach's. So the warden said that he couldn't let me stay there but he told me of a nearby private home where I could stay for only two marks. I found the place after just a little trouble. It was very nice with a refinished outside, and very neat and clean within. I unpacked and went back to Herb's. He was there, having received my note which I stuck in his keyhole. It turned out that he was here at 5, but in someone else's room so he didn't hear the bell. We talked and had some tea and supper, and then it was already 10:30! The time goes so quickly! So back to the house and a nice soft bed.

Monday, November 29, 1954

I met Herb this morning at 11, and we were together the rest of the day. Herb lives in a new and modern dormitory. It is a double room, with beds that double as couches, a balcony, a lavatory with hot and cold water, two easy chairs, two desks and chairs, a stool and a small table. All this for 32 marks a month! Why, Ed was paying 45 in München for half as much! We ate lunch in the Mensa, the equivalent of a student union. There was a lounge, a restaurant and a cafeteria. We chose the cafeteria, really a big eating room, where you can buy tickets for one or both of very cheap menus and get soup, boiled potatoes and red cabbage for 70 pfennig. That's pretty good. Herb gets seven free meals a week via some sort of a scholarship. The building also has student offices and so forth. The whole thing is quite new and modern.

Herb tried to explain it to me—it's a "Foundation" sort of a thing, an organization for the students. The buildings, and so forth, are owned and operated by this body, a student doctor is provided, and the whole thing is subsidized by the state (of Rhine-Westphalia). Everything is very cheap—there's a barber shop and beauty salon, and a laundry, too. More buildings are being planned to be built next summer. Next on the list is a girls' dorm. Herb's dorm also has a library, lounges, meeting rooms, and a bicycle garage, a kitchen on every floor and one larger one, and two rooms (a serving room and a lounge/eating room for the girls, and girls only! I guess it lets them get away from their minority feeling. In Bonn, there are lots more men than women.) Herb, being the president of this floor, got the passkey from the head resident and showed me all around.

We went to the University as far as Herb knew it. There is an Agricultural school and a Medical school, but they are somewhere else in the city. The University building is the old Palace of the Elector of Bonn. An enormous place, it's not entirely used; some of the building still needs fixing up and repairs enough due to age, war and lack of funds. The inside is not belied in the least by the outside. The inside is quite modern. We walked down Koblenzstrasse,where all the government is—the parliament, the Bundespost (post office), and many official residences and legations.

As darkness fell, we were walking along the Rhine. We saw one of those very large tugboats with seven barges in tow! There's not much evidence of war damage anymore in Bonn, but we did see a little. Then we had supper at the Mensa and hopped the trolley to my rooming house. I showed him all my souvenirs and we had a long talk. Then, as it was pretty late, we went back to Bonn. Herb's roommate was just in and we all three talked a while before I left. We also met today the president of AS&A, the local student government, and had tea with him. He was at Ohio State when Herb was at Wooster and met Lilibet Childs there. His English is in contrast to Herb's. His is Oxford, so much so in fact that he is often mistaken for an Englishman.

Herb is very interested, so his studies imply, in politics, and the local elections got a bit of his attention. The Christian Democrats (Adenauer), the Free Democrats and the Social Democrats are the three big parties. Herb tried to explain how they were different, and so forth, but it was all very dense to me. He explained all about his studies and how they were set up, and about the cases which they are given to ponder. It sounds interesting but not enough so to me.

Tuesday, November 30, 1954

I went to Herb's at noon, and we were together until 4. We went Christmas shopping and spent until 2 in the stores. Then lunch, then talk. The election turned out for the better, as Herb sees it. The Christian Democrats lost a few seats and the Social Democrats picked them up. This means, says Herb, that the Christian Democrats will have to give in a little on their Cultural policy. The main issue is separate parochial schools.

What did we talk about? Oh, everything in general. We discussed Mom, I told him all about Liz and he explained about his girlfriend. Just two guys together and getting closer.

I left Herb and went on to Köln. By the time I had eaten and packed it was 6:30. Köln is just a half hour from Bonn, but I missed a turn somewhere and found myself in the center of the city when I should have been in the north side. That, plus the brick roads (it was raining), and a long wait at the police office until they found out the Bickenbach's house number (for some reason I don't have it written in the address), combined to make me show up at their place about 8:30 p.m. They were expecting me for the weekend, but after consulting the map and the calendar, I'm a few days ahead of my former plans. They were just finishing supper,and the whole family was there. There's "Opa," Herr Neuman, Frau and Herr Bickenbach, Gerlinde (27—wow!), Uta (18—wow again!), and Edda (14—she'll get there!). They got quite a kick out of my whole rig, especially the little bells

I have on my zipper pulls. It wasn't five minutes before Gerlinde was trying on my helmet in front of the mirror, and Uta stuck a spray of evergreen on the side. Yessir, a real nice family. All seem to be in good health and good spirits. Edda is in school, Uta is going to stenographic school, and Gerlnde is the secretary at the Evangelistic Kirche. The oldest daughter, not home now but working in Köln, was engaged this past weekend. The house is filled with flowers because of it. Then, of course, it's Christmas time and the house has evergreens and Advent candles all around. Frau Bickenbach got talkative after the others had gone to bed and told of their escape from the Russians and eventual return to the home of her parents. They had quite a hard time. Now they have had their entire house again for the last three months. It's one of these "semi-separated" affairs like Ada and Harry have—they own half of the entire structure. The kitchen is in the basement and food is carried to the dining room above via a dumbwaiter. There's a small room off the dining room, separated by a curtain, and another small room used for storage. Upstairs is a large bathroom and three bedrooms and on the third floor I haven't been.

Wednesday, December 1, 1954

Gee! December is here! I can feel the icy fingers of winter down my back, but it's warmed somewhat by the warmth of Christmas thoughts. Today is Mom's birthday, too. Fifty-five years young—that's my Ma! I took a long hot bath this morning and washed out some things at the same time. My brown khaki shirt hasn't been washed since Graz, around the 20th of October, and its really dirty! I went all over it with a scrub brush. I had to, to get it clean! The Bickenbachs said it's what the students refer to as a "semester shirt." I won't talk about my jeans. Perhaps they're past redemption. The last time they were washed was at Karlsruhe, on our first visit there, and they've been through h___ since then! After lunch Frau Bickenbach and I went to Alteburg, a small town east of Bergisch-Gladbach. There's an old church there that is really a gem! It's very simple and plain, although not as much as Reims. It's all Gothic and quite big; a former Monastery was there. The windows are mostly checkered black and white with no color except for a small coat of arms of the donor in the corner. Later windows are colored but only in places. Most of these later windows are also checkered black and white. A large window in the back of the church is the most colorful. The church is used for Protestant services, too. This is because of a proclamation of the local ruler "way back when" saying that it could be used for both confessions.

Then we went across the road to the Märchenwald Fairytale Forest. This is a walk through the wood with stops at various little houses. Each contained a tableau of a different fairy tale. The first one, "Bruderchen und Schwesterchen" ("Brother and Sister," a Grimm fairy tale), had a real, live, young deer and a rabbit in the set. There are almost a dozen of them, "Hansel and Gretel," "Snow White and the Seven Dwarves," etc., etc. There were three where the story was acted out by puppet or dolls, worked by machinery for 10 pfennig in the slot. We went all around, then went into the adjoining cafe for tea. The lamps on the inside were each made of carved wood. The wall lamps depicted the "Seven Crows," with each carrying a little lamp in his beak, and the two chandeliers were each made up of seven figures walking along a log each carrying a lantern. The figures and the crows were all about a foot high and all hand-carved. Pretty nice!

We heard from the waitress that the "world champion" German soccer team had lost to England—much sadness here, I guess. We talked until our bus came at 6:30.

Mom's going to find another kindred soul when she comes over to Europe and visits Köln, I think. I was planning this night for "costume showing night," but Uta had a choir rehearsal, Herr Neuman went to bed early, and Edda had to finish schoolwork so it comes tomorrow night. We got out their wind-up phonograph and played my records. Darn! The record I bought in Salzburg is cracked clear through. Actually it is broken but the unbroken paper label in the center holds it together. Well, I'll save it anyway. Maybe I can make a copy. Herr Bickenbach gave me a flat piece of plywood to bind the records against so they don't get banged up anymore. There's nothing like locking the barn door after the horse is stolen! Happy Birthday, Mom! Here it is December 1st, 1954 in Bergisch-Gladbach.

Dear Folks:

I leave here Friday morning and hopefully get to Rotterdam Saturday evening. This gives me the 5th, 6th and 7th here. I'll try to write from there, and from NYC, naturally. I'll probably be home the 20th, 21st or 22nd.

Love, Ted

Thursday, December 2, 1954

Today Frau Bickenbach and I went to Köln. We saw the Kölner Dom (Cologne Cathedral), most of which is still being repaired. The attendant said that the windows were mostly broken during the war. It's a large Gothic structure with some beautifully carved woodwork. The organ and the structures supporting it are modern—doesn't fit in well with the style of things at all. We saw the doors outside—they were modern, too.

They made an air raid shelter nearby and came upon the site of the old Roman town. So after the war the air raid shelter became a museum. There were old Roman and ancient Christian gravestones there and the central work of art with a beautiful piece of Mosaic floor. There was a chart on the wall showing the sites of all the previous buildings on the site of the Dom.

We had coffee at a nice little cafe, and went shopping for Christmas cards. The streets are all filled with decorations but they only use white bulbs, no colored lights. We found the cards and quite nice ones, too. But the prices! Expensive! About 25 to 40 US cents for what would normally cost a dime at home. That's why the Germans don't send many cards I guess because in their wages/buying powers relationship it's even more expensive. The postcard types are cheaper so that's what I got.

Then Frau Bickenbach had to go home and I stayed in Köln for the afternoon. I mostly just wandered around looking at the store windows and decorations. The Kaufhof, the biggest department store, had a little show about the "Heinzelmännchen von Köln" ("The Gnomes of Cologne") which I saw, and the store was selling very good pfeffernussen, which I ate. I went to a music shop and listened to records. Their LPs here are more expensive than in the States. I managed to get back all right to Bergisch-Gladbach. Then Uta said she had to babysit so wouldn't be able to see my souvenirs (tonight was "show night"), but after supper when I was showing everything, she came in towards the last. Then she and her mother offered to sew patches on my ski jacket, so that was begun.

Friday, December 3, 1954

Gerlinde was sick in bed yesterday, so I didn't see her at all. Today everybody was up and gone before I was up. But it took me longer to get ready than I figured. Frau Bickenbach gave me some Deutsche Christmas cookies to take with me. I don't know where I'll ever find room for these cookies, but they'll probably be all crumbs by the time I get home anyway.

So I was still there at lunchtime. I saw Gerlinde long enough to say goodbye (she has some sort of recurring trouble with her stomach), and Uta was home for lunch, too. I got under way at 1, finally, and got as far as Roermond, just over the Dutch border, by nightfall. In the money-changing office on the border I came across some German paper money of one- and two-mark denominations. I stayed at the youth hostel in Beegden, a small place just outside Roermond. It was officially opened only in the summer but since they were home anyway, and I was only one, they kindly let me stay. I spent the evening sewing on patches. It's now 11 down and 23 to go.

Saturday, December 4, 1954

I got all set to go this morning, and when I kicked the motor over, the kicker lever broke! But luckily, there was a smithy just across the street from the youth hostel and he did a very neat welding job in no time at all, and I paid him less than a guilder for it. So I got on my way. I had to buy gas, and I was amazed at the price. It was 37 1/2 Dutch cents to the liter, about 2/3 the price in Germany! So I filled up, my last tank full in Europe, and came straight on to Rotterdam.

The Dutch have excellent roads and I'm glad they do! All day long there was a terrific wind. It nearly blew me down when it came from the side and I had to go in second gear when I went against it. Since I was traveling north and west and the wind came from the Atlantic, I never got a tailwind. All the roads are wide and not much brick is used. However, it was mostly dry today. There are well-paved and clean bicycle rights-of-way by every road, usually well away from the road, and entirely separate.

It's a real flat land and there's a noticeable lack of trees, especially along the roads. I saw people walking around in wooden shoes—they didn't seem to be unwieldy or uncomfortable, but I'll stick to leather, thank you! I got to Rotterdam about 3, but everything closes here at 1 on Saturday, so neither Holland-America nor American Express were open and I'll have to wait until Monday. To bad. Had I known this, I would have traveled farther last night. I would have liked to have had my letters today.

Sunday, December 5, 1954

The youth hostel was closed today but they gave me the address of a cheap hotel which turned out to be very nice, run by the Salvation Army. I spent all day sewing on patches—it's really beginning to look like something!

There was this Belgian fellow there (he spoke French, Dutch, German and English) who was very interesting, He was the father of a spastic baby (at least it sounded like that), just two years old, and is trying to find some way to get him to the States to cure him. He hasn't got much money so he's writing to some of the big magazines in the States, trying to get them interested in the case. He should try some TV programs, too. I sure hope he succeeds. We went to a movie together. It was an American film in English with Dutch subtitles: *Saskatchewan*—pretty good. During a break between the news and shorts and so forth, and the main feature, there was community singing. An electric organ played, and the words were flashed on the screen. Real nice! They ought to do that in America, too!

A US guy from Texas who is sailing on the ninth, came in the hotel, sent over by the hostel. So we three had a good time talking. Back at the hotel they gave us each a great big St. Nicholas cookie that's traditional here in Holland—we had coffee later on—very nice and cozy, with the management and guests all sitting together in the small sitting room/dining room combo.

Monday, December 6, 1954

First thing this morning I went to the American Express office and picked up the mail. There were a couple from Mom, a couple from the insurance company in England about renewing my policy—Ha!—and a nice card from Aunt Fritzi. I inquired by telegram as to what became of the $55 extra which Dad sent to Heidelberg. Later in the afternoon I went back and they said they had returned it to the sender. So—no extra money for me. I did get the 30 bucks for the bike and we went right away to Holland America and arranged for the shipping. They said they remembered Bob from his November sailing, and that in order to get his bike down to weight, he even had to take his petrol tank off. Well, I didn't have to go that far, but the windscreen, luggage carrier and saddlebags are now "hand baggage."

In going around the city, then, I walked, seeing as I had no means of transportation. Rotterdam is completely rebuilt, being almost totally destroyed by Hitler. It's a marvelous job, and one of the most modern-looking cities you'll ever see. Only a few of the old-style buildings are retained—as monuments or something, I suppose, to show what was. Later on, back at the hostel, who should show up but the lady from South Africa whom I met in Milano and Innsbruck! We had quite a time talking. Then we went down to the warden's to hear my phonograph records and those of the Texan (he moved back to he hostel, too), had tea, showed them some American toys the Texan had ("Slinky" and some "Silly Putty") and had a real good time. Tomorrow I sail. I have only seven guilders left so I'm going to be a real cheapskate on the boat.

Rotterdam December 6, 1954

Dear folks:

Now, I don't know how long it's going to take for that leftover $55 to reach you again. Possibly, you already have it. But I cashed my last Travelers Check and have only seven guilders left. I sure would like to see some of that "folding green" when I see Dad in New York. Also, if you address mail to:

Holland America Line
29 Broadway, New York City
Care of *New Amsterdam*
Arriving December 15th, 1954
Please Deliver On Board Ship

(all of that is necessary), and send a check or bank draft, I can cash it on board with the purser. Or a letter at the American Express office would do, too.

Love, Ted

§   §   §

A grand adventure! I wasn't particularly cognizant at the time of a presence of God as I traveled. But in retrospect I can see that He was with me every inch of the way. He has guided and protected me all my life, as my memoirs attest. So, dear reader, I leave you with this verse to contemplate:

Trust in the Lord with all your heart,
and do not lean on your own understanding.
In all your ways acknowledge Him,
and He will make straight your paths.

(Proverbs 3:5, 6)

CPSIA information can be obtained
at www.ICGtesting.com
Printed in the USA
LVHW081930181021
700771LV00013B/825/J

9 780975 393437